CONNECTING FATHERS, CHILDREN, AND READING

A How-To-Do-It Manual for Librarians

Sara Willoughby-Herb
Steven Herb

**HOW-TO-DO-IT MANUALS
FOR LIBRARIANS**

NUMBER 105

NEAL-SCHUMAN PUBLISHERS, INC.
New York, London

Published by Neal-Schuman Publishers, Inc.
100 Varick Street
New York, NY 10013

Printed and bound in the United States of America.

Library of Congress Cataloging-in-Publication Data

Herb, Steven.
    Connecting fathers, children, and reading: a how-to-do it manual / Steven Herb, Sara Willoughby-Herb.
        p. cm. — (How-to-do-it manuals for librarians; no. 105)
    Includes bibliographical references and index.
    ISBN 1-55570-390-9 (alk. paper)
    1. Libraries—Services to families. 2. Reading—Parent participation. 3. Children—Books and Reading. 4. Family literacy programs. 5. Father and child. 6. Fathers—Juvenile literature—Bibliography. I. Willoughby-Herb, Sara. II. Title. III. How-do-do-it manuals for libraries ; no. 105.

Z711.92.F34 H47 2001

2001018315

To Wayne Willoughby and Walter Herb,
our own wonderful fathers,
and
Genevieve McQueeney Willoughby and Barbara Homan Herb,
our extraordinary mothers

CONTENTS

PREFACE

Connecting Fathers, Children, and Reading: A How-To-Do-It Manual for Librarians examines the important relationship between children and fathers and explores the vital link among families, reading, and libraries. Traditionally, the efforts of librarians to involve families in children's learning have been restricted to mothers, essentially because of historical precedents in which mothers were at home and took primary responsibility for children in the preschool and school years. Today in many families both parents work and are attempting to share child-rearing responsibilities more equally. This practical need for more involved fathering is supported by recent research findings on the positive effects fathers can have on their children's development when they are engaged in active parenting. As more and more fathers take on important roles in their children's upbringing and learning and thereby help to redefine fatherhood for a new generation, those of us who work with children and families need to be better prepared to offer guidance and support

Our approach to this support should be flexible and varied, and needs to cover the whole range of fathering from the transitions of becoming a first-time parent through the many challenges of marriage and parenthood that shift and change as children grow and develop. Our guidance should range from the development of fatherhood in its earliest minutes during the pregnancy and in the newborn's scanning of a parent's incredulous face, all the way through to the joyful mentoring experienced in grandparent-hood.

The broad aim of *Connecting Fathers, Children, and Reading: A How-To-Do-It Manual for Librarians* is to assist librarians and others who are concerned with young children's whole brain development, their mental wellness and stability, as well as their language and literacy development, to consider ways in which they can involve fathers, and other significant males, in their efforts. As we shall see, when fathers become more actively involved in their children's literacy activities, benefits accrue for both children and their fathers. Our primary focus throughout this manual is how we can help fathers become involved in their children's foundation for literacy, often referred to as emergent literacy. It is absolutely critical to remember that although fathers can contribute greatly to children's development, the absence of a father should not lead us to believe that the family is dysfunctional nor the child disadvantaged. Family strength and child nurturance grow from many sources: mothers and grandparents, siblings, friends, extended family members, community mentoring programs, the neighborhood house of worship, family support programs, and caring neighbors. Our effort to include fathers in our programs is just one of the many important ways we can strengthen children's learning opportunities by collaborating with significant adults in their worlds.

In Chapter 1, "Understanding the Link Between Fathers and Learning," we consider some of the significant research findings on fathering, findings that point to the benefits our programming efforts hold for both children and their families. Though we must begin with the recognition that many of today's children spend little or no quality time with their fathers, our hope is that by including fathers and other male role models in our program efforts, we can strengthen our children's opportunities to benefit from father-child interactions.

Chapter 2, "Recognizing Diversity in Fatherhood Today," looks at fatherhood through two major lenses—the new important roles that fathers are playing (and should play) in the lives of their children and the diversity of special circumstances fathers are facing in today's culture from single parenthood to reconstituted families. The chapter concludes with three broad strategies that are supportive of the important new roles of fathering and sensitive to the diverse situations facing fathers in our society today.

Chapter 3, "Selecting Books That Reflect Good Fathering," focuses on the importance of children and their parents finding role models in children's literature and provides a set of ten guidelines that libraries can use to select children's literature supporting good fathering. A five-part annotated bibliography completes the chapter. This comprehensive resource examines good books portraying a diversity of fathers and fathering situations, dramatic play, story starters, dad discussion group books, and books focusing on children and fathers facing special circumstances.

In Chapter 4, "Involving Fathers in Their Children's Literacy Experiences," we suggest some general and specific strategies for working with fathers in libraries. The chapter explores the goal of literacy learning—the overall ability to incorporate speaking, listening, reading, and writing into all learning. Most of the chapter is organized into three sections that correspond with those family literacy practices that are the best predictors of success—parents and children *reading together*; parents and children exploring *writing together*; and parents and children regularly *engaging in conversations and storytelling*.

Chapter 5, "Reaching Out to Fathers Through Library Programming," focuses on how we can collaborate across our communities with other agencies and facilities. We look at what makes collaboration successful and suggest many agencies and strategies that might work in any community. If libraries can reach out with and through other agencies to share their message and approach with fathers whose families are not likely to be reached through in-house library programs the whole community will benefit.

Chapter 6, "Resources for Families and Libraries," contains several sections of resources including those focused on fathers, strategies for professionals who work with fathers and grandparents, child rearing and children's development, as well as useful Web sites that will help libraries partner with fathers to foster literacy.

Chapter 7, "Children's Books About Fathers and Fathering," creates an annotated children's book list about all aspects of fathers and fathering. Over 450 titles, many published in the last several years, are divided into dozens of categories to help libraries in their collection building.

In this country there are many fine institutions whose primary missions are to help people, but the public library remains a unique treasure in its mission to help all people to help themselves. At the library the young may find useful information, an amusing entertainment, and an opportunity to dream. Children may spend time seeking an answer to a homework question, laughing at a storyhour, or traveling to another planet through a book's pages. The cumulative effect libraries have on the whole life of a child is remarkable. Children learn to love books at libraries. They can learn to love learning. They certainly learn to become literate in the broadest, most glorious sense of the word. Libraries and literacy experiences for the young are bound forever from bookshelf to hand, from page to heart, and from story to soul.

Libraries need to enlist and encourage the help of parents—especially fathers—in this fine endeavor. We can help them learn to become good storybook readers, storytellers, and conversationalists for their children. We can teach them about the importance of encouraging imagination and curiosity as well as supervising homework, ensuring regular library visits, and helping their children participate in the library's reading programs. We know that children who have these experiences at home are more likely to develop competence in literacy learning and to do well in school. For children who are at risk for learning difficulties, this kind of family involvement is even more significant. These children urgently need to come to literacy learning through regular and frequent interactions with a supportive adult who encourages their explorations. A child's future is at stake and cannot be left to chance—we in the world of libraries must ensure that children find those supportive adults. The primary mission of *Connecting Fathers, Children, and Reading* is to support libraries in their missions to serve families where each member is a literate life-long learner.

ACKNOWLEDGMENTS

Our interest in gender influences on literacy development began with observing our two daughters' differential reactions to our reading aloud and storytelling habits at different ages and stages in their lives. Steven's tendency to get children excited immediately before bedtime vs. Sara's ability to calm and soothe was one of many differing approaches to literacy activities in our house. [Sara eventually prevailed in this more sensible approach to the daily bedtime ritual.]

Both girls had different views on what their parents should be reading to them and how they should be performing. Sara was not permitted to do voices of characters that differed too much from her own while Steven was given carte blanche. Steven was not allowed to read anything too sad or sentimental because of his tendency to get a little too caught up in the emotion.

Our eternal thanks to our daughters Annie Zannetti and Maggie Herb for being such great appreciators of books and stories, and for giving us the original inspiration for this book. And thanks also to Michael Zannetti for being a wonderful modern-day dad. And, to Sylvia Zannetti, we are so proud of your words, pictures, thoughts, and kindnesses.

Some of the original thoughts for this book grew out of our previous jobs as Coordinator of Children's Services for the Dauphin County Library System in Harrisburg (Steven) and Professor of Teacher Education at Shippensburg University and Nursery School Teacher at Rowland School for Young Children in Shippensburg (Sara). To all our former colleagues, we remember fondly the wonderful years we spent together. In particular, thanks to Lisa Murphy of the Children's Literature Council of Pennsylvania, and to the many excellent teachers and professors at Rowland, especially Judy Smith, Cindy Pimental, Charlotte Klein, Darlene Maxwell, Vonnie Rylant, Steve Ludwig, Kent Chrisman, with a special note for Jim Zullinger, a remarkably fatherly teacher. We also want to acknowledge the inspiration of our colleagues Donna Couchenour, Early Childhood Professor at Shippensburg University and the talented librarian Barb Bartels of Rowland School.

Traveling even further back in time, to the multitalented kindergarten teacher Rebecca Nelson, thanks for "My Hero," a fitting title for an excellent piece from our very own heroine. Rebecca was our nursery school student at the Precision Positive Preschool at Penn State's College of Health and Human Development 25 years ago.

At Penn State University, thanks to the University Library administrators Sally Kalin, Laurie Probst, Katie Clark, Bonnie MacEwan, and Dean Nancy Eaton; to Steven's supportive faculty colleagues in the Education and Behavioral Sciences Library—Rosemary Heffner, Justina Osa, and Carol Wright; and to the EBSL staff who have helped track down information over the years we worked on this book—Betty Arnold, Elaine Hannon, Pat Hermann, Eloise Ingram, Chuck Maurer, David Newbury, Barb Riegel, Harlan Ritchey, Sue Watson, and as always, most especially to the self-titled fearless leader of that wonderful group, Jenny Litz, who also served as an able reader of the manuscript. Thanks also to Jen Spence of the Pennsylvania Center for the Book for her terrific support on so many fronts, to Karen Schwentner of the Pennsylvania Center for the Book for her Web support, and to Tracy Weaver of First Book of Central Pennsylvania.

Special acknowledgment also goes to Diane Gingerich, who was instrumental in the early work on the massive children's book bibliographies. To the multitalented undergraduate teaching/research assistants Kara Robertson and Bethany Walk, thank you for your excellent past, present, and future work, with a special note of thanks to Kara for serving as a reader of the manuscript and for fact checking book and Web information; and to Bethany, whose work on Chapter 7 was critical to its successful completion. The patience award for this book goes to Charles Harmon of Neal Schuman—thanks Charles, for everything.

To our editor, Virginia Mathews, you always make our work so much better, but we wish we could meet your expectations more precisely because of our tremendous admiration for who you are in the world of literacy and most especially, for what you have done to transform that world.

Finally, we owe a huge debt of gratitude to Sally Driscoll, Reference Librarian and Instruction Coordinator at the Robert E. Eiche Library at Penn State Altoona for her extensive work on the children's book bibliographies in Chapter 7. Thanks very much Sally, it could not have been done without you.

As always, shared credit to all who are named above for any help our book delivers, but omissions and errors belong to us.

Sara Willoughby-Herb
Steven Herb

1 UNDERSTANDING THE LINK BETWEEN FATHERS AND LEARNING

In her book *Community Child Health*, Dr. Judith Palfrey notes that although the adult/child ratio in the United States has almost doubled during the last century (from 1.64 to 3.54 adults per child), children are not necessarily benefiting. Fewer children than ever before are growing up in two-parent families (58%); this number alone doesn't tell the whole story, as many of these children might not be enjoying the potential benefits of a two-parent family. As many as 16% of children growing up in two-parent families are actually living in reconstituted families, and they may or may not have a close relationship with both parents. In other two-parent homes, long commutes to work can create conditions more like those in single-parent homes (Palfrey, 1994). Surely, large numbers of children are not involved in regular, nurturing relationships with significant adult males in their environments.

In families in which parents are divorced, there is a far greater and predictable lessening of fathers' influence in children's lives (Weissbourd, 1996). This begins with the divorce itself; in 90% of cases, mothers are given custody of the children. From that moment on, "only one sixth of all children will see their fathers as often as once a week after a divorce, and close to one half will not see them at all. Several years after a divorce, fathers will be entirely absent from the lives of almost two thirds of these children" (Weissbourd, 1996:53).

It seems clear that whether we look at statistics on divorce or just examine the conditions of today's families, many children in our country are spending little time in the presence of and interacting with their fathers. As we join with other concerned professionals in focusing our services on preventing or remediating such situations, we can inform and inspire our program planning by examining what can be gained by children and their fathers when there is greater interaction between them.

MUTUAL CONTRIBUTIONS OF GOOD FATHERING

INVOLVEMENT WITH FATHERS BENEFITS CHILDREN

Research studies of children from one- and two-parent families have long substantiated the relationship between fathers' positive involvement with their children and the children's accomplishments, particularly in two areas: **socialization** and **achievement**. For this discussion, we refer to *involvement* as Ross Parke discussed it in his book *Fatherhood* (1996), characterized as a father taking responsibility for his children, being available to them, and interacting with them.

Children's Social Development

Researchers note that as fathers spend more time with their families, they become more attached to their children and more knowledgeable about them (Belsky and Kelly, 1994:254). Children's socialization is enhanced by interactions with these knowledgeable fathers; this is apparent from the first months of life and continues though adulthood (Parke, 1996). Many fathers engage their young children in playful interactions (playing surprise games, swinging baby around, tossing her into the air) that seem to make unique contributions to development. During infancy, while babies gaze for long periods of time at their mothers, they laugh and smile more at their fathers. Babies who have more contact with their fathers adjust better to strangers than do babies who have less contact; perhaps that physical play leads a young infant to be bolder. The positive effects of this kind of early play are still seen into the school years when researchers find that "popular children have fathers who are able to sustain physical play for longer periods and use less directive or coercive tactics" (Parke, 1996:137). Apparently, in playing with these knowledgeable and competent fathers, children learn to regulate their own emotionality and to understand and communicate emotional feelings with others. This important connection with a child's emotionality is seen again in adolescence when fathers, more often than mothers, nurture the youngster's increasing independence. In fact, the lasting effects of positive interactions between children and their fathers were noted in a 26-year follow-up of a child-rearing study, which found that the "most powerful predictor of empathy in adulthood was paternal child-rearing involvement at age five" (Parke, 1996:145-146).

Similarly, we can expect that some children raised without fathers are at risk for socialization problems, although these problems vary across groups of children (Parke, 1996). Problems are more pronounced among white than black children, and among boys more than girls. Observations in school settings indicate that boys from father-absent homes are more liable to be disobedient and unpopular, to have friends who are deviant, and to be sad and depressed. Girls from father-absent homes are more likely to have trouble getting along with peers, to cheat and lie, and to have difficulty in paying attention. In her book *The Trouble with Boys* (1994), Angela Phillips agrees that sons seem particularly vulnerable when raised without fathers. She speculates that perhaps mothers who are divorced find it more difficult to teach their sons about the goodness of being a male. One could conjecture that this would also be true of single mothers who have been deserted by the fathers of their children.

Children's Achievement

In Ross Parke's 1996 review of research studies on achievement, he notes that many children from single-parent homes appear to suffer academically. They are more likely to drop out of high school, to have lower test scores and GPAs, to have poorer attendance, and to have lower expectations concerning college attendance. Parke comments that as with socialization, father presence affects the academic achievement of boys and girls differently. In infancy, boy babies who were raised without their fathers spent less time exploring and examining new objects than those raised with their fathers. Girl babies profit more through the verbal stimulation that accompanies play with the father. In the preschool years, both boys and girls who had an opportunity to play with fathers who were skilled playmates showed evidence of enhanced cognitive development. As children continue through school, a girl's achievement is related to her father's friendliness to both her and her mother, and to his support of his daughter's autonomy and competitiveness. The highest-achieving boys are those with fathers who are nurturant and who can effectively discipline their sons without resorting to hostility.

In Phillips's study of how fathers' involvement affects boys, she notes that boys who have an opportunity to spend an average of two or more hours a day with their fathers are more often high achievers than those who do not. In addition, her studies show that the achievement of boys from working-class families is more adversely affected by father absence than is the achievement of their middle-class peers.

In summary, a father's involvement affects and enhances his children's developmental course. These effects are most apparent

U.S. Department of Education Report Reveals Connection Between Children's Success in School and Fathers' Involvement

An important finding from the 1996 National Household Education Survey conducted by the National Center for Education Statistics (Nord, Brimhall, and West, 1997), is the relationship between children's academic performance and their fathers' involvement in their education. These data were gathered from a sample of nearly 17,000 parents/guardians across a range of racial-ethnic and socioeconomic backgrounds who had children in kindergarten through twelfth grade.

Parent involvement in education was defined as the extent of participation in these four types of activities: attending a general school meeting, attending a regularly scheduled parent-teacher conference, attending a school or class event, and serving as a volunteer at school. Parents involved in three or four of these activities were categorized as highly involved, those attending two were categorized as moderately involved, and those attending one or none were categorized as having low involvement. Father involvement was studied in two-parent (including biological, step, and adoptive fathers) and in father-only families.

Findings regarding two-parent families indicate low levels of father involvement, with nearly half of these children having fathers who participate in one or none of the school activities yearly. Apparently in these families, the division of labor assigns school involvement primarily to mothers. While mother involvement in these families is strongly related to children's school success and adjustment, the addition of a highly involved father does matter, and increases the likelihood of success. Children whose fathers are highly involved in their education are more likely to get mostly As, to enjoy school, and to participate in extracurricular activities, and they are less likely to repeat a grade or to be expelled from school.

The typical single father is far more involved (nearly as involved as mothers from two-parent families) in his children's education as compared to fathers in two-parent families. However, differences between high involvement and low involvement of fathers in these father-only families are even more dramatic than differences seen in two-parent families. Students with highly involved fathers are nearly twice as likely to get mostly As as compared to their peers whose fathers have low involvement. Particularly noteworthy is the finding that among sixth through twelfth graders, those adolescents whose fathers are highly involved in their schooling are significantly less likely to be suspended or expelled from school.

Findings about highly involved fathers from both groups depict these men as being involved with their children in activities outside of their schooling as well. These activities include visiting a library, museum, or historical site—activities that also increase the likelihood of their children's school success.

Conclusions drawn by the researchers include the importance of making these findings known to families, and targeting father involvement as a way to enhance children's likelihood of academic success.

WHAT IS A FATHER?

The Herr Research Center at Erikson Institute is seeking a fuller understanding of what father care means in low-income, culturally diverse communities. The ultimate goal is to develop ways to help fathers remain anchored to their children and generative throughout their lives. When Professor Aisha Ray was asked if there are aspects of fathering and father involvement itself that are not being researched but should be, she replied, "Yes, many. I think one important issue is the definition of 'father.' When we look at fathering in America, we have to determine if we are discussing biological or surrogate fathers. One of the terms that researchers use to describe men who are not the biological father, but who have taken on the generative role of caring for kids, is 'social father.' And in all communities, including low-income communities, these men play an important role. So in looking at involvement, we must pay attention to the father's relationship status with the child" (Ray, 2000: 5).

in the areas of achievement and socialization. Differential effects are seen between boys and girls, across racial groups, and across socioeconomic groups. These data regarding the powerful effects a father's involvement can have on a child's achievement and socialization focus on the group but overlook the individual. Data can never substitute for the powerful memories of parents evoked in a grown-up child. One of our mothers has now reached the remarkable age of 94, and her memory of short-term events has all but disappeared. She forgets our visits less than an hour after they have occurred and doesn't remember what she had for lunch, or if she even ate lunch, just 30 minutes after her last bite. But she remembers listening to the World Series with her dad every October like it was yesterday. She remembers poems she was taught by her mother—poems from 85 years ago that she can recite without error. The effects of parents on how we behave, how we handle ourselves, and how we view the world are powerful and forever. Data will never fully measure what we've lost when we don't have that chance to form those memories, to make those permanent connections.

Many of the factors that make up successful achievement behavior are taught by both moms and dads and are critical in all forms of learning. How we persist in the face of challenges most often comes from our parents. How much self-control we have when faced with frustration is a powerful weapon in all sorts of learning throughout our lives. How long do we stay mad at some slight? How quickly do we apologize for whatever part we played in a transgression toward a family member? How long do we hold grudges? Are we able to be happy when alone? Are we able to find joy in words and stories and solving problems? Most of who we are comes from our parents. Much of our emotional strength, language play, and cognitive tendencies come from our early childhood experiences with our parents. A father's involvement in a child's life has profound long-term benefits for the child.

INVOLVEMENT WITH CHILDREN BENEFITS FATHERS

Successful experiences in fathering have positive effects on men as well as on their children. As with children, these effects differ from one man to another: effects of fathering on men vary across cultures and with younger and older fathers. In spite of these variations, however, there are similarities in the contributions fathering makes to men's lives (Parke, 1996). Of note are three particular areas of men's development that are enhanced by successful fathering experiences: emotional support and growth, maturing of direction/purpose in life, and increased feelings of generativity.

Fathers' Emotional Support and Growth

The emotional aspects of successful family life are often an important resource for fathers, as a sense of community and close affiliation grows scarce in the world of work. Studies of fathering today reveal that many men are indeed becoming more engaged with their children emotionally. Fathers report that nurturance and goal-setting are important aspects of their involvement with their children, that they take extra responsibilities in dealing with their children's problem behaviors, that they even view the playful leisure time spent with children as being of great importance to them (Parke and Stearns, 1993).

In her study of how society "teaches" boys to be men, Angela Phillips states that for men who are fortunate enough to have wives who stand back and allow them to explore the parenting of a baby, this can be the beginning of an emotional relationship unlike any other they have experienced: "For some men, an intimate relationship with a baby may be the turning point, the moment at which barriers start to come down. However, it is a moment that, for many men, won't arrive unless their partners have the courage to make a space in which it can happen" (1994:162).

Fathers' Sense of Maturing Purpose in Life

Emotional engagement with one's children and a father's own (increasing) maturity go hand in hand as men learn to father their children. Certainly, goal setting for one's children is based on the belief in one's own competence to nurture those goals. Research in this area indicates that fathers can be as competent as mothers in the many important areas of child rearing; even in infancy, fathers are capable of skillfully reading and reacting to baby's cues

CHANGING LEVELS OF INVOLVEMENT OF NONCUSTODIAL FATHERS
The National Center for Education Statistics report Fathers' Involvement in Their Children's Schools (Nord, Brimhall, and West, 1997), includes positive findings about children's opportunities for interaction with their noncustodial fathers. In 1996, these children were more likely to have contact with their fathers than were children of fifteen years ago. While only 31% of these fathers had any school involvement at all, their involvement had positive academic effects, especially for children from grades six through twelve.

(Parke and Stearns, 1993:159). In studying how marriages are affected by children, Jay Belsky and John Kelly observed that although it seems to take fathers longer than mothers to develop a strong attachment to their children, fathers do become "swept away" by their babies. In becoming more attached, fathers spend more time with their babies, learn more about them, and begin to feel more mature and grown-up themselves (1994:48).

The maturity and direction that fathering brings to the lives of many men is noticeable as a loss in the lives of some divorced and separated fathers. Phillips reported that fathers who lost contact with their children after divorce expressed feelings of their own unimportance as far as their children were concerned (1994:164). When Judith Wallerstein and Sandra Blakeslee (1989) interviewed parents ten years after their divorces, they noted that many younger divorced men appeared to be still adrift years later and had not easily moved into the more mature adult roles associated with being a husband and father.

Fathers' Feelings about Generativity

Ross Parke defines generativity in terms of a person caring about and engaging in activities that will improve the outlook for future generations; he believes that the enhancement of generativity is one of the most significant effects fatherhood has on men (1996:15-16). Research supports Parke's contention. In their studies of families who were strengthened by parenthood, Belsky and Kelly noted that babies can create a "new sense of family" and that children often bring people closer to their own parents, creating feelings of generational continuity (1994:48). Correspondingly, Wallerstein and Blakeslee (1989) noted this as a real loss among the divorced fathers they interviewed. These fathers felt that their own generational continuity was diminished as they lost contact with their children.

Considering these many ways in which involvement in fathering benefits men as well as their children, it seems appropriate to support programs that strengthen positive fathering. Such programs are bound to foster growth that is interactive and mutually beneficial, and that has positive effects on the whole family.

LIBRARIES, LITERACY, AND FATHERING

Public and school libraries have long endeavored to involve parents in their children's literacy learning; an emphasis on fathers is merely an extension of a well-explored path. Yet it is important to consider why this collaborative triad among libraries, parents, and children is especially useful in engaging fathers in their children's lives. We will discuss what we consider to be three important aspects of such a partnership.

First, reading aloud as an activity seems a good **prescription for developing fathers' new roles.** The very image of children and parents reading together conjures a relaxed, quiet activity, one that is indeed a break from the hectic routine of many families' daily lives. Dr. Judith Palfrey's experiences in child health care led her to conclude that families who are constantly "on the go" can negatively impact their children's development. Fatigue is more likely in these families, and little quiet relaxed time is spent together (1994:13). For fathers specifically, storybook reading provides an opportunity to develop a less traditional way of relating to one's child. As stories are read and discussed, fathers will become involved in their children's and their own sensitive and empathic responses. These are the kinds of experiences that Ross Parke contends modern men need to develop as they interact with their children (1996:68), and the kinds of experiences that build an attachment to one's child that Belsky and Kelly (1994) identified as a step toward becoming a more knowledgeable parent. Through these kinds of interactions, parents build intimate relationships with their children, relationships grounded in real knowledge of one another's feelings, thoughts, and behaviors.

We want to emphasize that it is the nature of literacy experiences themselves that provide this empathic link to others, a link that is not necessarily an important part of typical father-child interactions. Both Parke (1996:62) and Phillips (1994:176-177) note that even when fathers *are* involved with their children, their typical mode of interaction is more often physical and playful rather than verbal. In fact, many commonly reported father-child activities, such as fishing, playing with computers, and watching television, require very little conversation at all. Linking fathers to their children's literacy experiences, then, would broaden traditional father-child relationships in ways more akin to the newer roles required for today's fathering.

Second, literacy activities—especially reading aloud—can be viewed as an excellent **resource for fathers and fathers-to-be** as they search for guidance in defining their own ideas about fathering. A friend of ours who teaches a freshman composition course at our local college recently asked her students to write an essay about how they believe that their lives might be different from those of their parents. Although short on specifics, the overwhelming majority of her students, both male and female, wrote that they intended to spend more time with their children than their parents had with them.

Certainly, characters and incidents in stories help all readers define parameters and specific ideas about who we might want to be and how we might hope to behave as we travel through life. Young men are indeed searching for this kind of information. In his report *Today's Children: Creating a Future for a Generation in Crisis*, David Hamburg writes about adolescent parents, reminding us how unfortunate it is that adolescents' role models are largely chosen from the media or their peers. He urges us to consider that "one of the most important things we can do for adolescents is give them a clearer view of constructive adult roles and what it means to be a respected adult" (1994:183). Of course, the best role models are persons with whom we have close relationships, but images from literature can support and provide alternatives to our personal experiences. For example, the reading of a story in which a father is able to repress his own feelings of frustration to cheer up his child provides a fine example to emulate for both the young boy listener and the young man reader.

We can't assume, however, that just any random selection of fine children's literature will provide appropriate male role models (Stewig, 1988; Kortenhaus and Demarest, 1993). Later in this text we will discuss some characteristics to look for when choosing books to influence fathering, and we will recommend some specific titles. Well-chosen books can be excellent resources for males who are defining who they want to become in the lives of their children. Books are a readily available, portable, and relatively inexpensive resource as well.

Finally, the **library is an ideal community partner in supporting parenting.** Researchers and child advocates who are concerned with improving the welfare of children in the United States recognize that community-wide efforts must be made. It is not enough to focus intervention within any one type of agency, such as public schools or social welfare organizations. While researchers recommend the creation of family support centers within communities (Carnegie Corporation, 1994; Weissbourd, 1996), they also note the diversity of today's communities, and that throughout any given day, families interact with a number of community agencies and representatives.

In *Starting Points: Meeting the Needs of Our Youngest Chil-

ARE FATHERS' CONTRIBUTIONS TO CHILDREN'S DEVELOPMENT UNIQUELY MALE?

This is clearly not true in single-parent families with respect to children's educational achievement. In the National Center for Education Statistics report Fathers' Involvement in Their Children's Schools (Nord, Brimhall, and West, 1997), researchers examined both father-only and mother-only families. They found that in both of these situations, parental level of involvement is similar to that of mothers in two-parent families. Indeed, the parenting behaviors of single mothers and single fathers are more similar than not.

Papalia and Olds suggest that we need to study the effects of children having two parents or caring adults with whom they regularly interact: "The very fact that a child's two parents have two different personalities—no matter what these personalities are—influences development in unknown ways" (1996:283). Our research leads us to hypothesize that in many cases, a second concerned and caring adult could provide some of the interactions that research identifies as unique to the father's role.

---

dren, the Carnegie Corporation's task force states that "the problems facing our youngest children and their families cannot be solved entirely through governmental programs and business initiatives." Rather, we must mobilize whole communities to support children and families (1994:9). The task force's call to action includes four recommendations that the authors say are vital for improving our children's welfare. Two of these recommendations fit easily into our linking of fathers, literacy, and libraries: (1) promoting responsible parenthood and (2) mobilizing communities to support young children and their families. Our focus on fathering as a particular instance of promoting responsible parenting reflects the literature on fathering today in which "fathers are increasingly viewed as appropriate targets of institutional assistance. This type of institutional backing is necessary in light of the fact that fathers may need disproportionate support to maximize their potential for involvement" (Parke and Stearns, 1993:168).

Historically, libraries have served the diverse needs of children and their families. Today more than ever, public and school libraries are collaborating with a wide array of agencies in order to support the families they serve. Among their many national, state, and community partnerships are collaborations with Head Start, pediatricians, child care providers, public schools, museums, performance groups, businesses, service clubs, youth groups, and health care agencies. Certainly "America's librarians are ready to take—in some cases already are taking—a vital role in prevention and intervention with the families of young children" (Mathews, 1996:7).

We envision libraries supporting fathering, particularly through activities such as choosing and highlighting literature that is especially appropriate for fathers to share with their children; acquiring and promoting resource material related to fathering; encouraging read-aloud programs that involve fathers and other male role models in the community; encouraging fathers and other male role models to assist in children's literacy learning programs; and making certain that young males are exposed to literature that includes appropriate male role models. We will describe these and other programming ideas in more detail in later chapters.

2 RECOGNIZING DIVERSITY IN FATHERHOOD TODAY

The second half of the last century brought about many changes in our society. Among the more radical of these are the changes in family life. The long-standing historical roles of mothers and fathers within families continue to change from generation to generation as more mothers go to work, children are enrolled in group child care programs, fathers and mothers share their once separate family roles, and divorce and single parenthood are more common. Many of these changes can cause stress for parents and children alike as parents struggle to define their new roles and develop skills in performing them. In their study *The Transition to Parenthood*, Belsky and Kelly comment on the "quiet heroism of everyday parenting," noting that society gives very little support or acknowledgment for the selflessness required in becoming a good parent (1994:23). In this chapter we consider some of the diverse situations faced by today's fathers and, after doing so, draw implications about the kinds of understanding and support we might offer them so that they can better succeed in the new challenges of everyday fatherhood.

NEW ROLES IN FATHERING

In today's families, in which there are more single parents and more instances of both parents working, fathers are necessarily expected to be far more involved with their children. This involvement often includes responsibilities that men did not take on a generation ago, such as delivering children to baby-sitters, bathing and tucking them in at night, attending parent-school conferences, guiding social development, and assisting with homework. Many of today's fathers are the first men in their own families to be performing these new roles, and are often doing so without benefit of models or support. While it is important to point out that even fatherless men are often good fathers (Phillips, 1994), we recognize that many fathers experience stress because they are shaping a new kind of parenting with little guidance from their own families and from our culture.

Understanding the nature and challenges of these new fathering roles will help us as we plan to include fathers in our family programs. We are focusing on four of these new roles, and have chosen them because they represent fathering tasks that are both common and critical. We don't mean to imply that these are the only four important roles that fathers play in the lives of their children. We hope and trust that those people making a strong commitment to working with fathers will discover many other roles to support and promote in their libraries and communities.

FATHERS SUPPORTING MOTHERS

Research on fathering indicates that one important way in which fathers can positively influence their children is actually an indirect relationship, and involves their being supportive of mothers (Silber, 1989). That is, when a father helps out with household chores, when he is complimentary of his children's mother, and when he expresses approval of her parenting, the mother actually becomes more effective in her parenting. It is easy to understand how this indirect effect works. The father who, upon returning from work, takes over the care of the new baby for the next few hours is probably ensuring that a more rested, relaxed, and competent mother will feed and get the baby ready for bed that evening. However, society's or a particular family's expectations about the division of roles between parents might be incompatible with such a practice.

Being a good father in today's world involves being a good husband, and often being radically different from one's own father. In a study of 48 working-class fathers, researchers attempted to investigate whether early caregiving by fathers had a positive influence on children. Indeed it did, as they found that early caregiving by fathers enhanced their children's cognitive abilities by one year of age (Nugent, 1991). In addition, the research findings revealed interesting characteristics of these fathers who readily took care of their young children: they were also men who were younger and happily married, and had adjusted their own work schedules after the baby was born so that they could share domestic chores with their wives.

One can see the critical importance of this supportive role beginning as soon as a couple knows they are expecting; therefore, our efforts to reach out to fathers should reasonably begin with these new and newly expecting fathers, and it should include information about the positive effects of this supportive role of fathers within the marriage.

FATHERS AND NURTURING

As we pointed out in the first chapter, playful interactions with a father can provide important contributions to children's learning, but fatherhood today involves fully shared parenting and

Is Violence a Necessary Part of Maleness?

Statistics linking violent acts with males can be found nearly everywhere. In their report on violence and America's children, the Children's Defense Fund (1995) noted the results of a survey in which 40% of students in inner-city schools reported that one of their male relatives carries a gun. This same report cites data from the U.S. Department of Health and Human Services regarding firearms deaths: "Since the mid-1980s young Black males have suffered an epidemic increase in firearm deaths." In a recent newspaper article concerning the high rate of infant deaths being linked to teenaged mothers (Story, 1999), it was reported that these early deaths often come from violent behavior such as being shaken or thrown by a male caretaker (not necessarily the father). Some theories of child development even link the increased aggression that we see among male adolescents to biological patterns shared with other animals (Cole and Cole, 1996:626). Watching the television news in the last several years has shown us all that any public gathering place—a church, the mall, a fast-food restaurant, and even one's own school or workplace—can become a horrific scene of violence largely enacted by gun-toting males.

In her book—Boys Will Be Boys: Breaking the Link Between Masculinity and Violence, Myriam Miedzian writes that while it is true that boys are more aggressive and violent than girls from the earliest years, there is no biological evidence that this is a necessary outcome for boys (1991:72-74). Her research led her to conclude that the typical male biology (higher levels of testosterone and lower levels of the inhibitor seratonin) may be related to a higher frequency of behaviors such as impatience, impulsiveness, and irritability, and that these behaviors are likely rewarded in young males from an early age. In addition, research in child development identifies specific experiences related to high levels of aggression in children: being an unpopular or rejected child, spending large amounts of time in a negative environment, and living in violence-plagued neighborhoods (Seifert and Hoffnung, 1997:416).

Preventing Violence in Males

Miedzian (1991) and others (Gilbert and Gilbert, 1998; Kantrowitz and Kalb, 1998) make suggestions for mitigating violent behaviors in males. Among these are continued nurturance of males, building their self-esteem, deliberately constructing opportunities for males to succeed at the things in which they excel, and teaching them alternatives to aggression. It comes as no surprise to those of us who work in this field that many of their recommendations are easily tied to **literacy learning**:

- providing experiences in which boys are able to receive and give cooperation, comfort, and empathy,
- small group activities in which boys and girls share their experiences and interpretations of those experiences,
- listening activities, and
- engaging boys in literacy experiences that allow them to broaden their experiences and understandings (Gilbert and Gilbert, 1998:218-221).

demands more than these typical playful interactions. Fathers are expected to spend more time with their families and to have broader expertise in interacting with their children. This expertise necessarily includes nurturing children and creating and engaging in sensitive and empathic relations with children. Teaching children, introducing them to society's mores, and disciplining them in positive ways—all challenging tasks for any parent—can be especially difficult for some fathers. As we saw in the last chapter, research suggests that fathers should be more involved in nurturing their children's development because children do benefit from these activities.

Yet for most fathers there still exists a strong pull from the legacy of traditional fathering: good fathers were thought to be physically and emotionally strong, dependable problem solvers, good providers and protectors. Their care for the family was important, but not as tied to personal interactions as to connections between the family and the larger community. This legacy ignores the role of father as nurturer, and likely creates conflicts, especially for fathers whose own childhoods provided little or no opportunity for learning how fathers help raise their children. Isn't a father who is successful at his work, in spite of long hours away from his family, being a good father? In her book *The Trouble with Boys* (1994), Angela Phillips reminds us that even men who were taught to nurture may have had to suppress it as they stepped into and thrived in their workplaces. The tensions many men experience between expectations at work and their fathering certainly make it more difficult for them to take on added responsibilities with their children. In many ways, data reflect this work-family conflict; for example, only 2% of men who are eligible to take paternity leave do so (Biller and Trotter, 1994:12–13).

Ronald Levant, a psychologist who directs the Boston-based Fatherhood Project, notes that many of today's men have not been taught to nurture through their boyhood socialization as many girls have. Many boys never had to baby-sit or to cook, let alone be sensitive to others' feelings (Biller and Trotter, 1994:12-13). Learning to nurture one's children—guiding and interacting with them on a regular and personal level—appears to be a difficult and fragile task for many fathers, and one that we can attempt to support through family involvement programs.

FATHERS AND DAUGHTERS

A third new role in fathering is that of taking on increased parental responsibilities in raising one's daughters. Historical divisions in family tasks typically prescribed that fathers took responsibil-

ON FATHERS AND DAUGHTERS, FROM REVIVING OPHELIA: SAVING THE SELVES OF ADOLESCENT GIRLS

Fathers also have a great power to do harm. If they act as socializing agents for the culture, they can crush their daughters' spirits. Rigid fathers limit their daughters' dreams and destroy their self-confidence. Sexist fathers teach their daughters that their value lies in pleasing men. Sexist jokes, misogynistic cracks and negative attitudes about assertive women hurt girls. Sexist fathers teach their daughters to relinquish power and control to men. In their own relations with women they model a power differential between the sexes. Some fathers, in their eagerness to have their daughters accepted by the culture, encourage their daughters to be attractive or lose weight. They produce daughters who believe their only value is their physical attractiveness to men. These fathers undervalue intelligence in women and teach their daughters to undervalue it too.

On the other hand, nonsexist fathers can be tremendously helpful in teaching their daughters healthy rebellion. They can encourage daughters to protect themselves and even to fight back. They can encourage their daughters' androgyny, particularly in sports and academics. They can teach daughters skills, such as how to change tires, throw a baseball or build a patio. They can help them understand the male point of view and the forces that act on men in this culture.

The best fathers confront their own lookism and sexism. Fathers can model good male-female relationships and respect for women in a wide variety of roles. Fathers can fight narrow definitions of their daughters' worth and support their wholeness. They can teach their daughters that it's okay to be smart, bold, and independent.
(Pipher, 1994:117-118)

ity for their sons' behaviors while mothers were responsible for their daughters' development. However, fathers are now expected to help raise and provide guidance for their daughters as well as their sons (Parke and Stearns, 1993). This is especially the case in today's smaller families and, of course, in situations in which fathers are the sole custodial parent.

In spite of this expectation, most men still pay more attention to their sons than to their daughters. In fact, many men report having particular problems in effectively dealing with their daughters, especially daughters whose temperaments are difficult (Parke, 1996). Most fathers today have not grown up in a home where strong father-daughter interactions were modeled, and even among a father's own friends there might not be good models for fathering daughters. Hope Edelman (*Motherless Daughters: The Legacy of Loss,* 1994) has written a thoughtful and useful book about the special case of fathers raising their daughters alone, with empathy for both daughter and father. We can assist fathers in carrying out this new role by highlighting helpful resources as well as providing supportive opportunities for father-daughter interaction.

Yikes, That's My Boy

Once I was the proud father of two daughters. When guys I knew became fathers of girls, I welcomed them to the Dads of Daughters Club.

When they duplicated the feat, I congratulated them on joining the Double Dads of Daughters Club.

Then we let out that we had a third kid coming. After two girls, everyone assumed, I must really want a boy. The lone male in a houseful of females becomes a figure of fun, someone who will never get near a bathroom or a telephone.

An old gold miner I knew in California stood ready to impugn my masculinity if I became the father of three daughters. "You know," he said to me with narrowed eye and cocked head, "it takes a man to make a boy."

My dad, meanwhile, was big on the family-name preservation aspect of having a boy—you know, the archaic notion that women become Mrs. John Q. Husband, so it's up to the male child to keep the family name in play for another generation. With two older sisters and no male cousins, I was our Anglicized last name's last hope.

From what I've heard, my dad greeted my birth the way Mufasa greets the arrival of Simba in The Lion King—you know, the mountaintop, the offering up, the beam of light from the heavens. My sisters think my parents spoiled me rotten.

The idea of replicating my own family structure was not without appeal. Raising a boy with two older sisters would be like watching myself grow up.

Mostly, though, I championed girls. With two sisters and two daughters, I was used to girls. I liked what a guy I knew had to say about being the father of five daughters: "Little girls always love their daddies."

I thought of how few public meltdowns my girls had had, and how good they were at sitting still in theaters and on car trips. "Girls are great," I declared. "I've been around little boys. They're monsters."

At a playground with my daughter once, I felt like I was watching the whole history of the human race. The boys charged up the slides and jumped up and down on the swinging bridge, yelling and shoving all the while. The girls organized a tea party in the shade of the climbing structure.

Many of us boomer parents were surprised by such manifestations of "la difference." We thought it was all sexist socialization. We vowed to play trucks with girls and dolls with boys. I pitched to one of my daughters once. She batted with a pink purse dangling from her forearm. Then she got bored.

We don't get it: How can truck love be hardwired?

Ultimately, I took the 10-fingers, 10-toes position: Boy, girl—just give us a healthy baby. And lo, it came to pass that we had a son. He was your basic baby, at first. Now, though, at age 3, he's behaving in ways that give the Y-chromosome a bad name:

- Give him any two objects—socks, chopsticks, washcloths, potatoes—and he will make them fight to the death, with sound effects.
- Tell him to find something to do so you can make dinner and he'll pinball into the kitchen

---

Yikes, That's My Boy (continued)

---

walls and appliances, pratfalling spectacularly, with sound effects.
- Tell him he can't have candy before dinner and he'll call you a poopy butt.
- Serve him a meal and he will not sit, will not eat, will not keep his hands to himself, will not allow anyone to talk and will not stop banging.

In short, he's "all boy"—loud, violent and gross.
My older daughter thinks we spoil him rotten. My wife says, "He's going to outgrow this, right?"
Of course, I say. Look at me.
They look. With alarm.
(Frank, 1998)

DEALING WITH CHILDREN'S DISABILITIES AND DIFFICULTIES

The final new role we consider here is that of the father's involvement in helping raise a child with behavior or learning problems. Parents of children with special needs have many more responsibilities and concerns than do parents of normally developing children. However, a typical prescription for children with learning and behavior problems is *more* interaction with their families. Parents are usually included as "teachers" in the educational plans for their children, and are expected to help in many ways: by providing extra practice of skills learned at school, by helping carry out programs for rewarding or punishing children's various behaviors, and by helping to keep careful records of their children's behaviors. In addition, these parents must be prepared to be advocates for their children, often needing to make important educational decisions with little or no support.

Depending on a family's resources and problem-solving expertise, many of these demands can be daunting, and often take a toll on parental relationships. Mothers of disabled children note that their child preoccupies their lives in ways that they believe children's fathers do not experience (Bower and Wright, 1986). Fathers of children who have disabilities describe feeling ignored by school or social service personnel and getting information about their children in a "secondhand" manner from their wives (Smith and Luckasson, 1995:388). Providing guidance and assistance for young parents facing these kinds of stressors will do much to improve the developmental outcomes of their children as well as to strengthen the family.

One kind of guidance that seems important for these particular fathers is helping them discover new ways of engaging their children in play. Playtime with parents—often recommended by educators—can be very therapeutic, especially for younger children. As we discussed earlier, playfulness is a common attribute of father-child interactions among families in the United States. The kind of play typically prescribed for children with disabilities, however, is not the traditional fun-loving play that many fathers excel at, but rather play that involves closely observing and judiciously responding to children's behaviors. For example, parents might be asked to make certain that their child takes turns, or that the parents model play behaviors similar to that of the child's school friends. Fathers report that this "serious" play often reduces their enjoyment of playing and weakens their motivation to engage in regular play with their children (Parke and Stearns, 1993). In addition to learning new ways of playing, these fathers often need to learn new ways of disciplining their children. Children with learning and behavior problems often require much more patience, consistency, and positive interactions than do other children. As we stated earlier in discussing fathers and nurturance, these kinds of interactions are not part of the role modeling experienced by most of today's fathers.

DIVERSITY AMONG TODAY'S FATHERS

Concurrent with the increased expectations regarding fathering roles is a more diverse population of fathers, many of whom are not dwelling within the traditional two-parent, one-income family and most of whom have no real role model for their own unique fathering circumstances. Consider the numerous special populations of fathers today whose particular situations we will need to be sensitive to as we examine the new father roles and develop father involvement programs: expectant fathers, new fathers, stepfathers, fathers of reconstituted families, fathers of children with special educational needs, custodial and noncustodial divorced fathers, fathers who travel or are at work a great deal of the time, older fathers, teen fathers, custodial and noncustodial grandfathers, and incarcerated fathers. In addition, there are many men who are attempting to fill in for absent fathers. These men might work as volunteers in a variety of programs in schools, libraries, or other community agencies, or they may simply be caring and involved relatives, friends, or neighbors.

WHAT ABOUT THE CASE OF ABUSIVE FATHERING?

More than a million new cases of child abuse and neglect are reported yearly (Seifert and Hoffnung, 1997:329). In her discussion of trusting men to care for children, Miedzian notes that men are more associated with violent crimes than are women, and that nearly all cases of sexual child abuse are committed by men (1991:102-114). Although she cites several research studies showing a relationship between child abuse and fathers not participating in the early care and nurturance of their children, Miedzian cautions us that men who are very reluctant to get involved in caring for their children might fear their own inadequacy and might, in fact, be more likely to be abusive.

As we work on programs to involve fathers in their children's literacy learning, we need to be alert to fathers who are not well suited to these activities. Further, we need to be certain that our programming efforts don't leave out children whose fathers are not present or truly not competent enough to participate.

Whatever the particular circumstances of all these fathers and acting fathers, it is likely that most of the men are uniquely shaped by those circumstances; we cannot assume that the same kinds of programs or interactions will be appropriate for or benefit all of them. By examining the particular needs of some of these fathers, we can sensitize our understanding of how we can support the diverse fathering situations within our community programs.

DIVORCED FATHERS

We begin with this large group of fathers and recognize that there are, of course, great differences among these men. They might be single fathers, custodial fathers, fathers having joint custody, visiting fathers, highly involved fathers, or fathers who have little interaction with their children. Whatever their particular situations, the time right after divorce is a critical one and a time during which we ought to try to reach fathers. When fathers who are divorced lose a sense of their link to their children, they no longer see their children as a vehicle of their own generational continuity and then have less motivation to feed their relationship together (Wallerstein and Blakeslee, 1989). If one no longer sees future relationships as being critical, it becomes much more difficult to attach importance to relationships in the present.

Supporting a father's efforts in parenting at that time might be one way to prevent the very common retreat of fathers right after divorce. This retreat from their children's lives is not a predictable one, as it often occurs even in families in which the father has been close to his children and has spent large amounts of time with them. According to research by Biller and Trotter, what is most predictable is the discontinuity between father-child relationships after a divorce (1994:122). These researchers advise men that father absence is not a necessary result of divorce, and they must work especially hard to stay close to their children and to be a real partner in raising them.

A father's success as a partner in child rearing after divorce is enhanced when parents are able to prepare children for the divorce and when they are committed to supporting their children's need to love and admire both their parents. Ross Parke's 1996 research on how fathers influence their daughters' achievement demonstrates the importance of the father's respect for and friendliness toward her mother. Biller and Trotter advise fathers to "be careful how you talk about your children's mother . . . it can be very damaging for them to believe that either their mother or father is inadequate or worthless'" (1994:212).

Navigating through the complications of maintaining good parenting while divorcing is surely frustrating and often happens in the absence of any clear guidance. Any efforts we can make to educate fathers about these issues and to help them learn how to be effective parents after divorce will surely help confront the common feelings of just wanting to escape from the family (Phillips, 1994). In their study of how divorce affects families, Wallerstein and Blakeslee note that divorce is the "only major family crisis in which social supports fall away"; even grandparents are often afraid to get involved, and friends often urge divorced persons to get a new start with a better spouse (1989:7).

Even when these first steps are successful, life as a divorced parent rarely is easy. In Wallerstein and Blakeslee's 1989 study, divorce was nearly always followed by a reduced ability to care for children, to support them, to discipline and even play with them. Divorced parents have to redefine their own and their children's roles, develop new schedules perhaps now based on two households, and guide and support children's learning in a stable and dependable way even though opportunities for interaction with children are decreased. Learning these new ways of managing parenthood takes time, and the learning is most often trial-and-error as these fathers are once again exploring roles that were probably not part of their experiences while growing up. Ten years after divorce, Wallerstein and Blakeslee found many younger fathers still feeling "adrift" and a number of older fathers beginning to "lean on" their children (1989:27).

Naturally, children of divorce present their own difficulties, requiring great sensitivity from parents and making the everyday tasks of parenting yet more challenging and often stressful. In *The Kids' Book About Single-Parent Families*, Dolmetsch and Shih (1985) offer guidance for the many new problems these children face, among which are learning to get along with a parent whose behavior is different because of new responsibilities; adjusting to a parent dating; forming or keeping a close relationship with a parent one doesn't live with; the need to form closer relationships with other adults such as grandparents; sharing holidays; and not living with a same-sex parent. These challenges are not temporary either, but change and recur throughout a child's life. For example, when children of a divorce consider marriage, they see themselves as taking a real risk (Wallerstein and Blakeslee, 1989:297). The problems these children face are often magnified by society's expectations that children can adjust to their family's changes on their own, or that their difficulties are similar to the ones their parents experienced and, therefore, if their parents are adjusting, the children should be doing so also. Ten years after their parents' divorce, while many of the children became competent, happily adjusted adults, almost half of them were worried, underachievers, self-deprecating, or angry young adults (Wallerstein and Blakeslee, 1989).

Clearly, divorce has a pervasive influence on children. Children of divorce see themselves as survivors of a tragedy, and they actually expect their own children to be affected by it (Wallerstein and Blakeslee, 1989). We saw a striking example of how such effects might occur in one of our adult students who, during a class activity, was unable to remember anything about playing during his childhood, because "all I can remember about my early childhood is that my parents got divorced." An important conclusion for us is that supporting a father's parenting efforts necessarily includes guidance in understanding and dealing with the kinds of difficulties his children are experiencing.

STEPFATHERS AND FATHERING IN RECONSTITUTED FAMILIES

These fathers, of course, experience many of the situations described in the previous section, but reconstituted families have their own characteristics. Biller and Trotter report that almost five million children live with a mother and a stepfather, and that another million live with their father and a stepmother (1994:212-213). Life in these families can bring added problems as family members learn to form new relationships and live within a stepfamily. Although adults would like to believe that "what is good for adults will be good for their children," this is not always so (Wallerstein and Blakeslee, 1989:10). Researchers note that children in these families have more behavior problems, especially during the first years of the new marriage. Resentment and jealousy of the new parent are to be expected. Patience, understanding, and flexibility are daily requirements of stepfathers (Biller and Trotter, 1994:213-217).

Reconstituted families comprise 16% of the 58% of U.S. families with two parents (Palfrey, 1994). Accordingly, many of the fathers we work with are trying to parent two sets of children, all with individual needs and problems, and probably most with particular needs created by the divorce. Stepparenting is never automatically successful; it takes time to build relationships with stepchildren, just as it takes time to build a relationship with a newborn infant. As we work with stepfathers, our patience and understanding of the time and effort required of them will help nourish their interactions with their reconstituted families.

ADOLESCENT FATHERS

Although the rate of teenage pregnancy is slowing in the United States, it still is a major factor for consideration because our country has one of the highest rates of teen pregnancy among all the developed nations (Cole and Cole, 1996). Typical hardships that accompany teen parenting include needing to drop out of school to work and/or care for the child, poverty, changes in one's social and family life, less planning and preparation for parenthood, and a lack of time for transitioning into adulthood. In addition, the absence of a good father in their own lives is a frequent and difficult situation for many adolescent fathers. Yet many adolescents and their children do survive these difficulties and become strong families. In *Today's Children* (1994), David Hamburg suggests we not focus on the pessimism of statistics (that two thirds of all out-of-wedlock births are to adolescent parents), but rather we remember that a crucial task of adolescence is to do something worthwhile. Helping adolescents become good fathers would capitalize on this natural motive.

Many child care programs have been ineffective in getting fathers, especially young fathers, involved in their children's lives. The programs tend to focus on mothers and children, and it is easy to see why: the mothers are often the custodial parent. But it is important for all child-focused programs to examine their policies, programs, and attitudes toward fathers. Are they being invited and welcomed? Are special efforts being made to reach out to these men whose own lives would be positively transformed by becoming involved in their children's lives? The value to their children is immeasurable.

SINGLE FATHERS

Within this category are widowers, single men who are caring for or have adopted children, and divorced custodial fathers. Cer-

---

SINGLE-FATHER HOMES ON THE RISE

A recent summary of 2000 census data reports:

- In 2.2 million households, fathers raise their children without a mother. That's about one household in 45.
- The number of single-father households rose 62% in 10 years.
- The portion of the country's total 105.5 million households that were headed by single fathers with children living there doubled in a decade, to 2%.

"Thomas Coleman, executive director of the American Association for Single People, attributed the rise in single dads to a variety of reasons, including more judges awarding custody to fathers in divorce cases and more women choosing their jobs over family life" (Armas, 2001).

The article points out that single dads need just as much help as single moms, but may be less likely to seek help.

---

tainly the last group is the most common, as many more divorced fathers are now being awarded custody of their children.

Although research demonstrates that men are as competent as women at parenting, there are some concerns that many single fathers have. One of these relates to raising daughters; many in the larger culture see raising a same-sex child as easier. Biller and Trotter report, however, that the gender match with their children is not at all the most important aspect for successful single fatherhood. Rather, the two most critical tasks of fathers' parenting are that they are able to communicate well with their children and that they can create a home life that provides structure and security for their children (1994:204-205).

These tasks might sound difficult for a custodial father, but in fact, these men have a good track record for involvement in their children's learning. A positive finding about single fathers was reported in the Department of Education's Father Involvement in Schools project (Nord, Brimhall, and West, 1997): "Children living with single fathers or with single mothers are about equally likely to have parents who are highly involved in their schools— 46% and 49%, respectively. Both fathers and mothers who head single-parent families have levels of involvement in their children's schools that are quite similar to mothers in two-parent families and are much higher than fathers in two-parent families." This is surely a busy and motivated group of fathers who are likely to be very cooperative participants in our programming efforts.

GRANDFATHERS

For a growing number of grandparents, surrogate parenting has replaced or been added to the traditional roles of grandparenting. Rothenberg (1996) summarized the statistics on this recent phenomenon in a paper for public school personnel: 5.4% of children under 18 years of age live in their grandparents' homes, and in slightly more than half of these homes, neither of the child's parents is present. The importance of grandfathers in children's lives, whether or not they are custodial grandparents, is celebrated by Dawn Thurston in an article for *Mature Outlook* magazine. She notes four important roles (crony/friend, male role model, model for aging, and keeper of the past) that today's grandfathers can play and cites successful personal stories of men who exemplify those roles (Thurston, 1999).

For those grandfathers who have been obligated by the responsibilities of a second family, however, there can sometimes be great stress. Rothenberg (1996) notes some of these stressors and suggests approaches for those of us who are working with grandparents as parents. Strong emotions are a nearly necessary component of this situation. Grandparents feel a mix of appreciation for the opportunity to become close to their grandchildren, with resentment and anger over their increased responsibilities. Grandchildren experience strong emotions as well, often feeling abandoned, fearing instability in their lives, and finding visits from parents unsettling as often as they find them supportive. Rothenberg's suggestions for supporting grandparents include helping them connect to available services (particularly new services that have come into existence since their days of parenting), extending them a genuine welcome as our setting is likely different from the place they remember from the past, offering support groups and grandparenting classes, using inclusive language ("dear family" vs. "dear parents") at events and in correspondence, and going out of one's way to find out and use the names the children call their grandparents.

CONCLUSIONS

In summary, we recommend planning activities for father involvement that are supportive of the four important new roles of fathering and are sensitive to the diverse situations of fathers in our society today. Three broad strategies for those of us who work in literacy programs are discussed below.

BOOK SELECTION

We can take note of these new fathering roles as we examine new books for acquisition, story times, and "marketing/promotion," being particularly aware of portrayals of fathers who support their wives, fathers who are nurturant, fathers who are successful both at work and at home, and fathers interacting enjoyably and successfully with their daughters and their children with special needs. For example, when choosing stories in which fathers are caregivers, it is important to be certain that these are not all fathers who are out of work or choose not to work. We want to provide a balanced collection that also supports these fathering roles and allows every child, every dad, and every mom to find situations in children's books that look familiar and those that look new and interesting. We can look for stories that portray grandfather-child relationships, children's relationships with visiting fathers, and so on. When we ensure that such books find their way to today's fathers as well as to the young children who will be tomorrow's parents, we are truly supporting fathering in our communities and positively affecting the welfare of our children.

REACHING OUT TO FATHERS AND TARGETING PARTICULAR GROUPS OF FATHERS

Our support of these new roles is likely to be most effective if we are able to reach out to fathers, welcoming them and making them feel that their involvement in children's learning is important. In beginning these efforts, we should consider targeting new and expectant fathers in particular. By making contact with any parent at this time, we are more likely to be successful; their enthusiasm for being good parents is usually at its peak, and fathers and mothers are setting personal parenting goals.

In addition to targeting these new fathers, we need to remember the importance of timeliness in working with other groups of fathers. For example, making connections to recently divorced fathers might help keep them connected to their children. Our involvement with grandfathers who have recently taken on custodial roles will provide support for their attempts to learn fathering roles that most likely are quite different from those they practiced with their first family. In addition to being sensitive to their particular situations, we might consider offering programs that target these groups and connecting them with available services. Our efforts should have the added outcome of helping these "re-newed" parents feel less isolated.

My Hero

"Ms. Rebecca," says Emory as his hands hover about my kneecaps, "can I dress up?"

"Of course," I say.

We walk together to the big green box of dress-up clothes and begin to paw through the articles, feeling the different fabrics between our fingers. Emory, as usual, has trouble choosing. No, he doesn't want the blue coat. He shakes his golden head when I hold up the space suit. His nose wrinkles in disdain when I ask if he would like to be a chef.

"Who do you feel like being today?" I ask him.

"Mmmm . . . maybe the Real Robin," he answers, his eyebrows raised.

"What will you need for that do you think?" I wonder.

"You know . . . one of those thingys that goes on your back and your shoulders . . . a flying thingy."

"Oh! A cape?"

"Right!"

He is excited now. I shuffle through the clothes again and find what is actually a red apron, but no one has used it as an apron ever. It is always a superhero cape. I tie it, this flying thingy, around Emory's shoulders. He smiles in this quiet contented way he has, as if he hears music inside. Almost gently, he flies out of the room. I can hear him chanting, "The Real Robin . . ."

When he swoops back to me, I ask him about "the Real Robin." What does the Real Robin do? In typical adult fashion, I am assuming that the Real Robin is the sidekick to Batman. He's a superhero, right?

Emory says, "I really can't talk right now, Ms. Rebecca. I need to get home to my nest of baby eggs."

Oh. Rebecca, you fool . . . the Real Robin is "real" because he is a real bird. He's not flying around fighting villains and saving the city. No, no. The Real Robin is a bird with a family. He flies not because he has some terrific magic power, but because he is a bird; the cape serves as Emory's wings.

I watch Emory crouch down on the tile floor of the kitchen and begin to talk to a collection of pink cotton puffballs that we use as counters for a piece of math work. His hands hover over the puffballs, patting them. I don't want to disturb him by moving any closer, so I cannot detect the words of his crooning, but I have a feeling that puffballs are not actually puffballs at all; they are his baby eggs. Oh, this fatherly bird, the Real Robin, is better than any superhero I have ever seen. Now, I can hear him singing, cradling a puffball in his palm and gazing at it with the most parental of love. My sweet Emory, you are so right; some of the best superheroes are daddies.

—Rebecca Nelson, 1997

PROVIDING ROLE MODELS AND OPPORTUNITIES FOR LEARNING

Finally, we recommend considering the library and its programs as opportunities for children and families to observe and practice these new fathering roles. Clearly, our supportive involvement of fathers in their children's literacy development (reading and discussing stories, for example) would make them feel both competent and nurturant. Among the many opportunities we can provide are hiring nurturant males as professionals and volunteers in our settings, providing follow-up story time activities that involve children in role-playing these new father roles, and encouraging fathers' participation across a broad range of literacy programs.

3 SELECTING BOOKS THAT REFLECT GOOD FATHERING

One of the most important things we can do to support good fathers and help those who might need fathering suggestions is to call attention to and circulate fine children's books that also happen to contain examples of competent and caring fathers. The models that these books provide are useful for fathers, mothers, and children.

ROLE MODELS

MODELS NEEDED FOR FATHERS

While we have discussed father roles and the needs of today's fathers at length in the previous chapters, we note here an important finding about how today's successful fathers develop their own new approaches. Research indicates that many of these men construct their styles of fathering by gathering ideas from a variety of sources rather than by imitating one particular father that they know (Daly, 1993). These men report that they take note of interactions and techniques used by other fathers, and elect to try out ones that seem to fit their particular situations. Certainly, storybook fathers could provide unique learning opportunities for these men. For example, a father might decide to add a bit of humor to his children's bedtime routines after noticing the children's enjoyment of the father's antics in *Daddy Makes the Best Spaghetti* by Anna Grossnickle Hines (1986). Fathers' tendencies to gather good advice from what they see rather than what they are told provides a good match with much of the research on literacy learning, especially emergent literacy.

MODELS NEEDED FOR CHILDREN

Children, too, learn much about roles and expectations for fathers and mothers from their storybooks. When hearing a version of *Cinderella* (Delamare, 1993) in which the author explained that Cinderella's father was a merchant and out to sea most of the time, faces brightened and children around the circle remarked

Literacy Learning through Social Interaction

In our research paper Preschool Education through Public Libraries (Herb and Willoughby-Herb, 2001), sponsored by the U.S. Department of Education in a national study, Assessment of the Role of School and Public Libraries in Support of Educational Reform, we examined many learning theories and studies about literacy learning in order to inform literacy advocates in schools, libraries, child care settings, and homes about the best ways of constructing literacy environments and learning opportunities.

We discovered that important social interactions are at the heart of most literacy learning, which is facilitated when children have the following:

- Opportunities to participate in literacy activities that are guided and paced by a more skillful member of the child's social-cultural world (Vygotsky, 1978; Bruner, 1983).
- Opportunities for learning that enable the child to be an active participant, regardless of the modality (listening, looking, speaking) being used (Bruner, 1983).
- Opportunities for intimate learning; that is, learning with support from someone who knows the child well enough to make appropriate judgments about when and what the next learning steps should be (Bruner, 1983). An emphasis on parents as first teachers is certainly supported by this aspect of Bruner's theory.
- Opportunities to acquire positive literacy attitudes by interacting with and observing models who will be most influential for individual learners, especially those models who share similar characteristics with the learner, and whom the learner respects and admires (Bandura, 1977). The importance of acquiring a positive "literacy attitude" is amply demonstrated in much of the emergent literacy literature (Morrow, 1993:132-133).
- Opportunities for support for learning that reside not just in their families and schools, but also across a range of cultural contexts that directly and indirectly influence children's development (Bronfenbrenner, 1979).

While developmental and learning theories offer broad guidelines for evaluating and planning literacy programs, additional research findings about specific, effective practices could also serve to guide librarians designing programs. There is a large body of research addressing the topic of effective techniques in support of early literacy development. These practices are derived from literature reviews and from more than one study; practices that seem possible to adapt to librarians working with children, families, and caregivers; and practices that are related to the roles that librarians can reasonably serve.

Some research findings regarding children's books follow:

- Children's early experiences with children's books are among the most significant correlates with their success in learning to read in school. Specific aspects of these books, such as the interest level for children and ease of understanding and remembering the story, make the experience even more effective (Mason and Kerr, 1992; Morrow, 1993).
- Children are more motivated to request being read to, and to "read" or explore on their own, books with which they are already familiar or have heard or read before and have enjoyed (Brock and Dodd, 1994; Dickinson et al., 1992; Herb, 1987; Schickedanz, 1993).

Literacy Learning through Social Interaction (continued)

- There is a positive relationship between how much children have been read to and how well they will read (Lancy, 1994; Scarborough, Dobrich, and Hager, 1991; Wells, 1985).
- Storybook reading is a more effective influence on literacy development when children have opportunities to engage in conversation about the story (Mason and Kerr, 1992; Norman-Jackson, 1982; Pellegrini and Galda, 1994).
- Children also benefit from the opportunity to interact with on-the-spot literacy events in their everyday lives, such as watching for the McDonald's sign along the highway, finding a correct page in a catalog, or looking at one's own name on an envelope or name tag (Taylor and Strickland, 1989; Teale, 1995).
- Literacy is enhanced when adults join in with children's pretend or symbolic play; for example, playing restaurant or playing school (Norman-Jackson, 1982; Pellegrini and Galda, 1994).

FANNY'S DREAM

Fanny's Dream is a very special book about the relationship between a mother and a father. Caralyn Buehner's character Fanny Agnes thinks she is destined for her town's version of a royal ball as she awaits her fairy godmother one summer night. When her magical benefactress doesn't show, she marries Heber, a farmer who always remembers the dream she gave up for him. He tries to treat her like a princess at least once a day, but most of the time the loving pair share in all their parental and farming responsibilities. It is a picture book filled with humor and devotional love that is an especially noteworthy version of the classic Cinderella tale (Buehner, 1996).

---

with comments such as, "So *that's* why her Daddy didn't help her," "He would be so sad for Cinderella," and "He didn't know that stepmother was so mean." Obviously, Cinderella's ineffectual father in previous versions of the story had troubled these children. Young as they were, their thoughts about this story *did* include thinking about the father's role. Delamare's telling relieved their concerns and confirmed their beliefs that daddies are supposed to protect their children.

Storybooks can have a powerful influence on children's behaviors as well as their thoughts, providing them with scripts and actions for their daily role-play and with important images and aspirations for their future families. We have often observed the very direct influences of storybook fathers. Two examples from a group of nursery school children over recent years are illustrative:

- A four-year-old boy, dressing a baby doll in the housekeeping area, was very careful to gently pull the shirtsleeves over each of the doll's fingers one at a time. When his teacher stopped to watch him, he said proudly, "Teacher, aren't I being a good daddy?" The class had just read a storybook about new babies, *Twinnies* (Bunting, 1997), and had talked about the fact that in this family both the mother and father take care of the babies.

- Another four-year-old boy, a beginning and labored writer, joyfully wrapped up several presents for his doll baby's first birthday and wrote the baby's name on each gift. This play happened after reading *A Gift from Papá Diego* (Sáenz, 1998), in which a mother and father were both getting ready for their child's birthday.

As writer/educator Carol Bly has eloquently written, the uses of story are many and powerful. Stories expand our horizons by giving us the experience of *other*; they present the ideal case, show us how to despise evil, teach us courtesy and playfulness, and identify the fine feelings we have (Bly, 1991:2-4). Storybooks teach us ways of behaving and give us choices. The best ones do it without ever telling us they are teaching us; the stories go straight from our heads to our hearts.

A final point about children learning father roles from storybooks is related to concerns that some of us have about children who do not have fathers, whose fathers are away much of the time, or who have less than adequate fathers. At one time we also wondered about those children's feelings when meeting fun-loving, caring, very present fathers in literature. Would those children feel sad or angry, or would they tune out the story? We began by reading father books carefully in the presence of these children, trying to read their reactions sensitively. We found no cases of negative reactions, and instead, what appeared to be a great interest in storybook fathers. In fact, the two boys described above both lived in homes lacking a warm and caring father. We have concluded that it is children such as these who especially need the lessons about good fathering that storybooks provide. They are interested and ready to learn; it is up to us to provide them with opportunities. Our belief seems to be shared by author Mary Hoffman, who describes the storybook character Grace (*Boundless Grace*, 1995; reviewed later in this chapter) as "particularly interested in [stories] about fathers—because she didn't have one" (Hoffman, 1995:unpaged).

MODELS NEEDED FOR MOTHERS

Lastly, we consider it important that mothers and young girls be exposed to models of active and caring fathers. Research regarding the often separate parenting roles of mothers and fathers indicates that many mothers act as a "gatekeeper" between fathers and their children. That is, mothers decide when, how often, and in what capacity fathers should be involved with their children. Beitel and Parke (1998) found that a mother's attitude about her partner's competence influences how involved he will be in his young children's lives. We have seen evidence of this gatekeeper role during the sociodramatic play of preschoolers, when girls chase boys out of the kitchen or away from the sleeping doll babies.

Of course, observant and involved teachers talk with children and enforce equitable standards for play. But in support of the teachers' efforts, we have also seen the effects of a reading of *Daddy Makes the Best Spaghetti* (Hines, 1986). This book empowers boys to *insist* that they be allowed to cook and to help get the doll babies ready for bed. It also empowers the girls to insist that the boys be caring in their treatment of the "babies." And when a teacher ends the story with mention of using some of its ideas during playtime, children are even more likely to model some of its portrayals of parent roles.

The mother-as-gatekeeper role usually becomes even more pronounced when parents are divorced. Because divorce often strengthens mother-child closeness and weakens ties to fathers, a storybook such as *As the Crow Flies* (Winthrop, 1998) informs mothers that there can be closeness between children and their fathers even in a distant relationship. In addition, it shows mothers that a relationship like this can be important for a child's sense of well-being. For many divorced mothers, storybooks of this kind might be their only exposure to situations in which both parents seem to be most focused on the welfare of the child. This ideal situation presented in story can be a motivator for mothers, as surely as it can urge children and their fathers to imagine that there are other and better ways to handle divorce in a family.

THE FAR-REACHING EFFECTS OF CHILDREN'S LITERATURE

Researchers who have examined the presence and roles of fathers in popular children's books caution us not to expect to find fathers or positive father portrayals in just any random sampling of books (Otstott, 1984; Stewig, 1988; Parke and Brott, 1999). In their book *Throwaway Dads*, Parke and Brott write at length about the preponderance of storybooks in which the portrayal of fathers is stereotypical (e.g., father is authority figure, nonnurturant, rarely present) or simply negative (e.g., the bumbling or useless dad). These kinds of portrayals send an un-

One of the funniest picture books of the last two decades is Piggybook by Anthony Browne (1986). The very stereotypical behavior of the father and the two sons parked on their rears and calling for their supper was sure to draw laughs from our audiences of mostly women. When Mrs. Piggott temporarily departs and the three chauvinists are transformed into actual pigs, the story becomes even funnier as the boys and dad get what they have coming. We were rewarded for reading it at workshop after workshop by nodding, smiling wives and mothers, mostly as an example of how picture books can sometimes be better suited for adults than children. And one day a father came up after the workshop and asked us if there were better examples of fathering than that in picture books. It gave us one more example of how no single book is the solution to every problem and no single story should be counted on to represent the world. It helped remind us that everyone should be able to find themselves in children's books. Perhaps Piggybook is the right story to get a knowing laugh from a mom who handles far more than her fair share of domestic chores, but there are many others that portray sharing, helpful dads as well. It is the obligation of the library to provide that wider worldview, to provide literary models for all the citizens of the community.

fortunate message to the fathers who read them: that "men as fathers are peripheral players on the parenting stage" (1999:203). Parke and Brott's concern is especially directed toward young children who hear these stories, because child development specialists agree that children acquire stereotypes early. We can assume that children add to their understanding of cultural expectations from reading and listening to storybooks. On the positive side, however, these authors summarize what young children could learn about parenting roles if their literary experiences included books with more positive father portrayals: "Boys must come to understand that to be an active, involved, loving, nurturing father is a viable and important life choice, one that a man should be able to make without having to sacrifice his career or his self-respect. And girls must come to understand that a father's role in the family is as valuable as a mother's, and that it is one they, as future wives and mothers, can benefit from enormously" (Parke and Brott, 1999:83).

ENHANCING THE EFFECTIVENESS OF MODELING

Learning by way of imitating a model has been studied extensively by social learning theorists (Bandura, 1989; Miller, 1993). We will not review this research here, but merely report some of the findings that relate to our objective of encouraging children and their fathers to imitate desirable behaviors demonstrated by storybook characters. We have reframed these findings in a library/literacy context. The likelihood of the reader imitating the behaviors of a storybook character are enhanced when:

- the storybook character is rewarded for those behaviors (e.g., when the dad in story is able to resolve a problem),
- the reader perceives some similarities between the character and him/herself (e.g., a young boy is likely to imitate a character close in age),
- the reader has reason to respect the character (biographies of famous dads are useful for this),
- someone points out or talks with the reader about specific aspects of the behaviors being modeled, or
- the opportunity to experience the storybook model is followed by an opportunity to practice the behaviors.

Of course *each* of these conditions can't always and needn't always be present for successful modeling to take place; after all, we can't (and wouldn't want to) control content in storybooks. However, we can control the last two items on the list much of the time. In fact, we have suggested some ideas for *verbalizing* (talking about, writing about) and *practicing* the positive fathering behaviors in many of the books in the selected reviews that follow. Note particularly those in the Dramatizing and Story Starters sections.

GUIDELINES FOR BOOK SELECTION

Our suggestions for choosing books that portray fathering are based on both our research and experiences in our own communities; we expect that you will want to adapt or add to these based on your experiences with the families you serve. For the book lists at the end of this chapter, we have tried to focus on books that are easily obtained. The book lists in Chapter 7 contain some books that are out of print, but they are likely to be found in libraries. We begin by recommending the following broad considerations as you select father-relevant books for your collections:

1. Look for books that **characterize fathers as nurturant**. Craig Heller (1994) defines nurturant as expressing affection, being involved in day-to-day care of children, and playing with children. We broaden this to include fathers who are involved in positive disciplining of their children, who teach their children, or who engage in behaviors that exemplify their emotional connections to their children.

2. Look for books in which a **father's involvement results in a positive impact** on the family or on the story's outcome; for example, he helps solve a personal problem or he supports the mother's efforts in mothering.

3. Look for books that portray **fathers as being successful both at work and at home.**

4. Within your collection, try to achieve a **balance of books that portray fathers actively engaged with their daughters as well as with their sons.**

5. Choose books that **portray diverse fathering situations** (divorced fathers, single fathers, stepfathers, grandfather caregivers, various working fathers) **and diverse fathers** (variety of races, cultures, ages). Remember that we are more likely to imitate persons who are in some aspects like us; we want to find storybook dads who resemble the dads we serve.

6. Choose some books that **portray other nurturant males,** such as teachers or relatives who are contributing to children's lives. Nurturant brothers and uncles are especially appropriate models for young boys learning about their role expectancies.

7. **Be aware that among the small number of books in which fathers are featured, a larger than realistic percentage of them may portray fathers who have problems** (fathers who are out of work, who are alcoholics, who are abusive, and so on). It is very important for libraries to own quality literature that deals with such problems honestly, but it could also skew the collection away from positive fathering images. That doesn't mean libraries should avoid those types of books, but it does mean libraries should carefully select books that represent the positive side of fathering as well.

8. Be certain you have included books that are purely entertaining or fun; after all, **fathering isn't all seriousness.**

9. Choose some books that **portray dads who are traditional, yet grappling with newer roles and values.** These will provide a readily identifiable model for many of today's fathers.

10. Finally, look for **books that portray fathers benefiting from fathering**: a grandfather enjoying sharing reminiscences with his children or grandchildren, or a father being cheered up or encouraged in important choices by his children.

STORYBOOKS WITH POSITIVE FATHER IMAGES

In the annotated book selections that follow, we describe the books and their stories, and we mention attributes based on the aforementioned guidelines. The books are organized into five groups based on potential uses.

The first and largest group could be considered a starter collection of books that depict a variety of successful fathers, the importance of fathers in children's lives, and fathers who enjoy and care about children. These would be ideal acquisitions for elementary school and public libraries. The next two groups focus on books that more easily lead to activities involving creative dramatics and story writing. We consider it important to point these out because of the relevance of these two activities in helping children and adults to learn from the role models in the stories.

Next, we include a group of books that might be useful for a fathering group, to inspire discussion, storytelling, and thinking about the impact of fathering. Our last group, a counselor's collection, includes books that might be shared with one child or family for a specific purpose. They address difficult subjects, and some are fairly didactic in their approach. It is important to remember, however, that not every problem or tough situation in life can be solved through the sharing of a book on that topic. Sometimes the last thing a family may need is a reminder of the troubles they are facing at home, while another might feel absolute relief that they are not alone in the world. We provide this section in acknowledgment of the broad and varied needs of every library's unique community.

GENERAL COLLECTION THAT PORTRAYS DIVERSITY IN FATHERING/FATHERS

Nonfiction Books

Hands. Lois Ehlert. 1997. New York: Harcourt Brace.
A great interactive and durable book for toddlers and preschoolers, this colorful volume includes depictions of things "my father" and "my mother" do with their hands. The parents' roles lean in traditional directions, but it is clear that they share responsibilities. A good choice for lap reads, story times, or a unit on "My Family."

Lots of Dads. Shelley Rotner and Sheila Kelly. Photographs by Shelley Rotner. 1997. New York: Dial.

A photographed collection of dads who represent a variety of races and cultures, but who are engaged in similar kinds of activities with their children: lifting, helping, working, and playing. This would be a great lap book for children at home or at school. It would also be an interesting book to peruse a bit before or after reading a storybook in which a father is a main character. It would certainly stimulate conversation about the dads children know as well as their ideas about what dads do.

Big and Little. Margaret Miller. 1998. New York: Greenwillow.

This concept book about contrasting, descriptive adjectives is illustrated with clear, attractive family photographs. Illustrations include both mothers and fathers with children, boys and girls in traditional and nontraditional activities, and racial diversity. A bonus is the size and simplicity of the print; beginning readers will soon learn to read the large words on each page. Finally, we bet that the photos accompanying "Big boy, little boy. Read to me" will make any young boy long for a baby brother to read to!

Single Fathers

I Live with Daddy. Judith Vigna. 1997. Morton Grove, Ill.: Albert Whitman.

This father-daughter story about a girl who lives with her daddy includes some of the stresses of single parenting that both parents and children experience. The girl's mother has promised to go to a Writer's Day at her daughter's school, but doesn't get there in time because of unexpected events at work. The girl is, of course, very disappointed. We see her father comfort her without criticizing her mother, "Maybe she had to work . . . She loves you very much." The story is a bit didactic, but would likely be of great interest to a child and father in a similar situation. This book would also be useful for a discussion starter, maybe for school counselors working with children who need support because of divorce, or for high school classes learning about marriage and family life.

The Father Who Had 10 Children. Benedicte Guettier. 1999. New York: Dial.

This rollicking story is vividly illustrated with scenes from the daily life of this very busy dad. This is a great example of fathering not being *all* seriousness! This book offers a humorous and exaggerated portrayal of the trials any single parent of ten children might experience—for example, children running wild as their father tries to dress them—but the story also highlights that nearly universal feeling of missing one's children even while being given a needed respite from them. Night after night this father has been building himself a boat and planning to sail around the world. His mother comes to take care of the children, but by the second day this guy is so lonely for his family that he sails back to get his children. Parents will find this entertaining; children will find it comforting as well.

You and Me, Little Bear. Martin Waddell. Illustrated by Barbara Firth. 1996. Cambridge, Mass.: Candlewick.
A sweet book about a day in the life of Little Bear and his father. The focus of this book is not that this is a single father, but rather that a father and son's life together can be special even in its "ordinariness." The events depicted include Little Bear helping his father with chores, Little Bear playing while his daddy finishes working, his tired daddy accidentally falling asleep, and daddy waking up and having fun playing with Little Bear. Father Bear is definitely a capable parent who enjoys his role. This story and its illustrations convey a warm, comfortable, and caring family even though it is just "you and me, Little Bear."

Children Visiting Fathers

Priscilla Twice. Judith Caseley. 1995. New York: Greenwillow.
Priscilla drew herself twice in a picture of her family, on one side with her mother and on the other with her father, because "they both need me." In this well-told story, we are introduced to Priscilla's parents as they are getting divorced. We see the difficulties Priscilla faces (and solves) as she learns to spend alternating weeks with each parent. The illustrations are bright and interesting; they include Priscilla's own drawings that seem to parallel her feelings about her family life. The story is not didactic, although much can be learned from it. The humor and caring in Priscilla's family make good food for thought.

Fathers Visiting Children

As the Crow Flies. Elizabeth Winthrop. Illustrated by Joan Sardin. 1998. New York: Clarion.
This fine picture book portrays a divorced father who lives seven states away "as the crow flies." A school-aged boy, Michael, is the main character in this story, and his father has come for his yearly visit. As the story unfolds we see this wise and caring father's successful efforts to maintain a supportive, emotional relationship with his son. There is much to be admired about this father:

his ability to make the visit special, yet to incorporate important parts of his son's world and its routines; his sensitivity to Mikey's feelings and his accompanying ability to engage his son in meaningful conversation; and his ability to comfort his son by telling him that their distance apart is really only "two seconds as the heart beats." The book is also filled with depictions of reading: father and son, together and apart.

Fun-Loving Dads

Pete's a Pizza. William Steig. 1998. New York: HarperCollins
This book is full of fun from start to finish, using humor that appeals to children and adults alike. Pete is not in a good mood, so his dad "thinks it might cheer Pete up to be made into a pizza." He proceeds to knead, stretch, and whirl the dough that is Pete, and to sprinkle on toppings (checkers for tomatoes, paper for cheese). When it is time to cut the pizza, the pizza runs away with the pizza maker in pursuit. It is clear that this "pizza-making" dad is quite adept at dealing with a moody child, and enjoys the efforts himself. What a wonderful story time piece! Older parents and grandparents raising their grandchildren will appreciate that the mother and father in this story are definitely middle-aged. And children and parents alike will be tempted to play the pizza game themselves. The spontaneous playfulness of this father would be a good model and discussion starter for a dads' group. Dads might invent their own variations on this activity—our son-in-law's version has our granddaughter being made into a taco and wrapped up in her favorite blanket.

Caregiving Dads

Cowboy Baby. Sue Heap. 1998. Cambridge, Mass.: Candlewick.
The father in this story, "Sheriff Pa," helps cowboy baby pick up his room and get ready for bed. This dad has competently contrived a game to make cleanup time a real success. Each toy retrieved becomes a prop in the ongoing dialog about cowboys out on the range. This father's clever storytelling does the trick; cowboy baby seems to enjoy the whole affair and is asleep when his mother comes by for her goodnight. This is a large format book with bright pictures, and would be a good choice for story hour. It just might provide participating fathers with a good idea.

Down the Road. Alice Schertle. Illustrated by E. B. Lewis. 1995. San Diego: Browndeer Press.
In this story a young girl's father shows empathy and creative parenting when he discovers that Hetty has accidentally broken all the eggs she had been sent to buy for breakfast. When Hetty

doesn't arrive home as expected, her father finds her sitting in a tree. Hetty confesses, and her father immediately realizes how sad and ashamed she is. He says, "I see. And you climbed up into the tree to think it over . . . There's no finer place than an apple tree to think things over." Her father smiles and climbs up beside her; later they convince Hetty's mother to join them. As one might guess, apples soon replace eggs on their breakfast menu. This beautifully painted story offers a fine substitution for scolding or punishing a child who has made a mistake.

Mr. Bear's New Baby. Debi Glori. 1999. New York: Orchard.
The brand-new baby bear is crying and can't get to sleep. Although mother and father bear take turns taking care of the children, baby's dad is working hard to soothe her. He rocks and pats and cuddles and walks her. Children will enjoy perusing the illustrations—the bear household is delightfully child-centered with diapers, toys, baby care guides, and gift cards strewn about. The story line involves neighboring animals bringing items that might quiet baby down, so children easily become involved in guessing what will be brought next and what will "do the trick." This is a great interactive story-time choice, and children are likely to compare ideas about who gets up to quiet babies during the night—mommies or daddies.

Traditional Dads Coping with Changed Values

The Bat Boy and His Violin. Gavin Curtis. Illustrated by E. B. Lewis. 1998. New York: Simon & Schuster.
This beautifully narrated and painted story tells about how a boy and his father resolve their differences concerning the son's career aspirations. The father's hopes for his son are clearly traditional and probably reflect some gender stereotyping, but each tries to understand the other and the story reaches a satisfying resolution. Along the way, we learn about the last days of the Negro Baseball Leagues. The issues and feelings portrayed have a wide application for fathers and sons today.

Big Bushy Mustache. Gary Soto. Illustrated by Joe Cepeda. 1998. New York: Knopf.
In this father and son story, we meet Ricky, a boy who works hard to be like his father and to get his father's attention. His father, however, is most often busy or inaccessible. Ricky volunteers to take a particular part in his school's play about Cinco de Mayo so that he can wear the mustache that looks just like his father's. He loses the mustache, which does get his father's attention, and his father resolves the problem in a way that reflects his

concerns for his son's being responsible and his sensitivity for his son's feelings. An added feature of this story is its use of Spanish words sprinkled throughout the text. Also, most parents reading this book could not help but consider how important it is to pay attention to and really listen to their children.

Blended Families

Mountain Wedding. Faye Gibbons. Illustrated by Ted Rand. 1996. New York: Morrow.
In this fun-filled story, a widow and widower's wedding day is filled with feuding children. Among the many calamities of the day is one so big that it brings all the children together in a unified effort that predicts a future of more cooperation. The story is told from the children's viewpoint, but it also depicts patient, though hassled parents.

We're Growing Together. Candice Ransom. Illustrated by Virginia Wright-Frierson. 1993. New York: Simon & Schuster.
This story is told by one of two sisters whose Mama has remarried. It begins, "I have a new Daddy." The story, set in a rural environment, tells of the natural, unhurried development of a bond between the girl and her stepfather. The stepfather is an excellent model of patience and caring. Because the family's new home is where he grew up, we also see how he and his mother gradually share their family's values and stories. This story creates a memorable picture of how the cultivation of human relationships is similar to the cultivation of nature.

Multicultural Fathers

A Gift From Papá Diego/Un Regalo de Papá Diego. Benjamin Sáenz. Illustrated by Geronimo Garcia. 1998. El Paso: Cinco Puntos Press.
A young bilingual boy lives with his family in El Paso, Texas. His birthday is near, and his grandfather, Papá Diego, is coming from Mexico with a special present. The story celebrates the special role of grandfathers in families. The illustrations are done with clay and painted with acrylics. Birthdays and visiting relatives are universal themes, making this story and its lovely illustrations accessible to any child.

Going Home. Eve Bunting. Illustrated by David Diaz. 1996. New York: HarperCollins.
It is Christmastime and Carlos and his family are going to Mexico, where his parents were born. In the story Carlos comes to understand why his parents still consider Mexico their home, even

though they moved to the United States so that their children's lives would be more promising. The father portrayed in this story is clearly an equal partner in parenting, works hard and sacrifices on behalf of his family, cares about the extended family, and is still in love with his wife. The brightly painted pictures and Carlos's narrative description of the trip influence the reader to celebrate this strong and caring family.

So Far from the Sea. Eve Bunting. Illustrated by Chris K. Soentpiet. Boston: Houghton Mifflin.
This father-daughter story depicts a Japanese American family visiting grandfather's grave for the last time before moving to Massachusetts. He was buried at the relocation camp to which he was sent during World War II. Laura and her father experience different feelings about the visit; the differences are resolved as Laura decides what memento she will leave at the gravesite. This story is a good example of a father and daughter discussing feelings, individual perceptions, and resolving differences.

The Longest Wait. Marie Bradby. Illustrated by Peter Catalanotto. 1995. New York: Orchard.
The family in this story is African American, and the time period is probably early in the twentieth century. This story is a clear example of a father who is dedicated and successful both at home and at work. Thomas's daddy is a mailman, and has gone out to deliver the mail during a ferocious snowstorm. Thomas and the rest of the family keep busy, but they are clearly worried. When he finally returns home with stories of the storm, Daddy is tired and has a fever, but upon seeing the concern in his son's eyes, he hugs him and reassures him by talking about playing in the snow the next day. The next day the father watches from his window, smiling as his sons play with their sled. This book would be a good inspiration for telling family stories, such as those about interesting jobs or heroic times.

Grandfathers, Uncles, Big Brothers, and Other Nurturant Males

Alfie and the Birthday Surprise. Shirley Hughes. 1997. New York: Lothrop, Lee & Shepard.
Fans of Shirley Hughes's other Alfie books will enjoy meeting up again with Alfie's neighbors, the McNallys. In this story, Mr. McNally is the focus, and he and Alfie clearly have a close relationship. Mr. McNally's old cat, Smoky, has died. Alfie leads the concern about Mr. McNally's sadness, suggesting they all give him a surprise birthday party. The birthday gift from Mr.

McNally's daughter will be a new kitten, and Alfie has to take care of the kitten for a whole night and day to keep it a surprise. The story ends with the party, where we see Alfie's pleasure in cheering up his friend. This story is also a good example of a young boy being caring and nurturant—with his neighbor, with his sister, and with a rambunctious little kitten.

The Piano Man. Debbi Chocolate. Illustrated by Eric Velasquez. 1998. New York: Walker.
This is a good example of a grandfather's role in passing down family history. The grandfather in this story played the piano for silent films and studied with the likes of Scott Joplin and Jelly Roll Morton. The story could prompt an exploration into the kinds of jobs children's grandparents held.

Beautiful. Susi Gregg Fowler. Illustrated by Jim Fowler. 1998. New York: Greenwillow.
Uncle George, a great gardener, is the focus of this story. He has taught his nephew to garden. After they plant flowers together, Uncle George says that he is ill and must go away for treatment but, "I'll be back when they are ready to bloom." When he returns, Uncle George is very ill and stays to live with the family. When the flowers finally bloom and the nephew brings them to his uncle, their beauty brings a real if temporary happiness to Uncle George and probably an important memory for the boy. This touching story is a sensitive portrayal of the child's feelings about this cherished member of his family.

What Baby Wants. Phyllis Root. Illustrated by Jill Barton. 1998. Cambridge, Mass.: Candlewick.
In this story, brother is the hero. The story begins, "Mama was tired, but baby wouldn't sleep." Enter a string of relatives trying to satisfy baby with outlandish ideas, such as a big sloppy kiss from a cow, and a woolly sheep pushed into the crib to warm the baby. Children at story time will enjoy the exaggerated solutions, and they can easily be led to the reasonable conclusion drawn by baby's brother. After reading the story, use a baby doll to let children take turns acting out how they would get baby to stop crying. Be certain to give boys and girls equal turns and affirmations.

William's Doll. Charlotte Zolotow. Illustrated by William Pène Du Bois. 1972. New York: Harper & Row.
This classic book is available in paperback. Its story is a wonderful argument for boys being allowed to have dolls "so that when he's a father . . . he'll know how to take care of his baby and feed

him and love him . . . so that he can practice being a father." This is a good book for children to check out and share with their families; it is also a good read for those "gatekeeping" little girls who try to chase the boys out of the housekeeping area.

GOOD CHOICES FOR DRAMATIZING

More, More, More Said the Baby. Vera B. Williams. 1990. New York: Greenwillow.
The three love stories within this beautifully painted and told collection will give children lots of ideas about how to play with and talk with (one of the rare books to do this) their baby siblings and their baby dolls. Even though we typically think of this as a book for toddlers, preschoolers also love it. They love remembering being babies and they love playing with babies. After reading the book, talk a bit about which story the children enjoyed best and why. Have some dolls on hand and ask children to take turns acting out one of the caregiver roles from the book. This gives you a chance to affirm some good mommy, daddy, and "grammy" behaviors.

When Daddy Took Us Camping. Julie Brillhart. 1997. Morton Grove, Ill.: Albert Whitman.
This small, simple story portrays a father who appears to be giving his wife some time to devote to the new baby, and perhaps herself, by entertaining his children for the day and an overnight. His children (a boy and a girl) clearly enjoy the entire camping activity, from the preparations and packing to the return home, at which point the reader discovers that the entire camping expedition had taken place in the backyard! We see the father playing with his children and teaching them many things about nature and camping. This storybook will certainly give children (and maybe their mothers too) ideas about planning a similar outing with their own fathers. You might gather some props for role-playing at the library; send home a picture and a note about the story so that children whose parents were not at story time will remember to tell their families about it. A great summer reading program choice, and probably a good idea for parents who aren't really the "camping" type.

Where Did Josie Go? Helen Buckley. Illustrated by Jan Ormerod. 1999. New York: Lothrop Lee & Shepard.
This is a newly illustrated song/story about a family playing games together. Dad joins in and is an important part of the fun. The story line is simple and the illustrations clear and inviting, so children could easily act out parts of this family's play. They will

especially enjoy the end of the story when the family falls into a restful, comfortable, and snuggly pile. Act out some of it at story time and suggest that the children try it again at home.

What Mommies Do Best/What Daddies Do Best. Laura Numeroff. Illustrated by Lynn Munsinger. 1998. New York: Simon & Schuster.

In these back-to-back stories, parenting tasks are portrayed through baby animals pictured with their fathers and mothers. We readily see that many of those are the same tasks that our fathers do: love, care, play, teach. Read both sides during the same sitting. There is no gender bias in these stories. Both mommies and daddies "take care of you when you are sick . . . hold you when you are feeling sad." After the story, you might call on groups of three children to pretend to be babies and parent animals from the story, having both parents take care of the baby. Make up a list of situations for the animal families to act out: puppy returns from being lost, kitten is sleepy, colt has hurt its foot. Praise children's caregiving behaviors, mentioning that both daddies and mommies take care of their children. For a craft after the story, children could make a baby animal and talk about how they will take care of it at home, as you recognize them for being "good daddies and mommies." As a further extension, children could be encouraged to practice these gentle, caregiving roles during their play with miniature animals and during their dramatic play when they pretend to be animals.

See also *Tell Me Something Happy Before I Go to Sleep* (Dunbar, page 49).

GOOD CHOICES FOR STORY STARTERS

When the Big Dog Barks. Munzee Curtis. Illustrated by Susan Avishai. 1997. New York: Greenwillow.

This story is likely to interest children ages three through six or seven. Its simple text and accessible illustrations will draw children into the story of what this little girl's mommy and daddy do to protect her. We see a father who is sensitive, patient, and responsive to his young daughter's emotional needs: "On a stormy night, when thunder comes, Papa holds me." After the story, children could draw pictures of their mommies and daddies calming their fears. Adult helpers could write sentences under the pictures and post them on a bulletin board. The caption "What Daddies and Mommies Do to Help Us" would probably attract the attention of library users and maybe give some ideas to passing fathers.

Tell Me Something Happy Before I Go to Sleep. Joyce Dunbar. Illustrated by Debi Glori. 1998. New York: Harcourt Brace.
Willa the little bunny can't get to sleep, so her older brother, Willoughby, helps her by giving her many happy thoughts to replace her fears. The illustrations are large and lovely, and the bunnies' expressions are charmingly easy to "read." Most children will be able to identify with Willa's problem getting to sleep. Willoughby's solution is also one that many big brothers and sisters could try. As a follow-up to this story, children could make suggestions of happy thoughts to take to bed. Make a list of these to post (make copies if children would like them, sending a note along to their families about the connection to the storybook); encourage children to draw pictures to illustrate the happy thoughts. Children would also enjoy taking turns pretending to be Willa (who tells why she is afraid to go to sleep) and Willoughby (who gives her a couple of happy thoughts to think of instead).

Boundless Grace. Mary Hoffman. Illustrated by Caroline Binch. 1995. New York: Dial.
Fans of Hoffman's *Amazing Grace* (1991) will enjoy this book, and will also find out why there is no father living at Grace's house. Grace's father went back to Africa after her parents split up; there he remarried, began another family, and had little contact with Grace. Grace visits her father for the first time, and although she experiences many stresses along the way, the visit has a happy ending. In this father-daughter story we see the impact a father can have on a child's life even when separated by distance and time. Storytelling, an interest of Grace's, is an accompanying theme. At the beginning of the story, we learn of Grace's particular interest in stories about fathers. Later, in Africa, Grace's father asks if she would like to hear a story "about the papa who loved his little girl so much, he saved up all his money to bring her to visit him." Grace returns home lamenting that there aren't "any stories about families like mine that don't live together," and so she decides to make one herself. Grace's story will be about a family that lives happily ever after, just not all in the same place. This book could easily lead to a writing activity in which children write family stories—their own, those of families they know or have imagined, or their thoughts about an ideal family.

See also David Adler's *The Babe and I* (below).

A SELECTION FOR A DADS' DISCUSSION GROUP

The Babe and I. David Adler. Illustrated by Terry Widener. 1999. San Diego: Harcourt.

This story introduces children to the Depression as well as to the famous baseball player Babe Ruth. The story is narrated by a young boy who sold newspapers to help earn money for his family, and actually sold one to the Babe. But the real story here is of the relationship between the boy and his father. The boy's decision to sell papers was motivated by seeing his father selling apples on the street, although the father had not told his family that he lost his job. The reader's sympathy toward both the son and the father makes us hope that they will eventually talk about the situation, which they do. Toward the end we are told that this is a story about "dad and I both working to get our family through hard times." Fathers will recognize this man's embarrassment over losing his job, and that issue might lead to related discussions: the historical role of father as primarily a breadwinner, boys thinking that they must always be strong, males finding it difficult to talk about emotions. This might also be a good starting point for telling stories about men the participants admire, about families getting through the Depression or other hard times, or about father-son relationships. Older elementary school children might also find this a good story starter book.

Daddy Calls Me Man. Angela Johnson. Illustrated by Rhonda Mitchell. 1997. New York: Orchard.
This delightful book holds four poems about a young boy named Noah. His everyday interactions with his family and the accompanying feelings are beautifully depicted in the large paintings and in well-crafted, spare poetry. The special bond between Noah and his dad is apparent in the first poem, wherein Noah lines up his shoes by his daddy's—"call them all our shoes." But in the last poem we understand the depth of that bond; Noah tells us of the new baby sister that "everybody comes to see." We suspect that he might be jealous, but he still shares his room and toys lovingly with her, "Then Mama calls me sweetheart and Daddy calls me man." Fathers will appreciate this depiction of their traditional role in providing a male model for their sons, but discussion could be extended to the importance of their daughters learning about what makes someone a true "man."

See also *The Bat Boy and His Violin* by Gavin Curtis (page 43), *Down the Road* by Alice Schertle (page 42), *Pete's a Pizza* by William Steig (page 42), *Father's Day Blues* by Irene Small (page 52), *The Summer My Father Was Ten* by Pat Brison (page 69), *The Longest Wait* by Marie Bradby (page 45), *We're Growing Together* by Candice Ransom (page 44).

A SELECTION FOR THE COUNSELING CENTER/ PARENTS' SHELF
Gay Father

Daddy's Roommate. Michael Willhoite. 1990. Boston: Alyson.
A young boy's parents have gotten divorced and his father now lives with his partner, Frank. The cartoonlike drawings and explanations of daily life in their home are simple and clearly didactic: "being gay is just one more kind of love, and love is the best kind of happiness." The message focuses mostly on the relationship between the two men rather than on the son, although the illustrations show him participating in many activities when visiting his dad. While not a perfect story, this book might be useful as a discussion starter for families or children with gay parents. It is one of the few children's books to portray a gay household, so it lets those children see other families like theirs.

Often, as the children's book field conveys relationships or characters for the first time, the books are more didactic than later stories will be. A good example was the huge spike in the publishing of books with disabled characters following the 1975 passage of the Education for All Handicapped Children Act (PL 94-142). It was about a decade later when disabled kids began appearing in stories that were not simply a spotlight on the child's disability. *Daddy's Roommate* is not a story about a family in which there is a gay relationship; rather, the relationship is the focus of the book. As such, the book might not necessarily satisfy a child's need to know whether and how other such families resolve situations associated with having a parent or parents who are gay.

Widowed Father

After Charlotte's Mom Died. Cornelia Spelman. Illustrated by Judith Friedman. 1996. Morton Grove, Ill.: Albert Whitman.
The author of this book is a social worker, and her experiences with children and families are evident in the messages presented here. Charlotte is a school-aged child who has just lost her mother. Her father is sad, busy, and emotionally distant. When Charlotte has a problem at school, it brings her feelings to her father's attention, after which they participate in counseling. This book is more instruction than story, but any parent or child reading it would easily see the importance of sharing feelings, getting support from family and professionals, and understanding that healing takes time.

Father and Child Separated through Divorce

Father's Day Blues: What Do You Do About Father's Day When All You Have Are Mothers? Irene Small. 1995. Ann Arbor, Mich.: Borders Press.

Cheryl struggles with writing an essay about Father's Day because her father doesn't live with her anymore. This frustration leads her to wonder about her own worth, thinking that not having a father makes her life not as complete. Through conversations with her mother, and through writing her essay, she resolves these issues. We see her gradual realization that she is special and unique, and that "your father is your father all the days of your life."

Good-Bye, Daddy! Brigitte Weninger. Illustrated by Alan Marks. 1995. New York: North-South Books.

Tom is both sad and angry about having less time to spend with his father now that his parents are divorced. On a day when he is even too upset to say good-bye to his father at the end of a visit, his mother tells him a story (through his teddy bear) about a bear child who had a similar problem. The story bear's mother uses sympathy and explanation to calm her child and to suggest saying good-bye next time, and it helps Tom feel better too. This book might be helpful for children in similar situations, and for mothers and fathers coping with children's feelings about visiting.

Adoption

Let's Talk About Adoption. Fred Rogers. Photographs by Jim Judkis. 1994. New York: Putnam & Grosset.

Although fathers are not the focus of this book, we include it here because the photographs include a diversity of nurturant adoptive fathers who are wonderfully involved in family activities. The book focuses on helping children feel secure about their adoptive families, allowing that they might want to learn about their own situations, and suggesting ways for them to express their own feelings. The words are gentle and inviting rather than directing, just as Mr. Rogers explains the many goings-on around his neighborhood.

Violence in the Family

Hear My Roar: A Story of Family Violence. Dr. Ty Hochban. Illustrated by Vladyana Krykorka. 1994. Toronto: Annick.

Hochban based this story on his research and work with children and adults who have been abused or have witnessed family violence, and he views the use of his book as primarily preventive. The afterword includes suggestions for reaching out for help from Canadian health professionals. The family portrayed in this story is represented by bears. The father becomes violent and abusive as he begins to drink more. The little bear's mother finally talks with the family doctor, and we see her begin to take steps to help herself and her son, Lungin. Lungin is assured that his father does love him, in spite of his behavior, and this seems to be true in this story. Unfortunately, this is not the case in all homes, but the author does point out that even though the reader's family might not be like this one, there are lessons to be learned within it. The 32-page book has five chapters, which could be read and discussed over five different sessions; this seems important for such a difficult subject. The writing and illustrations seem to be equally accessible to children (perhaps as young as kindergarten) and adults.

4 INVOLVING FATHERS IN THEIR CHILDREN'S LITERACY EXPERIENCES

Since we first began our studies of fathers' effects on the growth of children's literacy skills (Willoughby-Herb and Herb, 1992), research on fathering has expanded, taking a generally important place in studies of children's development. At that time, however, it was typically recognized that two of the most important contributions fathers made to their children's development were (1) that they supported the mothers' child-rearing efforts (mothers with supportive husbands were often better mothers), and (2) that fathers interacted in uniquely playful ways with their children. We found the father's role as a playmate to be of particular interest in our own work in family literacy. Research indicated that when this playfulness was a part of young children's everyday lives, children experienced more emotional highs and lows, were more willing to take chances and be open to new experiences, and tried harder to master certain new skills.

FATHERS AS NATURAL LITERACY PARTNERS

Certain outcomes of the playful father role, when applied to designing best practices for literacy education, might create important benefits for children's literacy learning, for example:

- Children should experience sheer enjoyment of literacy when being read to by a playful parent; this would then become a rewarding activity for children. Word play, tongue twisters, word games, word puzzles, and just plain silliness should be part of every child's early literacy experience, and dads are a natural provider of that kind of fun. The mislabeling of something the children know to be true amuses even the youngest children. Even infants know how to have fun under such circumstances.
- Children's experiences with risk-taking should lead to their being willing to risk errors while attempting to read a word

or to predict the outcome of a story. Risk taking also involves trust, the kind of trust that tells a young child that Dad will catch her every time she jumps into the deep part of the pool, that Dad knows when to stop teasing before feelings are hurt, and that taking chances (with parental guidance) is fun and rewarding.

- Children who have learned to work harder when playing with their fathers have already experienced the connection between effort and success that will help them to be active participants in learning to read and write. Sometimes fathers may reward this "working harder" behavior because they do require more creativity from their kids to engage their attention. Ideally, a father should be paying close attention to what his child needs, how hard an effort his child is able to deliver before frustration, and the level of reward needed to continue tasks.

- Children's experiences with emotional highs and lows should eventually enhance their ability to share deep emotional feelings (fear, sadness, ecstasy) with characters in stories. Fathers often push children up on the humorous or fun side, but they should also encourage the honest expression of all feelings. Too many dads are still uncomfortable with sadness and tears in their children, especially their sons. Empathic sadness is a trait worth encouraging; a dad who shows compassion is a great model for teaching compassion.

Father play and literacy play seem to connect in a perfect alliance, but we can't assume that fathers *do* engage in literacy activities with their children. In fact, in many families, activities such as storybook reading, writing thank you notes, and helping children with homework are considered primarily a responsibility of mothers. Perhaps these attitudes are related to long-standing gender differences in literacy accomplishments during schooling. The National Center for Educational Statistics (1998) reports that females outscore males in reading performance across all age groups, and they have "outscored males in writing proficiency at all grade levels since 1988." These data suggest that many fathers feel much less comfortable than their spouses as literacy partners for their children. Assuming that this is so, we need to develop strategies deliberately designed to involve fathers in their children's literacy learning.

It is important to note that our goal is not for father involvement in literacy activities to replace mother involvement, but rather for it to be a shared partnership. In 1996, researchers using telephone interview techniques (National Center for Educational Statistics, 1998) reported that 80% of three- to five-year-olds were read to three or more times per week. Approximately 38% of them visited a library at least once in the preceding month. We hope that one result of father involvement would be to increase the frequency of our children being read to and having the opportunity to visit libraries.

HOW LITERACY INVOLVEMENT BENEFITS FATHERS

An important benefit of involving fathers in their children's literacy learning, and one that is relevant to our discussion of fatherhood today, is that it provides an opportunity for fathers to explore and engage in important fathering roles. Significant in light of today's newer fathering roles is the opportunity it creates for engaging in a nurturing relationship with their children. Just consider how sharing storybook reading together can be a richly nurturant experience, encompassing

- shared attention between father and child,
- taking turns listening and speaking,
- asking and answering questions,
- father observing and being sensitive to his child's responses to the story, and
- father encouraging his child to make predictions about the story or even try to figure out a word.

Surely, when these kinds of activities are successful, they provide powerfully binding experiences between a father and his children—experiences that might buffer parent-child *dis*connections during more difficult times in family relationships.

Imagine the increased self-esteem felt by a father whose children enjoy the read-aloud sessions so much that they request longer and longer story times or that "*Daddy* read!"

Our goal in this chapter is to suggest ways of engaging fathers in a variety of literacy-related activities with their young children. We begin by consulting research findings about how to involve parents in family literacy experiences.

Involved Fathers Tell about Sharing Literacy Experiences with Children

Researcher Robert Ortiz (1994) interviewed thirty-three fathers about (a) their reasons for reading and writing with their children, and (b) what methods they used. These fathers reported that their reasons for involvement were related both to their assuming more child care duties, including helping with homework, and to their responding to their children's questions and interests. Among the activities these fathers engaged in were:

- nightly storybook reading
- daily homework time
- weekly library visits
- regular reading "together" time
- writing personal letters
- writing/reading words found at work
- reading print at church
- writing in the sand at the beach
- reading menus
- writing associated with home repairs (e.g., 9 inches, 2 feet 9 inches (2'9"), or four 2 by 4's)
- keeping scores
- playing video games

The success these fathers experienced led Ortiz to conclude that fathers can be fine literacy role models and teachers, and that we just need to encourage them to engage in literacy activities.

FINDINGS REGARDING FAMILY LITERACY PROGRAMS

Since the early 1970s, a number of researchers and practitioners have designed and evaluated programs to teach parents to assist their children in developing literacy skills (Sulzby and Edwards, 1993). Their findings, while not specific to fathers, provide important guidelines for us, and we have incorporated significant findings into our approach.

Sulzby and Edwards reviewed descriptive research on family environments and what parents can do to encourage their children's literacy learning. It is important to note that they were careful to include studies that represented a broad range of families, for example, those that included low-income and minority families. Therefore, we can assume that these techniques will be effective in our work within varied communities. Three critical family practices emerged from their studies:

"DADDY, TALK!"

[I]f initially they were little more than excuses to sit with Kate in our arms between naptimes, books were soon enough one of our liveliest pleasures, a part of our day together that, unlike any toy, grew along with us, keeping pace with all the changes of those first two years. And now that we've left them behind, along with the backpack and diaper pail and stroller that seemed such permanent fixtures in our daily life, I look back on these first-word or early picture books as something much more than the mere forerunners of enchantment I had originally assumed them to be.

Curious enough, it is not the pictures that come first to mind, but rather what one might call the picture-book voice. I might never have thought of this as a "voice" at all, in the same league with the magical story voice I'd felt cheated out of when I first sat down with these books, if it weren't for a happy misstatement on Kate's part, long after I had forgotten to wonder why it was we were bothering to study all those xylophones, yaks, and zebras. Almost two, and soon to put first-word books aside, Kate had taken to bossing us around the apartment with her new found powers of language: "Daddy, walk!" she would order, or "Mommy, sit!," and a variety of similar commands which for a time made up our daily paces. But when she crawled into our lap with a book it was never "Daddy, read!"—though that was the word we'd always used ourselves—but rather "Daddy, talk!," or, with a subsequent leap of grammar, "Talk it!"

Well, of course. What I had persisted in thinking of as reading was simply talking about pictures, or more often than not talking for them, bringing them alive. Unlike the soothing lullabies and sing-song nursery rhymes that make up our bedtime rituals, picture books were active, wakeful pursuits, full of discovery and animation. We barked and mooed and roared our way through the pages, plodding like elephants with our feet and plucking juicy red apples off the trees; we slurped out of spoons and flew with our hands like airplanes and birds. For whatever else they may have been, whatever their role in building vocabulary and teaching letters and numbers, these books were above all occasions to talk—to range around among words for the sheer fun of it, talking balloons here and skunks there, and a fat 'possum mother hanging upside-down from a branch with all her teeny-tiny baby 'possums on her back!

—David Pritchard, 1983/1984

- Parents and children *reading together*, along with the practice of repeated readings of the same content.
- Parents and children exploring *writing together* (both "pretend" writing and real writing, but for a purpose, e.g., writing a thank-you note).
- Parents and children regularly *engaging in conversations and storytelling*.

In this chapter, the family literacy experiences we are recommending are framed by those three critical practices identified by Sulzby and Edwards, with separate sections on reading, writing, and storytelling activities. In doing so we have limited our rec-

Dads and Sons: Sharing Good Books and Good Times

How important are books to fathers and their children? Here is a wonderful example of the larger purpose behind shared literacy experiences as seen through the eyes of a ten-year-old, an eight-year-old, and their dad. Books change lives daily. Books make life worth living always.

"We need literature because without it we couldn't make technology. We use literature to solve problems. Authors will write about pollution and other things, so hopefully people will realize how serious these problems are. Books can tell you about the past, like when there were knights roaming the land. Books can also tell you about your great, great, grandfather. That's not all, books can also help you learn a different language.

"You can also take a break from technology with a book. It's fun creating books. Most books build up your imagination. Also books have a big advantage, they're not expensive. Books are more real to me than movies.

"I always daydream or have dreams that I'm the main character or his friend. Technology is half bad because of guns and missiles or atomic bombs. Literature can't kill anyone but it can help some people by calming you down.

"Books also helped me. I came to a foreign land and books saved me. I read this one book that was about prisoners of war. I thought I had it hard off, geez, you should have seen what they had to go through. Suddenly I felt like living in another country was a luxury. Now when I feel lonely, I just pick a book."
—J. Conor Spink, age 10

"To get technology, you need books.
You can take a book anywhere.
Books are a lot cheaper.
Literature helps build your imagination.
It is fun creating books.
We can remember the past through books.
We can also learn different languages through books.

"Last year my family moved to Costa Rica. We are pretty isolated from any friends. So we need books to read. At night it sometimes gets pretty scary so a good book gives me company."
—Casey Spink, age 8

Finally, from a dad who happens to help kids learn how to read as a vocation:

"As I typed the boys' words, I kept hearing the echo of the words of Barry Lopez in Crow and Weasel, as Badger explains to the both of them that the true purpose of stories is that they become the means with which we care for each other. As a teacher, I know that I can help kids obtain the skill to accurately convert print into spoken and/or mental language without using literature as the medium of instruction. I further know that I can even teach kids to successfully comprehend texts and to correctly express their thoughts through writing with-

Dads and Sons: Sharing Good Books and Good Times (continued)
out the aid of timeless stories. What I can't do as either a teacher or a dad, without the assistance of inspired literature, is to help kids (yours, mine, or theirs) care deeply enough about what is written on the page by others so that they will quest to understand the potential meanings behind the words, or to have thoughts which are so passionately felt that it dearly matters to them to be able to express them both vividly and correctly. Boiling it down for me as a dad and as a teacher, I can only say that because I know that my students will go on to other teachers and my own kids will grow up and form their own families, I need and use literature for the only reason that, in the end, really matters—love. When my students have graduated out of my reach and my kids have outgrown the need of my care, when all of the facts of my lessons have been forgotten and the toys of our home have been discarded, the stories which I've shared with my students and which my wife and I have shared with our sons will remain with them, throughout all of their times of exultation and moments of hopelessness. And as Barry Lopez reminds us through Badger, 'Sometimes people need stories more than food to stay alive. That's why we put them in each other's memories.' Sharing literature is the only means that I know of to care for those whom we love when they move beyond our reach and live beyond our time with them." —J. Kevin Spink, 2000 Anchorage, Alaska

ommendations to the kinds of parent behaviors that research shows are actually effective in promoting children's literacy skills. In addition, we have made an effort to prescribe activities that are "father-friendly," that is, we specifically recommend activities that

- provide a logical match for the positive contributions that fathers *most naturally* make to their children's development (particularly activities that involve playfulness and challenge), and
- provide positive opportunities for fathers to practice some of the *new roles* expected of them in today's world (particularly nurturance/teaching of one's children).

GENERAL STRATEGIES FOR WORKING WITH FATHERS

Before describing specific activities for engaging fathers in their children's literacy learning, we would like to offer some general strategies that could be employed in most libraries. In general, these practices are ones that make our settings more welcoming and inclusive toward fathers.

1. Use father-directed or at least inclusive language in all publications dealing with family programs, for example in posters, flyers, and announcements placed in media. Examples of this inclusive language are "Dear Families," "Fathers, mothers, grandparents, caregivers invited to attend," and "All interested adults invited." Also, remember to connect fathers/males to libraries when you are producing videos or any pictorial graphics. Use this inclusive language also in everyday conversations with children and families: "Maybe your daddy or mommy could read more of this to you."

2. Make your environment one that "calls out" to fathers:
   - Construct an occasional bulletin board of special interest to them, such as one that features good books on fathering. *The Father Factor: What You Need to Know to Make a Difference* (Biller and Trotter, 1994) and *Working Fathers: New Strategies for Balancing Work and Family* (Levine and Pittinsky, 1997) are good examples. Father's Day and Grandparents Day are two occasions when these would certainly be seasonally appropriate.
   - Occasionally preset your library's computers to one of the fine fathering Web sites, such as fathermag.com (www.fathermag.com/) or Father's World (www.fathersworld.com), or bookmark those sites as recommended for families.
   - Make and distribute bookmarks especially for parents that include recommended books and Web sites for fathers.
   - Conscientiously greet fathers who bring their children to the library, and occasionally compliment them on their children's behavior; remember that many fathers feel uncomfortable and novicelike in managing their children's behaviors.
   - Be supportive of fathers' efforts to help their children locate and use library resources.
   - Make certain that your setting is physically comfortable for adults who are not accustomed to sitting on small furniture.
   - Invite fathers as well as mothers and caregivers to remain during preschool story times—there is much to be learned through observing a good children's librarian sharing stories.

3. When doing community outreach, be certain to schedule it

during hours and on occasions when fathers are more likely to attend; for example, if you work with local schools, it would be good to get your message out during a beginning-of-the-year open house or PTO meeting; as the year goes on, parent attendance often diminishes, this is especially true for fathers. Also, try to pair your efforts with already popular community events such as childbirth classes, or set up a booth or display posters at fairs and along parade routes.

4. Always be sensitive to children who, for one reason or another, do not have the benefit of father involvement. Sensitivity to families must include our conscientious determination to do nothing that would make any child feel uncomfortable or inadequate because his or her father did not participate in a particular project. We must always anticipate that some fathers will be unable or unwilling to participate, and have alternatives in mind. For example, if you are having children research stories about "My First Shave," suggest they might ask their fathers or grandfathers or uncles *or even* . . . (this "or" is your planned alternative and might include one or two of the males in your library or school).

5. Examine your library's current practices and create an action plan and team to develop goals and approaches that match your own resources, but that represent an effort toward involving more fathers and males in the literacy world of our children.

6. Finally, get this important message out to all of your staff. One of the best ways any of us can help men become good fathers (and in our case, good literacy-supporting fathers), is to *give positive attention to the boys and young men who come into our libraries.* A warm greeting and an effort to help them feel welcome and comfortable now will surely increase the likelihood that they will return with their children in the future. Furthermore, the caring and positive interactions we model will strengthen their capacity to be nurturant toward their own children in the future. In her book *The Trouble with Boys*, Angela Phillips makes a poignant case for young men needing the voices and support of adults outside their immediate families: "Those people who are so anxious to glue the family back together would perhaps do better if they looked around at the young men on the periphery of their own lives and asked themselves, 'When did I last give any of my time to listen to a young man who was not my own son?'" (1994: 207-208). Even

more compelling is James Garbarino's conclusion based on his in-depth study of young men and boys who have committed acts of violence, and what society needs to do to prevent this growing phenomenon. He states, "At the heart of the matter is whether a young child is connected rather than abandoned, accepted rather than rejected . . . " (Garbarino, 1999:34).

LITERACY LEARNING THROUGH READING TOGETHER

CHOOSING THE RIGHT BOOKS

Because we view our task as one of guiding fathers toward reading to their children, as with any teaching task, we ought to begin by selecting content with which our "learner" is most likely to succeed. The number one "don't" from Jim Trelease's chapter on "The Do's and Don'ts of Read-Aloud" is "Don't read stories that you don't enjoy yourself. Your dislike will show in the reading, and that defeats your purpose" (Trelease, 1982:68). We want fathers to enjoy and be successful in reading to their children, so we want to first find books they will like reading, and then suggest parent-child joint reading activities that fathers might also enjoy.

We begin this section with some thoughts about how we can try to get pleasurable reading matter into the hands of fathers. We can't identify books that *all* fathers will enjoy reading, but we can select ones that many fathers are likely to find satisfying. Two kinds of books that seem natural candidates for this category are books that contain the kind of playfulness (described in Chapter 1) that characterizes many fathers' interactions with their young children, and books that portray fathers in a positive manner.

The Playful Father

One child development text discusses this topic under the heading "Fathers and Other Playmates." The authors (Scarr et al., 1986) acknowledge that babies become attached to their fathers as readily as to their mothers, but that fathers are not *just* good mother substitutes. They provide distinct kinds of play experiences for their young children. Researchers find that fathers differ from mothers in that they engage in more physical play, and often invent new and unusual games (Yogman et al., 1977). When interacting with infants, fathers devote a larger proportion of that time to play than do mothers. And infants, in their play with fathers, show higher states of excitement as well as more complete withdrawals of excitement than in play with their mothers—higher and lower emotionality. The breadth of the types of play varies considerably, but play is universally wonderful for both parent and child.

Some time ago we began to consider the relevance of these data to the task of choosing books for fathers and children. We noted that much early reading is playful in nature—finding pictured objects, making animal noises, remembering words. At that same time, we interviewed some fathers and a male first-grade teacher concerning the kinds of books they especially enjoyed reading to children. We quote the teacher here because his statements included concepts brought up by the other men we interviewed. He began with this caution: "I'm afraid this will sound sex-stereotyped to you!" He went on to say, "I like action-packed books, ones with dialogue so I can change voices, ones with discrepancies and illustrations that make you have to think. I like reading the kids stories that are really goofy and silly, but I also like reading ones that play on the kids' emotions, stories that make them sad."

Do these descriptors sound familiar? The parallels to research on fathers at play—physical play, emotional highs and lows—are worth noting.

Do children appreciate these aspects of playing with fathers? In one research study with toddlers, two out of three children chose to play with their fathers when given a choice (Clarke-Stewart, 1978). A student of the first-grade teacher we interviewed told his baby-sitter, "I don't know why, but I feel like I want to own every book Mr. Z reads us in school."

Certainly there are lots of fine children's books containing the elements of good stories listed previously: Mitsumaso Anno's interesting picture books, Chris Van Allsburg's intriguing and mysterious stories, Jack Prelutsky's and Shel Silverstein's funny and playful poetry, Robert Munsch's silly tales. We have listed many others in Chapter 7. For now, we describe five particular storybooks that are appropriate for story-hour selections, and when checked out should interest fathers as well.

Abiyoyo. Pete Seeger. Illustrated by Michael Hayes. 1986. New York: Macmillan.
This book tells the tale of a little boy and his father who gain control over a terrible giant through their wit, magic, and music.

The story begs to be enacted, as Pete Seeger has so often done—to be sung, danced, faces made, voices dramatized. And the inside note from the author on the value of storytelling is touching; it motivates the reader to tell the story creatively.

Are You My Daddy? Carla Dijs. 1990. New York: Simon & Schuster.
A pop-up book with the familiar and ever popular story line about a lost baby animal looking for its parent. Clever, sturdy, well engineered, and simply illustrated, this book is especially suited for reading to toddlers. Their daddies can enjoy making the animals' heads move as they talk, and mimicking varied animal sounds and movements.

Bea and Mr. Jones. Amy Schwartz. 1982. New York: Bradbury Press.
This is a wonderfully funny story about a kindergartner and her father who are tired of their days at school and work, respectively. The pictures and words are full of discrepancies that keep the reader and listeners giggling: Bea sitting at a conference table dressed in her father's business suit, Bea's father being a whiz at the colored lollipop game played in kindergarten as he answers, "Vermilion red, I believe."

The Car Washing Street. Denise L. Patrick. Illustrated by John Ward. 1993. New York: William Morrow.
This book's joyful text and illustrations describe a whole neighborhood of families enjoying a hot summer Saturday morning by washing cars. Naturally, accidental sprayings as well as purposeful water battles find their way into the story. Fathers and children reading this book might just be motivated to have some car washing fun themselves.

The Football That Won . . . . Michael Sampson. Illustrated by Ted Rand. 1996. New York: Henry Holt.
This great parody on "the house that Jack built" is about "the football that won the Super Bowl." Football-watching or -playing fathers will love reading about the Dallas Cowboys winning the big game: the rhymes and illustrations are filled with interceptions, fumbles, crunches, cheerleaders, and even a blimp. Besides enjoying the fun of the rhyme, a reading father might be motivated to engage in a bit of a lesson on football—explained or demonstrated. Another fun football picture book is *The Dallas Titans Get Ready for Bed* by Karla Kuskin and illustrated by Marc Simont (HarperCollins, 1986).

HAVING SOME FUN WITH GENDER STEREOTYPES: "THE MANLY SUMMER"

John Saunders is a doctoral student in speech communication at Penn State University, but in a former life he was the children's events coordinator for a bookstore in Memphis while finishing a master's degree in communication. He thought it might be fun to celebrate the concept of "manliness" by creating a series of bookstore programs. He writes:

The theme for the summer kids events 2000 at Davis-Kidd Booksellers in Memphis, Tennessee, was the "Manly Summer." We had three months, three events, and three heavy machines. Once a month, we did a dirty manly event. The main reason for this was that I was the only male storyteller in Memphis who worked in a bookstore. Also, most story times were either gender neutral, or targeted to little girls with Madeline, Maisy, and such. So I took it upon myself to specifically target the boys and try to get some dads to come out to Saturday morning story times. The girls were NOT excluded at all; in fact, most of the girls present at all three events really enjoyed the big, heavy machinery.

The first event I did during the "Manly Summer" was on Father's Day. I dressed up like a construction worker. We sang some songs and I read What Daddies Do Best by Numeroff (1998). Then we went outside where I had a Bobcat (a small bulldozer) waiting. The operator started it up and drove it around and then I got into the shovel part. He lifted me up and I did a few manly poses. Then we shut the Bobcat off and locked it down so that it wouldn't move anywhere. We put a hard hat on each child's head and put dark make-up under their eyes. Then each child got to sit in the driver's seat (some with parents and some without) and we took a Polaroid of each child in the driver's seat doing something dirty and manly to give to their dads for Father's Day. The kids loved the machinery and they loved having their dads at the program.

The second Manly event was in July. We sang some songs and read I Love Trucks (Sturges, 1999). Then we went outside where two tractor-trailer big rigs were waiting, courtesy of a truck rental company. Each child had a turn climbing into the cabs and playing in the sleeping compartments. The children were also permitted to honk the incredibly loud horn. To add to the Manly theme, the kids got out of the cabs and we popped the hoods and started them up so the kids could see a heavy-duty motor in action. Most of the kids had never seen such a big truck before.

For the third event, I had contacted the local education branch of the Memphis Fire Department. We sang songs and I read My Fire Engine (Rex, 1999). Then we went outside where a hook and ladder truck and a pumper were waiting. The Fire Department people talked to the kids briefly about fire safety and then let them put on some of the gear, climb all through the trucks, and see how fire trucks work. They even let some of the kids turn on the lights and honk the horn. One of the firemen put the ladder all the way up and he climbed to the very top. Every child also received a fire safety coloring book, a Memphis Fire Department sticker, and a toy Fire Department car.

The three events were very fun and very different from the standard bookstore programs. I did actually have several dads start attending all events as a result of this special foray into "manliness." It helped change the story-time stereotype of just the mothers bringing the kids to a book event. I also found that the mothers and the little girls in attendance very much enjoyed the activities (John Saunders, personal communication, October 8, 2001).

Positive Father Portrayals

The positive contributions fathers make to their children's learning have only recently made a noticeable entry into the professional literature on child rearing. It is no wonder then, that what we read about fathers in the popular press is frequently critical. How often we read about fathers who spend little or no time with their children, who abandon families, who refuse to pay child support, who abuse their wives and children. It must be difficult for good fathers and for young and aspiring fathers to hear so many tales of fathering gone wrong.

As we mentioned in Chapter 3, it was our use of Anthony Browne's *Piggybook* (1986) that helped us learn our lesson when a good-natured father, still smiling from the story, asked if there weren't some books for his children that portrayed fathers in a kinder light. That father's question inspired us to search seriously for authentic instances of positive fathering in children's books, although the idea had been emerging for some time, based on our observations and experiences in the world of two-working-parent families. More and more fathers are escorting their children to story hour (especially evening programs), handling bath and story time at home, and helping to raise their children. For those of us who are promoting children's books and reading, shouldn't we consider whether our services are responsive to this new and growing clientele—reading fathers? And shouldn't we be more careful to see that these men come in contact with books that depict effective and caring fathers?

As fathers begin to occupy a more prominent position in family stories written for children, we can now find many examples of stories in which fathers are not Browne's Mr. Piggott, but rather are important contributors to the physical and emotional well-being of their families. A sampling of these types of stories follows; many others are included in Chapter 7.

Dad's Back, Messy Baby, Reading, Sleeping. Jan Ormerod. 1985. New York: Lothrop, Lee & Shepard.
This series of books for toddlers stars a creeping baby and the baby's dad. The dad is a playmate, but he is also obviously a caregiver. He shows admirable patience in his interaction with his child, who reminds us of the expression "terrible twos." His periodic frowns and tired face tell the reader that he can be annoyed, yet he treats his baby with loving consistency. In *Messy Baby*, the reader watches Dad pick up toys, books, and food from the floor of Baby's room while Baby is crawling behind him, undoing all. Dad finally turns around, looks exasperated, then re-

covers and hugs the baby, saying, "Never mind. Let's start again!" What a fine lesson in developmental expectations and caregiving for any father or grandfather reading this book.

Daddy Makes the Best Spaghetti. Anna Grossnickle Hines. 1986. New York: Houghton Mifflin.
A sweet and funny book, this one gets its charm from the daddy's personality. He's really quite a guy: he picks up his son at day care, does the grocery shopping, cooks, and plays jokes to the amusement of his family. The story and pictures portray a loving and realistic picture of a working family, and celebrate an energetic and caring father.

The Summer My Father Was Ten. Pat Brison. Illustrated by Andrea Shine. 1998. Honesdale, Penn.: Boyds Mills Press.
A girl retells the story of her father's boyhood misbehavior, when his and his friends' antics resulted in the destruction of an older neighbor's prized tomato garden. Her father had made fun of Mr. Bellavista as well, partly because he couldn't understand his Italian language and ways. The father felt very guilty and searched for a way to say he was sorry. There began years of gardening with Mr. Bellavista, gardening for him when he went to live in a nursing home, and gardening in memory of him each year when he plants the spring garden with his daughter. This story is a fine example of a sensitive father passing down wisdom to his daughter. Children will empathize with both the father and Mr. Bellavista.

I'll See You When the Moon Is Full. Susi Gregg Fowler. Illustrated by Jim Fowler. 1994. New York: Greenwillow.
A young boy helps his father pack for a business trip. Abe shares his concerns about missing his daddy, and wonders when he will return. Daddy shows Abe the sliver of moon outside his window, and explains that he will return when the moon is full. Abe promises to draw a picture of the moon each night while his father is away. The satisfying nature of this explanation is summarized by Daddy telling Abe, "You can always count on the moon, and you can always count on me."

You're the Boss, Baby Duck! Amy Hest. Illustrated by Jill Barton. 1997. Cambridge, Mass.: Candlewick.
Baby Duck is having a terrible time until Grandpa Duck saves the day. Grandpa senses Baby's jealousy about the brand-new baby, so he greets Baby Duck with a kiss, a remark about how some people make too much of a fuss over babies, and an invita-

tion to escape for a while and help him cook. Grandpa Duck is truly modeling the importance of the "crony/friend" grandfather role mentioned in Chapter 2. The message about Baby Duck's need to feel important is clear but not didactic in this lighthearted, expressively illustrated story.

SUGGESTED ACTIVITIES AND STRATEGIES TO ENCOURAGE READING TOGETHER

1. Have yearly workshops on the "Hows and Whys of Reading Aloud" to children, and explicitly invite fathers and other male caregivers. Many of the research findings in our first and second chapters would help motivate men to read to their children, so consider including a bit of research motivation. Make certain that the content you share differentiates how we read to children across a range of ages; for example, touching and pointing with infants and toddlers, reading and paraphrasing with preschoolers. Prepare short, simple take-home information. You might also want to invite a reading or elementary education curriculum coordinator from your local school district as a copresenter to emphasize the importance of reading aloud in children's academic achievement.

2. Select and circulate books that might attract fathers. At story hours and library classes, we often arrange displays and briefly "pitch" books that children might enjoy checking out. We suggest that now and then you include some books that their fathers might enjoy reading as well. For example, many fathers might be tempted to peruse biographies of sports figures or books about the Olympic games (especially during the Olympics). And certainly, if you know about your children's fathers' occupations and interests, you can be more particular in your book choices: "Matt, your Daddy drives a truck doesn't he? He might like reading this book about trucks with you. He can probably even tell you something that isn't in this book." And, if Matt chooses to take the book home, "Let me know what you and your daddy think about this one." Chances are, Matt will *make* his daddy read the book!

3. Mention and include pictures of fathers in outreach mate-

rials. If your library produces book lists or brochures for community partnership activities, remember to sprinkle books depicting fathers throughout them. If you prepare book lists for teachers who do family units, take care to include books that portray a diversity of positive fathering, and make mention of what is unique about these books.

4. Include father books in reading kits. Many libraries send selections of books to other agencies, such as shelters, doctor's offices, and child care centers. We could add portrayals of good fathering to the various other concepts we consider in assembling these collections.

5. Remember that we are selling reading to the dads themselves, as well as to their children. Use catchy graphics, bold colors, and creative approaches to grab the eyes of dads who are on their way to their favorite section of the adult side of the library. One March we set up a couple of fans to keep an inside-the-library kite in the air in front of a display of outdoor activity books for families. What father hasn't huffed and puffed up and down a field, demonstrating the fine art of lofting a kite skyward for the benefit of a son or daughter? Consider a family film and book festival as a good way to pique the interest of fathers. Choose film genres that might have a higher dad appeal: comedy, biography, action-adventure, space exploration, or western. Set up displays of children's books on similar subjects, and encourage browsing and checkouts after the film. Andrew Glass's *Bad Guys: True Stories of Legendary Gunslingers, Sidewinders, Fourflushers, Drygulchers, Bushwhackers, Freebooters, and Downright Bad Guys and Gals of the Wild West* (Doubleday, 1998) is a great example of such a book. Consider adding a short review of some of the books available, or have staff members serve as readers' assistants. Refreshments are usually effective in encouraging families to linger.

6. Include men as Readathon participants. When planning these celebrations of reading, be certain to invite children's fathers and well-known men in your community. Also try to get your local newspaper to publish photos of them reading, and definitely save those photos for your own publicity.

7. When designing parent-child projects to be done at home, try to develop ones that might attract fathers as participants. A simple example of this strategy is a project in which children are to interview more than one adult about, for

---

Museum Day Project and Father Participation

At Shippensburg University's lab school, the nursery class ends one of its units each semester with a celebration to which all family members are invited. Because the children typically choose the units as well as what they want to learn more about, this idea originated with the children, but it happened to be very successful in involving their fathers.

In one particular unit, small groups of children chose an animal to study. Their activities included reading about the animal, constructing a museum-like exhibit with a realistic habitat and stuffed animals or other models, preparing a brochure of interesting facts, advertising with posters and invitations, and hosting their families' tour of the exhibit. Children made tickets, signs, and refreshments. One boy was so taken by the unit that he wrote a poem about his animal—penguins—and wrote a story that linked three of the animals. We proudly made copies of his work to share.

It was clear (from comments of children and parents) that this project had captured the attention of many more fathers than usual:

- from the very beginning, as children took books home so that they could browse and think about which animals they wanted to study,
- through their "homework," for which they had to read and write down a fact they found interesting about their group's animal, and finally,
- on open house day, when fathers were eager to walk around and examine the exhibits, talk to their own and other children about how they had constructed the displays, and read and comment on the Interesting Facts brochures.

It was clear that they found each exhibit interesting and were not just politely visiting each area.

Since this project was last implemented, Jeffrey Mousaieff Masson's book The Emperor's Embrace: Reflections on Animal Families and Fatherhood (1999) has been published. Although this book is intended for adults, we recommend adding this kind of information if you choose to try this project. In fact, you might have girls and boys research the separate roles of parents in the animal families, and choose animals that are good mothers and fathers. Masson's book is a good starting reference for helping children find examples of good fathering: he describes varied ways in which penguins, wolves, beavers, prairie dogs, and pigeons are good fathers.

---

example, their taste preferences. Remember, too, that you might inspire more father involvement if your projects contain some traditional male interests. For example, design reading-connected projects that involve

- measuring. (How much of a blue whale would fit in your bathtub?)
- using tools. (Check the thermometer at your bedtime: Is it as cold as *Fifty Below Zero* by Robert Munsch? (Annick, 1986)

- science experiments/learning. See box on page 72 for a description of a successful father—and the rest of the family—involvement science project.

8. Assign rereading projects to send home, as a second adult will likely need to help. Remember that repeated reading is one of the most effective ways parents nurture their children's literacy, so we ought to devise activities in which the child is to ask two different people to read the same selection to him or her. In your note or explanation of who those readers might be, be sure to mention specifically fathers, grandfathers, or older brothers. Depending on the children's writing skills, they could record who read to them and make a smiley face or frown to represent whether that adult liked the story or not. You might consider allowing a limited number of these rereadings to count as points in your reading clubs.

9. Gather lists of "Fathers' Favorite Reads." Ask children to interview fathers, uncles, grandfathers, older brothers, and other males regarding their favorite childhood books. Compile a master list, post the findings, and locate as many books as you can for browsing and borrowing. This makes a nice activity to do near Father's Day or Grandparents Day or National Library Week. Including mothers, aunts, grandmothers, and sisters is a great way to open this activity to the child's whole family.

10. Buy multiple copies of some of the good father-image books. If you or the teachers or caregivers you work with are in the habit of purchasing multiple copies of books so that several children can check out books that they enjoyed hearing, do include some selections with good father characters. Some titles well loved by the young children we know are *Daddy Makes the Best Spaghetti* (Hines, 1986) and *I'll See You When the Moon Is Full* (Fowler, 1994).

LITERACY LEARNING THROUGH EXPLORING WRITING TOGETHER

Research on helping young children learn to be writers indicates that particular kinds of experiences are more useful than others in nurturing their motivation and ability. When we encourage parents to support their children in learning to write, our emphasis should not be on helping them teach their children how to form letters and spell words. Rather, it should be on helping children learn to

- explore with and try to draw the common graphic symbols used in drawing and writing (e.g., learn to make circles and horizontal and vertical lines),
- use these graphics as symbols (e.g., use circles and straight lines to make a sun, a flower, or the letter B),
- use symbols in meaningful ways, such as props for play (e.g., hang up a sun picture to represent morning or write the word "out" as a sign for—Doctor Is In),
- use print in varied ways (e.g., printing your name on a list to get your turn, writing the word "love" to express a feeling), and finally,
- understand that print records make our language permanent (e.g., writing your name on a sign-up list means that your turn will not be forgotten, writing people love notes means that they can read them often and remember that you love them).

Therefore, in this section we will focus on activities that are playful and/or center on using print in a meaningful way. Parents may indeed find themselves helping their children draw letters or spell words correctly, but we don't ever want parents to feel that children have to do it perfectly. Although our emphasis will be on activities that are more playful than didactic, there are many concepts that children learn when we draw and write informally with them: color names and shades, quality words such as light and dark, shiny and dull, hard and soft, large and small. And during those times when children ask us to show them how to make a letter, they learn additional concepts: left and right, top and bottom, straight and curved, round and flat, and first, and next, and last. When children have these kinds of experiences at home, they are so much more prepared to participate in the formal kinds of teaching that they will encounter in school.

FATHERS AND CHILDREN'S WRITING

The approach to writing we just described is clearly one that matches the playful father role. Our challenge will be in finding ways to integrate writing into the play that fathers are already doing with their children. This is not unlike the task of early childhood teachers who attempt to invite children to integrate literacy into their play instead of counting on children to go to the literacy center to practice it. There is ample evidence that children enjoy writing and reading what they've written when it is presented in this context. We remember that children (especially some boys who engaged in traditional gender-based play) enjoying writing in the following situations:

- When they had built a large wooden airplane after hearing Peter Spier's *Bored, Nothing to Do* (Doubleday, 1978). Their writing included drawing many buttons and gauges to tape to the plane's instrument panel, drawing a map to guide the flight, writing tickets to sell to the passengers, and making pilot's badges.
- When they had built a dog kennel after seeing the film *101 Dalmatians*. Their writing included dog names taped to each kennel, a booklet showing the tricks the dogs could do, labels on food containers, and a **"Do Not Disturb"** sign for when the dogs were sleeping.
- when they decided to be detectives after reading about how to find animal tracks. Their writing included drawing various footprints to be taped about, maps, Xs for marking locations, and scribble notations in their handmade "Detective's Notebook."

With this kind of playfulness in mind, we suggest trying the following ideas for involving men and fathers in writing together with their children.

SUGGESTED ACTIVITIES AND STRATEGIES FOR INVOLVING FATHERS IN LITERACY LEARNING THROUGH WRITING

1. Create a treasure hunt. You will need some kind of "treasure" for this activity (perhaps a coupon from one of your sponsors, or a trinket of some sort). This activity could be used during a story hour that typically attracts a number of fathers, or for a special workshop on literacy for fathers or another men's group such as Big Brothers. If children are attending, begin with a story that features a lost object or a treasure hunt, such as a chapter from *The Seven Treasure Hunts* by Betsy Byars (1991). In either case, *briefly*

explain the importance of families engaging in enjoyable writing activities with children, and tell participants that they will be making treasure maps, a great example of such an activity. Divide your group so that each mapmaker family will have a partner family of map readers. Send the map-reading families to another area of the library, and distribute a "treasure" to each mapmaking family, along with paper and pencils. Instruct them to hide the treasure and then draw a map for their partner family. After inviting the others back and conducting the hunt, reverse roles.

2. Hold a craft-making project at your library or center for families to make a wipe-off memo board or chalkboard. At the beginning of the activity and again at the end, remind parents of how important it is to write with children, and suggest several ways to include children in using the memo board, such as using it for reminders, shopping lists, sweet notes to children, and so on.

3. Write or draw a story about when you were young. This ninety-minute activity is a good one to do near the end of a program, when parents are comfortable with you and around one another (toward the end of a summer reading program or a school year, for example). Try to schedule an event for the children to do in a separate room (watch a filmed story, make crafts). Briefly talk to parents about the importance of writing with and for their children, and suggest that they know some stories that their children would enjoy—stories about themselves when they were young. Begin their thinking by telling one yourself. In our family, our children have enjoyed stories of making Halloween mischief, close escapes, things we had imagined incorrectly (like thinking all cats were females and all dogs were males), and favorite summer vacations. Even young children get a kick out of thinking about their parents being "bad," making mistakes, being naive. Ask if anyone in the group has any ideas and share them briefly. Then allow the parents to "incubate" the idea while they make a blank book for their child. (Books can be stapled, sewn, or bound with a bookbinder; covers can be decorated in any way. Always prepare directions and materials ahead of time.) When books are made, provide supplies—pens, pencils, markers, old magazines, maybe a book or two on drawing, some dictionaries—and let parents begin recording their "stories." At the end of the hour (some will not yet be done, but they can finish at home), invite the children back so that their parents can read/tell the stories to them. Suggest

that children can write a story of their own in the book too, and maybe there's room for a grandparent or sibling to add one. Then serve refreshments. We find that this is hard work for parents, but how memorable these books and stories will be. We guarantee you will be thanked for this one.

4. Initiate a cooperative animal design project when parents accompany children to story hour. Read a story about a mixed-up animal, such as Eric Carle's *The Mixed-up Chameleon* (Crowell, 1975). After enjoying the silliness with the children, have each parent-child pair reach into a hat to choose an animal part they are to draw (ears, eyes, one back leg). Make these cards ahead of time, making certain to have as many body parts as you expect children/families. Some extras you can add if the numbers are greater than expected are a decoration to wear around the neck, a bowl of food to eat, eyebrows, eyelids, ribbons for the tails, antlers, or warts for the chin. Put out piles of supplies—markers, crayons, paper, scissors, tape, glue, and other scraps—and tell folks to find a private place and work secretly. When everyone is done, gather together and assemble the animal. Talk about the silly parts of it, then suggest that families gather in groups (three to five groups will work well) to think of a name and explanation for the animal. Ask one parent in each group (remember the fathers) to write their suggested name and explanation so that it can be posted in the library.

5. Make a vehicle when parents have joined their children for story hour. Read a story that has a vehicle in it— a fire truck, for example. (Wouldn't it be great to have a fire truck visit, too?) For the follow-up activity, make 3-D cardboard vehicles, attaching wheels with paper fasteners. Demonstrate how to make doors for equipment storage. Let children and their families (hopefully some dads) work together to color and write on their take-home trucks. On models you make to show possibilities, include several kinds of writing and drawing: engine number, company name, numbers and words on various gauges; ladders, hatchets, hoses, first-aid kits, and other equipment.

6. Make paper airplanes. This project can be linked to nonfiction books about planes, air, aerodynamics, and making paper airplanes. Invite someone with paper-airplane-making expertise to demonstrate (try a high school science teacher or student). After the demonstration, allow children and parents to experiment and make their own air-

planes. Encourage them to write and draw on the planes, including names, numbers, destinations, and logos. The more they write and draw on the planes, the more recognizable they will be when retrieving them after the races! Do have a series of races after the planes are completed, but emphasize the fun rather than the competition.

7. Make greeting cards around holidays such as Valentine's Day, Mother's Day, and Father's Day. Set up a station with materials, equipment, and directions. If you have access to computers with writing or drawing programs on them, this would be a fine way for families who don't own home systems to learn about using computers. Also, this kind of writing is likely to interest many machine-loving fathers. Otherwise, you might assemble rubber stamps, markers, and collage items, and produce some varied samples to stimulate ideas. Display related books for checking out after the craft activity.

The next group of activities we suggest are "homework" or take-home projects. They are not lengthy, nor do they require expertise in working with children. Still, we need to remember that not all children will get to do them at home, so be certain to plan alternatives. If you are working with children who haven't yet been to school, they might not remember to do the projects themselves at home, so it is best to announce the project to their families.

There are various ways to handle these take-homes. You might do them with parents at the end of story time; in a school library, enlisting help from children in upper grades; or you could ask your male volunteers to help with these projects in the library. You might have a Parent and Child Together Night once a month during your evening story times, and use these activities at that time. You might do the activity with volunteers and children at the library, but send home directions for doing the project again or in a varied way with the family at home. Some families that share a family night together each week are looking for ideas of things to do, especially during long winters or rainy seasons.

8. A name-writing activity requires minimal involvement, but is a good beginning. After reading a book containing concepts about length (for example, in *Rumpelstiltskin* the long names are interesting to children), give each child a piece of graph paper with large squares. Tell them to take the paper home and ask each person in the family to print his or her name on the paper, one letter per block, and to

bring it back for the next story time. At the next session, talk with children about number and comparisons and whether anyone has a family member with a name as long as Rumpelstiltskin's. Guide children to cut the name strips they brought back, rearrange them according to length, and make a decorative frame so that their work can be displayed at home or in the library. Have extra graph paper on hand for children who have forgotten or didn't have a chance to finish the project at home.

9. Write about a building project. Read a story that has a building theme, for example *Changes, Changes* by Pat Hutchins (Simon & Schuster, 1971). Allow four or five children at a time to take home a set of Legos or other building toys. The children's task is to build something cooperatively with a parent or older sibling at home, and then write down what it is and one other thing about it. Hopefully, dads, brothers, granddads, and other males will be willing to help with this homework.

10. Find public print in the workplace. Read the children a story that has public print in its illustrations. You might choose a storybook with print here and there (such as Elizabeth Winthrop's *As the Crow Flies*), or a book that has print as its primary focus, such as Tana Hoban's *I Read Signs* (HarperCollins, 1983). After reading and discussing the story, look back through the pictures for the signs and other public print in the pictures. Take children on a walk through your building or around the room, to find other words they can read (make certain that at least some are low enough for the children to read and see well enough to copy). Then give them pencil and paper and ask them to write down some of those words. Provide two blank word cards and a prepared direction sheet to take home to their parents, requesting that parents write down one or two words that are posted where they work. In your note, be certain to mention that this will work for parents who are stay-at-home moms and dads as well. Remind parents of the assignment as they pick up their children. Make a bulletin board for displaying the results. Children will love finding their family's word cards posted at the library. This project can continue for a few weeks, as everyone brings in cards.

LITERACY LEARNING THROUGH STORYTELLING AND CONVERSATION

STORYTELLING

Throughout most of human history it would seem quite unnecessary to explain the importance of storytelling to people. For most of our history, storytelling was the only means of communicating what was important from one generation to another. Stories provided the rules and the laws and the consequences for not following them. They connected us to the natural and supernatural world and rewarded us for taking care of our families and our neighbors. Stories answered our questions and provided comfort. Stories explained the world and how we should make our way through it. They connected us to everything that came before us and allowed us to dream of the future. Storytelling is our oldest form of entertainment, our longest-running teaching tool, and the most important way we learn who we are within our family, our town, and our culture.

All those attributes still ring true, but it might be a little harder to identify the stories and the storyteller's role in today's electronically dominated culture. A quick look at the critically acclaimed books, films, and television shows will yield one answer: great stories still lie at the heart of great art. A second answer can be found in the schools; the best teachers are those who can use stories to communicate with all the children in their classrooms. The remarkable teachers also allow the children to find their storytelling voices.

But it is the third traditional role of stories that matches best our goals in this manual. Storytelling tells us who we are in our family, our town, and our culture. From the stories of our births to how we cure hiccups, we find that family stories still provide guidance on how we lived and should live our lives. (Sometimes the family stories provide plenty of motivation to try to live our lives quite differently!) From the stories of the brave and foolish things family members have done over the decades, we learn to take pride in who we came from and delight in the occasional stumble everyone needs to make to live a life worth living.

The stories we tell about ourselves become our lives. They are how we present ourselves to our family and the outside world. These recounted incidents of our lives become our most critical memories of who we once were, and perhaps help guide present and future decisions as well. As Oliver Sacks once said, "Biologically, physiologically, we are not so different from each other;

historically, as narratives—we are each of us unique" (Sacks, 1987:111).

Long before we turn to reading and writing, we are helping our children become literate through oral language, the stuff of stories. We sing and chant to our babies. We pull on toes and blow warm air onto squirming bellies while we name and rhyme. We swoop and toss and help our children to listen to the playfulness of words. We listen to our baby's earliest gurgles and coos and reply as best we can because we know how important those first stories and conversations truly are. Storytelling lives on as the foundation for all future literacy pathways. The richer the storytelling environment in a child's life, the more choices he or she has with words and ideas. Even in homes where books are rare and reading is a challenge for a parent, storytelling is possible and essential.

Certainly, storytelling is an important path to literacy no matter what one's age. Tim Jennings (1986) tells how storytelling helped a group of difficult high school students develop the motivation to learn to read. These particular students thought that being read to was childish, so their teacher was unable to use this activity to nurture their desire to read. They did enjoy hearing folktales, however, and eventually developed a desire to read them themselves—and to be read to—for hours each day. Storytelling using traditional stories was the perfect catalyst for these students.

Storytelling apparently serves children well for purposes other than academic literacy. Susan Engel (1995) observed and studied children telling their own stories; she concluded that storytelling does much more for children than "add color to the day." According to Engel, learning to make sense of the world, learning to solve problems, making and keeping friends, and constructing a sense of one's self are among the important outcomes of children's storytelling. Engel's examination of storytelling also focused on what it is that allows children's storytelling to flourish, and she found two important influences: (1) having confidence in talking, and (2) "joyousness" in telling stories. A child's confidence and joyousness in storytelling come about from particular kinds of adult interactions, ones that we want to foster as we work with fathers or any parent:

- to be attentive listeners,
- to listen actively and respond to what children are saying,
- to see that children are exposed to a variety of ways of telling stories (e.g., Grandpa's rambling stories, Aunt Jenny's "lesson" stories),

- to permit children to tell stories about things that matter to them (be it a television show, a fight at school, or a pet's death), and
- to remember not to overcorrect, dismiss, or make fun of what children say.

The connection between good fathering and storytelling is pointed out on *Dads Can* (www.dadscan.org), a Canadian Web site with the goal of promoting "responsible and involved fathering." One of the site's recommended "10+1 tips" for fathers is *"Tell Your Story*: Your history, and that of your parents and your own family, can be interesting to your child. A young child often feels the world began at his/her birth. By your reflections on your past, you provide your child with the intriguing sense of history and of past generations. You need not tell all the details of your history, but only those which leave your child with the feeling that you too were once a child and you grew up and became an involved father."

With particular groups of fathers, we might actually be more successful in involving them in storytelling than in reading aloud to their children. Data from telephone surveys conducted by the National Center for Educational Statistics (1998) indicate that among children between the ages of three and five years, nearly 80% had been told at least one story during the preceding week. This percentage was reflective of children regardless of whether or not they were enrolled in preschool programs, their families were poor, or their parents were not well educated. On the other hand, these factors did influence children's likelihood of being read to or taken to a library.

CONVERSATION

Conversation and storytelling often go hand in hand, but here we refer to conversations between parents and children that have purposes other than storytelling. During conversation, parents listen to children's ideas, answer their questions, instruct children, ask them questions, explain things, reflect on children's interests and activities, lead them to think, and show them how to use language for thinking. Recent research on parent-child language indicates that the quality of verbal stimulation and conversation in a child's home has a powerful influence on the child's later learning (Hart and Risley, 1995; Snow, Burns, and Griffin, 1998). Children with fortunate language environments experience mealtime conversations, adults and children recounting the day's activities, adults paying attention to what children say, and adults who enjoy playing with language (making silly rhymes, telling jokes, singing). We need to model these kinds of interactions for parents and support their learning how to initiate them.

Sometimes, however, children are not very talkative themselves. We have discussed techniques for helping to support children's oral language elsewhere (Herb and Willoughby-Herb, 1994); these might be useful strategies when working with parents who have real difficulty stimulating and carrying on conversations with their children. For many parents, however, a good and comfortable setting for learning to support their children's conversational skills is in storybook reading. We can do much to teach these conversational skills by inviting parents to observe and later assist in our own storybook reading and discussions.

SUGGESTED ACTIVITIES AND STRATEGIES FOR INVOLVING FATHERS IN LITERACY LEARNING THROUGH STORYTELLING AND CONVERSATION

1. Hold a family storytelling workshop. If possible, invite a speaker or guest who enjoys telling family stories to model this technique. Share with the participants the many benefits of storytelling. If you know the participants well, you might do a bit of "round-robin" storytelling in small groups. Some possible topics are our family's most unusual expression and where it came from, the origin of our family's surname, our family's most unique character, and the second most embarrassing thing that ever happened to me as a child (no one ever tells the most embarrassing!). Your program might also include sharing:
   - **storybooks** in which there is family storytelling, such as *This Is the Bird* by George Shannon (Houghton, 1997), *Sister Anne's Hands* by Marybeth Lorbiecki (Dial Books, 1998), The *Basket* by George Ella Lyon (Orchard, 1990), *Tell Me a Story, Mama* by Angela Johnson (Orchard, 1989), *Up North in Winter* by Deborah Hartley (Dutton, 1986), and *The Year of the Perfect Christmas Tree: An Appalachian Story* by Gloria M. Houston (Penguin, 1988).
   - **ideas of other family storytelling topics**—stories of love

gained or lost, stories about family heirlooms, humorous antics of family pets, great physical feats or dangers, immigration/emigration, remembrances of family members now deceased, holiday rituals, food rituals
- **preservation of family lore**—making homemade books (for example a recipe book with photos of the original cook, photocopies of the original writing, photos of family gatherings); making a memory box (with photos or trinkets inside, along with a written piece about the items); making a "Book of Days" with photos and remembrances placed at appropriate places; making video and audio records; organizing storytelling sessions, complete with an appointed historian, at family reunions; and of course, a variety of artistic expressions, such as writing songs and poems, painting pictures, stitching quilts
- **resources/books** to stimulate family storytelling, such as Anne Pellowski's *The Story Vine: A Source Book of Unusual & Easy-to-Tell Stories from Around the World* (Simon & Schuster, 1984) and *The Family Storytelling Handbook: How to Use Stories, Anecdotes, Rhymes, Handkerchiefs, Paper & Other Objects to Enrich Your Family Traditions* (Simon & Schuster, 1987)

This activity is an ideal one for recruiting grandparents, so do encourage their attendance too. A favorite topic for grandparents is to tell about a family member who was an important part of their past, but not their children's. Such remembrances would be a nice addition to the family's "Book of Days" mentioned above.

2. Model how to converse with children, by making talking time a part of every story time. Research clearly associates the quality of conversations children experience with their subsequent literacy development (Snow, Burns, and Griffin, 1998:148). Story time (with a craft or follow-up activity) is a great time to demonstrate to fathers and other caregivers present how to:
- ask thought-provoking questions about stories,
- introduce a new word or concept,
- prompt children to think about a concept, and
- respond positively to a child's effort even when the content isn't accurate.

Remember that this kind of engagement with story that we habitually encounter is not necessarily a part of children's or their parents' own family experiences. And it is certainly not part of the traditional view of fathering.

3. Model how to carry on social conversations with children by talking with them before and after story time, not just during the planned program. The more of this you do, the better you will become because you will learn more and more about the children. Simple conversations can begin about a stuffed animal a child is carrying or a craft project. Conversations about the world of sports and movies are appropriate too, when you know the children's interests. Remember the importance of helping children and their families feel confident in their talking, and demonstrate techniques such as patience in waiting for a child to formulate an answer, refraining from laughing *at* a response, speaking at the child's eye level, and listening sincerely and responsively. Again, this kind of conversation might not be part of a typical father's experiences.

4. Work different methods of storytelling into events and story times at which fathers are participants. Let fathers know that there are many ways to tell stories, probably a different one just right for each father. For example, we have found that some dads just love audience-participation types of stories that allow them to be raucous and rambunctious with their voices or their bodies. Other fathers love puppets, while still others like to do draw talks or provide the kinds of silly answers a draw talk might call for: "And, his nose was made of a . . . ?" "snow blower!," calls a father. "OK, a snow blower, a snow blower. And his nose was made of a snow blower, and his name was Aiken Drum!" Librarians should always keep in mind that they are demonstrating techniques fathers can use at home at the same time they are providing excellent literacy activities for the children.

5. Use a broad array of storytelling models available through audiotapes, videos, and community members. The National Storytelling Association has some wonderful videos families might borrow for entertainment (and indirect storytelling tips). Books on tape provide another model for storytelling and expressive storybook reading. Encouraging community members to be storytellers at the library presents another kind of model. Seeing other people tell stories live often leads to an "I can do that" view of storytelling, especially when the models are fellow community members just sharing stories informally. Having a

joint storytelling marathon activity might be a fun way for the whole town to tell one big yarn. Open on a Friday night in summer with "Once upon a time . . ." and simply invite the next person to come up and continue the narrative. Watch while it gets simply crazy, especially from the input of young children. Have an ending ready so the town can eventually go home to bed.

6. Work with teen parents. A special population of fathers and mothers requiring special attention are those who became parents while still in high school. Storytelling can become a way of encouraging conversation when questions and answers are not yielding much information. Our storyteller colleague Marcia Bowers successfully worked with teenagers several years ago through the sharing of birth myths or birth stories (Bowers, 1993). Where did these teens come from? What were they told of their arrivals and what could they tell about their own children's births? Many details that were shared pointed to the challenges these teens faced and the hard lives they were living as young parents, but the stories also provided an opportunity to take some pride in accomplishments with their children and some common ground among the teen parents. Life is always a little easier when problems can be shared with people who know exactly what you are going through.

7. Invite older boys and girls to present short book talks (on their favorite books at that age) to younger children who attend story hours. Not only will you be giving these young adults a chance to talk about a literature experience, but you will also undoubtedly influence some new reading choices among your young readers.

8. Celebrate Father's Day with a storytelling event. During June, invite fathers and other males in your community to tell real-life stories to accompany read-alouds during story time or to accompany reading themes going on in your library. Some topic examples are "The Time We Were Snowbound," "Surviving the Flood/Tornado/etc. of ____," "My First Camp-out," "Getting Used to My Baby Sister." Of course, a similar program in May for mothers would be great too.

9. Celebrate a family history month or week with children. This is often an eye-opening activity for families, who may not have thought of their own families in the context of history. The idea is to give children a family history-gathering project. When you explain this to your children's families, emphasize information coming from both mothers and

---

POP POP HOMAN AND THE START OF A STORYTELLING LIFE

My story begins in Stony Creek Mills, Pennsylvania, the oldest of three sons and the oldest grandchild on my mother's side. My grandfather had waited twenty-five years for another chance with a boy. His only son had died in his first week of life and as his four daughters became married adults he constantly encouraged them to have children. My mother was first and I was born on a snowy Easter morning, ten days past due and following a very difficult labor. (No one who knows me will be able to resist a smile at the ten days past due, but I do hope few will smile over the difficult labor!)

My new parents were as happy as new parents could or should be and the extended family behaved in exemplary fashion, but it was my grandfather who stole the show. Stories are still told of his joy at this event. The last twenty months of his life were the first twenty of mine and he made me feel quite special. He beamed at every move, laughed at every antic, and smiled back at every smile. He also encouraged me to misbehave, tease, and talk. Talking was my strength. I began telling tales as soon as I could and enjoyed the laughter of my audience soon after. As I grew older and became a brother, I acted as preschool translator for Paul's unintelligible uttering. I couldn't really understand much of what he said either, but he seemed to like the stories I told our parents about what I thought he had said. When David came along and I entered school, I began telling both brothers bedtime stories about elementary school. A frequently requested favorite was about a boy named Denis who pooped the floor. I knew my audience.
—Steven Herb, 1990

---

fathers. We have done this project in a variety of ways:

- having children participate in a show-and-tell about when their parents were little. Some of the wonderful outcomes were a father teaching his son how to play marbles and then the son teaching his friends; and a father taking his son to his grandmother's attic to find his favorite set of books, *The Hardy Boys*, and then the son devouring the stories.
- having children share a story of their parent's mischief. Some great stories were told here too: A little boy acted out a thrilling scene of his mother pulling the knobs off the TV set so her brother couldn't change the channel. He began, "Back in the olden days, there was no such thing as remote control."
- having children tell or write about a favorite member of their family.
- having children write the biography of one of their parents. Our fourth grade teacher did this recently and posted the illustrated biographies in the school hallway. The mothers and fathers were charmed and delighted to read

the content that their children chose to tell about them—silliness, near-tragedies, interesting jobs. This became a good prompt for more storytelling by parents, "I had my arm broken, too!"

10. Hold a workshop for grandparents. Berry Brazelton says, "The power of the past is what makes grandparents' wisdom and memories both painful and supportive" (1992:429). Helping grandparents find ways to share family history and communicate in special ways with their grandchildren will also guide them to focus their memories in ways that are supportive of their children's families. Some activities and practices you might share for grandparents communicating with their grandchildren are sending postcards regularly; using a particular color ink or stamp so that even children who can't read know that "this is from Grammy!"; sending photographs of the children's parents when they were little, along with a few sentences about that time; sending a joke along with every letter (grandfathers especially like this one!); using e-mail; and taping storybook reading. Surely, the participants will also want to share their own successes with one another, and some might even want to meet regularly to work on family storytelling projects.

Storytelling is as old as we are as a people, but as new as the baby born seconds ago. It will be that baby's pathway to literacy as it has been for all children who hear stories on their way to learning to talk, to read, and to write. It remains a remarkably powerful tool for communication, education, and entertainment. Storytelling never needs to be upgraded and is unaffected by the digital divide. It is there, ready and waiting to be used by anyone willing to say, "Once upon a time."

5 REACHING OUT TO FATHERS THROUGH LIBRARY PROGRAMMING

In the last chapter we described how libraries might extend their in-house programming efforts to include fathers, thereby involving them in their children's literacy experiences. In this chapter our focus is on how we can collaborate across our communities, with other agencies and facilities, so that we can share our message and approach with fathers whose families are not as likely to be reached through in-house library programs.

THE NATURE OF SUCCESSFUL COLLABORATION

Collaboration is always important in helping us extend our reach, but in some situations it is the most appropriate way to involve families. Certainly, all programs that aim for family involvement must reflect a cautious sensitivity to diverse family situations, family abilities and stresses, but in reaching out to some families, this sensitivity expertise is essential. For example, not all parents are equally suited for "teaching" their children, nor are all children equally easy to "teach" using typical interactions and techniques. Furthermore, other family stresses such as economics and parental discord may be so pervasive that they preclude a parent's ability to work with us on a project at any given time. Therefore, when we work with at-risk families, we ought to coordinate our efforts with staff from other agencies (Head Start, family and youth services, special education service providers), perhaps in coordination with their family involvement programs.

We begin by considering the nature of collaboration itself, an activity that can be successful or futile, exhilarating or frustrating. When successful, however, the positive outcomes of collaboration are many:

- It enhances efficiency of community services because it prevents duplication of effort.

- It allows us to bring our efforts to families we don't typically meet (e.g., at-risk parents), through working with professionals who already have established a trusting bond with those families.
- It enhances our effectiveness by bringing together the resources and experiences of many others.
- It means we can do more and reach more people using fewer of our own resources.
- It expands and renews our own expertise through our work with others.

Research on effective collaboration can further our understanding by identifying characteristics related to its success. Sometimes community collaboration requires us to extend our horizons, to adopt a creative approach in seeking support. Edwards (1991) reported on her success with a "Parents as Partners in Reading Program," in which nonmainstream parents were taught to carry out effective storybook sharing with their children. Her summary discussion of the effective elements of the program begins with a list of people and organizations in the community whose cooperation was critical: the Ministerial Alliance, business leaders, grandmothers, bus drivers, school and library personnel. She tells of a local priest who spoke about the importance of literacy (as a "tool of faith") in a sermon, and of the owner of an area bar who attended the training sessions, transported parents, and even helped arrange for child care.

Particularly useful is research that identifies effective professional behaviors, as we can actually strive to practice these strategies. Successful collaboration in an early-intervention program, for example, was associated with these characteristics among the persons involved:

- a high frequency of contact with one another,
- flexibility (e.g., in scheduling),
- sharing of information,
- consistency, and
- a focus on cooperation vs. competition (Dinnebeil, Hale, and Rule, 1999).

We advise you to give careful consideration to these findings as you develop programs or choose from the various projects we suggest in this chapter. Begin your collaborative efforts with organizations whose personnel are already familiar to your staff, and with whom you can expect to develop a cooperative sharing relationship marked by consistent yet flexible efforts. As Edwards's research points out, however, don't overlook support from non-

FOCUS ON PARTNERSHIPS: THE FATHERHOOD PROJECT

The Fatherhood Project is an activity sponsored by the Families and Work Institute, and described in its publication New Expectations: Community Strategies for Responsible Fatherhood. This fine resource contains guidelines and program tips valuable to anyone wishing to develop programs for involving fathers in their children's lives. The advice is based on successful practices, and it ranges from suggestions for initiating programs to strategies for sustaining programs. Chapters provide details from exemplary programs that illustrate the strategies suggested. Literacy involvement is recommended as a "tip" for getting and sustaining men's involvement. "Literacy skills make it possible for parents to experience one of the great pleasures of parenthood—reading to their children—" (Levine and Pitt, 1995:44).

One chapter lists nearly 300 programs and organizations across the country that are involved in fatherhood initiatives. The project maintains updated information regarding these efforts. Among the organizations identified as strong collaborators are several having a presence in most communities: YWCA, United Way, Salvation Army, Boys and Girls Clubs, Planned Parenthood, and, of course, public schools and religious centers. See further particulars at the conclusion of this chapter.

traditional sources in your community. Finally, once your collaboration has begun, remember to monitor your own practices of effective professional behaviors.

POSSIBLE STRATEGIES FOR COMMUNITY COLLABORATIONS

1. Make a presentation on the father's role in children's literacy development at one of the predominantly male organizations in your community (Lions Club, Kiwanis, Police Athletic League, fraternal organizations). Bring along copies of Armin Brott's books on fathering (see Chapter 6) as well as some of the books he recommends for reading aloud to children. If possible, have a male from the library's staff deliver this presentation; researchers find that many men feel more comfortable talking about these kinds of topics with other men. Naturally, offer your cooperation if group members wish to take on this topic as one of their community involvement projects.

2. Obtain permission to make a bulletin board or display a poster in a lobby or public place where fathers might spot

it and have time to reflect on its information. Post an eye-catching picture of a father reading to a child, along with brief text capturing the important benefits of fathers and children reading together. Depending on your audience, include some data, such as:

- In 1995, the average four-year-old in the United States spent only 42 minutes a day under his or her father's care (Olmsted and Weikart, 1995).
- Researchers find that in today's young families, children whose fathers read to them frequently are more interested in books and they pay attention to them longer (Lyytinen, Laakso, and Poikkeus, 1998).

3. Attempt to connect to grandfathers who are acting as parents by contacting local retiree groups and area religious leaders. Encourage them to survey their members' interests in activities for grandparents regarding children's literacy development. Make certain that the advertisements include a pitch to grandfathers as well as grandmothers, and that your hosting organizers know of your interest in and reasons for attracting grandfathers.

Consider cosponsoring a Grandparenting/Reparenting Support Group if your community does not have one. Rothenberg (1996) recommends these strategies as particularly useful for such groups:

- Collect and share resource information.
- Assist grandparents in helping children adjust to the stress of new living arrangements.
- Arrange for respite care during the group meetings.
- Invite agency personnel to explain the kinds of community services available to these families (it's likely that many more are available since these folks last raised children).

And surely, grandparents who are led to read children's literature with their grandchildren will come to see the many ways in which storybook sharing helps them and their grandchildren: spending a quiet, thoughtful, sitting-down time together; getting to know one another better; making connections to one another's pasts as well as dreams for the future; and helping children learn to read, converse, and solve problems.

Remind these grandfathers about the importance of sharing their own experiences with their grandchildren. They can teach them games (marbles, for example) and tell them interesting stories of their own lives, giving them an education not available to children of younger parents. In fact, we might suggest these men share kinds of information about themselves that are related to their own resilience, thereby providing a model of resilience for their grandchildren. The following topics, derived from a questionnaire, would provide important storytelling fodder for the group:

- Tell about times when you overcame problems or stresses in your life.
- Tell about brothers, sisters, or other family members who helped raise you.
- When you felt upset or in trouble, to whom did you turn, inside or outside your family?
- Tell how you cope with stress now.
- Tell about times when you helped others (Rak and Patterson, 1996).

4. Host a workshop for fathers (in the workplace) on ways to keep in touch with their children even though they travel or are separated. Contents for this workshop might include:
   - taping storybooks (sending a tape of your voice along with a paperback book),
   - tape-recording a story about your youth or your remembrances of a special time with your child or your family,
   - using a special color ink, rubber stamp, or sticker on each of your letters, showing that this is a special kind of writing for you.

If your community includes a military base, this would be an especially useful presentation because many of these fathers travel regularly. Many workplaces have a human resources officer who plans programs designed to enhance the welfare of their employees and families; this person would be a good contact for you. Plan to begin the workshop by reading aloud one of the children's books suggested in Chapter 3 to emphasize the importance of fathers in children's lives. Take along some good read-alouds and tape recorders for instant checkouts.

5. Connect your efforts with young men in your community. Consider enlisting help from student volunteer groups from your local college, or organizations such as Big Brothers or Save the Children's Mentoring Program. Suggest their participation in a Homework Help Night at the library, read-alouds, and other library programs as part of their yearly activities. Ask to speak at a Big Brothers meeting, to share the importance of men reading aloud to children, and to inform them of and invite them—along with their—"littles"—to special library events. Take along applications

for library cards as well as brochures about upcoming programs and events.

6. Arrange for college students to be pen pals. Make contact with a local college professor who teaches courses in reading education, language arts education, or English education. Ask about the possibility of arranging for a pen pal matching with a group of children who visit your school or public library. This gives you an opportunity to find a male pen pal for children who have fewer opportunities to engage in literacy activities with males. Have writing days during your library time so that you can send the letters to the professor. At Shippensburg University in Pennsylvania, this is a standard component of certain courses in teacher education, and college students eagerly look forward to mail from their pen pals. In addition to typical pen pal exchanges, these students share experiences with books they have read and content they are learning about. The experiences are profitable for the teachers-in-training, as they come to know about the literacy abilities and interests of real children, and the children enjoy a special opportunity to send and receive meaningful mail.

7. Collaborate with preparation for childbirth or parenting programs at your local medical center. (See "Catching New Fathers" for related information.) This kind of meeting often attracts nearly as many fathers as mothers, so it is an especially good venue for sharing our support for fathering. Parents-to-be are doing many things as they get ready for the baby; among these preparations is the construction of stories about the new baby and themselves as parents. Perhaps you already meet with these families to introduce them to the resources your library has to offer them. If you have a brochure about the importance of reading to children, make certain it includes fathers, and do bring copies along. Along with this introduction to your services and to the importance of fathers and mothers reading to their young children, you might emphasize two other ideas: (1) the importance of parents "conversing" with babies by singing, talking, making eye contact, and taking turns making sounds, and (2) the notion of a child starting life as a member of a family and an extended family, making this a time to begin thinking about meaningful family lore, such as finding out some of the family's baby-related rituals (how to soothe a crier, songs or poems to chant, attracting baby's attention).

You might want to talk about traditionally differentiated

Catching New Fathers: A Caution

The birth of a first child is often a critical time in a marriage. In spite of their best intentions, few couples accurately perceive the changes a new baby will bring to the marriage. We can't expect that new fathers will immediately adopt these new roles we have been discussing within the family. And, especially early on, fathers and mothers won't necessarily share the same level of eagerness about the care and nurturance of the baby. We recall a colleague, soon to be an excellent father, making an appointment and having to change it saying, "I keep forgetting we have a baby now." This is something his wife, although also a busy professional, would never have said! Belsky and Kelly (1994) reported that among the couples they studied, it often took longer for the father's love to take a strong hold and soar, and that fathers often needed more time than mothers in order to explore what did and didn't work when interacting with a newborn child. We should caution ourselves not to rush to judgment about the motivation of these newest fathers and to be patient with their need for extra time in developing interaction skills.

mother and father roles, and to speak of this as a time when the new family might diverge from those traditional roles (for example, fathers today *do* change diapers). This is also a good time to share fathering resources with the fathers in the audience.

8. Collaborate with high school home economics teachers. These teachers usually teach a unit on parenting and/or baby-sitting; it is usually required for both male and female students. Suggest a storybook reading or storytelling project for these students, offering the library's resources and maybe even your guest "lecturing." You might invite some of the students to share their skills during your regularly scheduled story times. In their book on fathering, Ross Parke and Armin Brott (1999) argue for providing formal parent education early in children's lives. This kind of content would give young men an opportunity to learn about and practice some important parenting behaviors, as well as prompt them to think about what they want to pass on to their own children in the future.

Many schools require students in home economics classes to have a short preschool teaching experience. If your area school district is one that does so, discuss the importance of males modeling an interest in books and reading, and suggest some books for the males to read aloud at circle time, along with some suggestions for playing with the ideas in the books.

Writing Personal-Social Stories for Children with Special Needs

Carol Gray (1998) has developed a technique for helping children with autism-related disorders that involves the writing of social stories for the children. These stories can be written by parents or teachers, and involve clearly describing particular situations for children, giving them information about others' perspectives of the situation, and giving information about what the child should do or say. These personalized stories can be used for a variety of situations, such as teaching a child about going to a friend's birthday party, going to restaurants, or going to the doctor's office. Photographs or drawings can be used to illustrate the stories. Parents might be interested in working together to write these stories for their children. Parents with computer expertise can contribute to that part of the task, those with verbal skills to the sentence writing, those with artistic skills to the drawings. While these stories have clear educational value, they will also become important memories for the children and parents; they will be stories of the important events in their children's lives.

---

9. Working with your local special-education agency/educators, hold a parent workshop on reading storybooks and telling stories to children with special needs. Storybook reading and talking about the story provide a good framework for parents to help their children learn many language and social skills. Research shows, however, that young children with disabilities are not read to as often as other children (Willoughby-Herb and Vaughan, 1996), and they miss the many fine parent-child interactions and the language stimulation that accompany this activity. We can demonstrate storybook interactions as well as share particular books that are appropriate for children with various kinds of disabilities. Remember to include storytelling as an important literacy activity for these parents too. Many parents find that storytelling based on day-to-day life experiences is a good way to teach their children some of the "scripts" that they have difficulty remembering. For example, taking turns telling the story of "What We Do When We Go for New Shoes," or "What We Do at Snack Time at School," will help children remember what they are to do and say in those situations. The information in the box above describes a recently developed technique for using personal stories to help children with autism. Workshops on these topics might be held jointly with your local early-intervention providers and/or special-education service providers. Try to identify fathers as well as mothers who can model the successful techniques they have discovered.

10. Contact your local Boy Scout or Boys Club to inquire whether baby-sitting, child care, and reading are among the topics covered in any projects the group conducts. Share your interest in encouraging fathers and young men to become more involved in children's literacy, and your interest in assisting with a possible collaborative project.

11. Work with father support groups in your community. Again, offer to do a presentation, ideally with modeling by male staff members. Consider, too, that some fathers in this group might not be custodial fathers; sharing with them the various weekend and summer vacation activities sponsored by your library could be a very effective way to involve them in literacy activities with their children.

12. Inquire about local services for teen fathers, and offer to provide a workshop for them. High schools often have programs for teen parents; contact the guidance office. Tichenor, Bock, and Sumner (1999) described a literacy program for twenty at-risk teenage parents. This program was designed and carried out collaboratively among a public librarian, a high school English teacher, and university practicum students. The at-risk students were taught about high-quality children's literature in their English classes; the public librarian provided the books for examination and taught them how to share the books effectively with young children, and the practicum students helped the high school students on a one-to-one basis. At the end of the class, each student wrote an original children's story. Results of the project included improvements in the students' reading and writing abilities. Although the author makes no mention of fathers having been involved in this project, this is certainly one that ought to be extended to fathers as well.

13. Target adolescents in foster care, another important group. Often these young people have little modeling or training in skills related to family life and child care. The Children's Defense Fund reported that "an estimated 20,000 young people leave foster care at 18 or 19 each year with no formal connections to family; they have not been returned to birth families or adopted" (Children's Defense Fund, 1999). If possible, arrange to have some separate sessions for the males and females, with training done by same-sex staff members. You might encourage them to read aloud to younger children in their homes, or to volunteer at your library, in order to practice their newly developed skills and understanding about reading aloud. Collect some

---

FOCUS ON PARTNERSHIPS: PTA FATHERS' COMMITTEE

Ian Elliot (1996) describes a father involvement project in Little Rock, Arkansas, that developed as a result of a PTA group sponsoring a fathers' committee. The "McDads' Club" at McDermon Elementary successfully involved fathers in a range of school activities: helping out in the classroom, homework support, playground renovation, and making presentations about vocations and professions. Among the findings the project coordinators made for maintaining father involvement was stressing the possibility of short-term as well as long-term involvement. More dads joined when there was an expectation that they would re-evaluate their time commitment periodically. One of the projects that stimulated interest for these fathers was bringing authors to school. Certainly, this activity might provide a fine avenue for collaboration between libraries (public and school) and fathers in the PTA.

---

storybooks as well as young-adult books that are particularly relevant to the lives of these children.

14. Contact family counselors and family physicians in your area, and apprise them of the resources you offer families. If you have made bookmark lists of good father books and resources, take copies to be distributed through these services. Offer to provide a display and a regular selection of read-alouds in their offices. Literacy advocacy through the medical profession is a successful national and regional model. People, especially younger people, tend to listen to their physicians so that a "prescription to read" to their children is often highly successful advice.

15. Contact high school counselors and teachers of family-living courses, sharing your resources and book lists. Identify young-adult novels with strong father roles, and suggest these be considered for book reports.

16. Work with local elementary schools on a joint literacy project aimed at parent involvement. You might supply materials about fathering to school personnel, and offer to hold a children's program at the library just for children whose parents are attending the program. See the "Focus on Partnerships" sidebar for a description of a successful PTA dads' group.

17. Contact child care providers and Head Start programs in your area. Most of these professionals plan a literacy program at least yearly, and family literacy is now a major emphasis of Head Start. Offer your assistance, sharing your interest in reaching out to fathers as well as mothers. The Library-Museum-Head Start Partnership, developed under the auspices of the Center for the Book at the Library of Congress and in collaboration with the Association for Library Service to Children (a division of the American Li-

Reclaiming Lost Boys

James Garbarino has spent more than 25 years studying the impact of violence on children and youth around the world. His book Lost Boys: Why Our Sons Turn Violent and How We Can Save Them reports his understandings based on lengthy interviews with boys who committed acts of lethal violence, and on his expertise in interpreting child development research. He identifies and brings understanding to situations likely to make a boy become violent, and he helps us understand ways in which we can work to prevent our boys from resorting to acts of violence.

Experiences with Literacy. Among the antidotes Garbarino recommends is literacy experiences. The following passage from the preface to his book illustrates the striking resemblance between approaches recommended for these young men and our knowledge of the real contributions literacy can make to any life. "Sitting behind closed doors week after week with boys who have nowhere to go, I gained a new appreciation for the value and the power of reflection, introspection, reading, and an open heart . . . I came to understand better than ever before the power of one's story, the value of one's personal narrative in making sense of experience, no matter how dark that experience may have been. And I came to appreciate as never before the critical importance of taking time, of being given time, and of feeling included." Garbarino's propositions can only strengthen our own resolve to bring the gifts of literacy to children whose lives can truly be changed through such encounters.

Experiences with Fathers. Garbarino presents startling data about the welfare of young people in America: in 1990, as many as 25% of American youth suffered from severe depression; in a 1992 survey, 35% of city-dwelling sixth to twelfth graders reported worrying that they would not reach old age because they will be shot; mental health researchers find that 20% of today's youth are sufficiently troubled and disrupted developmentally to require professional intervention.'Parental abandonment is cited as one of the significant factors related to the problems today's children experience. In presenting data specific to fathers, Garbarino reports that violence in boys is related to either of the following situations: the presence of an abusive father in the home or the absence of a caring and resourceful father. These boys miss the feelings of safety and unconditional love that a caring father could bring to their lives. Statistically, children whose mothers are involved with a man who is not the child's biological father are particularly at risk for child abuse of all kinds.

Experiences that Redirect and Reclaim. Garbarino's work with violent boys has led him to believe that the community can and should support these young at-risk boys early on. He is optimistic about ways a community and its institutions can help: providing emotional support for parents whose sons are demonstrating problem behaviors, seeing that children and their parents get professional help, and making efforts to find stable homes for all children. A fourth suggestion is one that we can incorporate into our own programming efforts: to commit ourselves to presenting these children with experiences that meet their developmental needs by providing them with stability and continuity in their other relationships in the community.

Garbarino says that "social health comes from stability, security, affirmation, time for

---

Reclaiming Lost Boys (continued)

socialization, economic equality, a good home for the spirit, a whole community, and democratic public institutions that protect human rights." By including these elements in our program plans for families and youth in at-risk neighborhoods, we take important steps toward becoming a social anchor that might contribute to a child being reclaimed (Garbarino, 1999:xi, 150).

---

brary Association), has produced an excellent manual entitled *The Library-Museum-Head Start Partnership: Books Change Lives*. It provides a detailed guide to carrying out collaborative literacy programming in Head Start programs and other settings. (See the Resources on Child Rearing and Children's Development section of Chapter 6 for ordering information.) Chapters include (1) Motivation to Read, (2) Materials Selection and Acquisition, (3) Activities in the Classroom, (4) Family Literacy: Building Bridges from Head Start to Home and Community, (5) Training/Education for Parents, Other Caregivers, and Teachers, (6) Community Collaboration and Resources, and (7) Examples of Head Start and Early Childhood Programs Carried on by Libraries and Museums.

18. Meet with professionals in your local juvenile justice and child welfare services. Offer support to their staff or directly to families by hosting presentations and providing book selections. In his book *Lost Boys: Why Our Sons Turn Violent and How We Can Save Them* (see review on page 99), James Garbarino draws conclusions about successful programs for violent boys. In discussing the fact that traumatized and abandoned young people often feel that life is meaningless, he cites psychologist James Pennebaker's research findings regarding the crucial importance of reading and writing in "the process of reclaiming violent and troubled boys, because they can find new alternative models for themselves in the positive lives of others" (Garbarino, 1999:227-228).

19. If there is a prison in your area, make contact with persons providing literacy activities. Suggest your support in helping fathers make taped stories to send to their children, in providing a read-aloud library for use during family visits, in encouraging writing to their children and getting involved in family storytelling. These kinds of activities will likely help fathers as well as their children, as many of these young

Breaking Barriers with Books

Name of Project: Breaking Barriers with Books
Director: Margaret Humadi Genisio
Address: Department of Reading
University of Wisconsin Oshkosh
800 Algoma Boulevard
Oshkosh, WI 54901
Target Population: Children, preschool through age 12, of men incarcerated at a 1,440-bed medium-security prison.
Mission/Goals: Breaking Barriers with Books' focus was on "the creation of long-lasting positive memories between father and child." The program goals were:
to provide the child with opportunities to enjoy literature with her or his father in much the same way as one would at home,
to provide the child with opportunities to strengthen paternal bonds, building positive memories,
to enhance a sense of paternal empowerment by giving fathers a strong information base to use in book sharing, and
to provide a model for a self-directed parents' support group, led by fathers, that could be replicated in the future.

Program goals were monitored by direct observation, interactive journal writing with the fathers, and documentation of continued program activity at the prison. The three programmatic components were (1) an instructional component, (2) the parent/child visitation, and (3) the parent support group meetings.
Results: The director found, through the journal entries of participants, an increasing use of book-sharing strategies, reflection about participation in the program, benefits to children, enhancement of parenting, and a sense of active fatherhood. Genisio remarks, "Fathers worked long hours to write in their journals, create extension activities, explore new children's literature, meet and take ownership of the program, focus on the parenting they were able to achieve through book sharing, and plan the way they might continue the program activities in the future" (Genisio, 1996:98). Breaking Barriers with Books received a Barbara Bush Family Literacy Grant.
Comments: In recent years some libraries, usually in concert with literacy programs, have been experimenting with prison-based reading programs for both fathers and mothers. We have talked to a few of the innovators behind such programs; there is no mistaking that this is one of the more challenging outreach projects a library can undertake, but it is also the most rewarding project for all involved—the prisoners, their children, and the library (Genisio, 1996).

men are examples of the "lost boys" Garbarino has studied. If you decide to try this kind of outreach, you will find Glen Palm's 1996 research in parent education with incarcerated fathers to be useful in planning your collaboration. Palm's findings include the importance of helping these men maintain contact with their young children, and of finding ways to express care and concern for their children. Other resources for this kind of program are:

(1) *F.A.T.H.E.R.S.* (Curtis, 1995), a project developed by the State Library of California that involves, among other objectives, teaching incarcerated fathers how to use children's books for teaching and making connections with their children, and

(2) First Book's (www.firstbook.org/) collaborative project with the Washington D.C. Family Literacy Project designed to develop parenting skills in mothers behind bars. Sheila Matthews, who is serving 15 to 45 months for possession to distribute cocaine says, "When I was drugging, I lost my kids . . . I'm glad that I can be a mother again and that [my son] will accept me." At the end of the program, each child received a free book from First Book, which, according to Kyle Zimmer, chief executive office of the nonprofit group, was "born out of a commitment to giving disadvantaged children their first new book." Department of Corrections Director Walter Ridley said the combination of the books, the story time, and the visits for mothers and children has a ripple effect: "Reading leads to a lot of opportunities, because people begin to feel good about themselves."

20. Contact the directors of your local literacy-related community agencies, offering your motivation and resources for getting fathers involved in reading aloud to their children. Organizations such as a Literacy Council, Head Start's Even Start family literacy program, and your local First Book advisory board would all leap at a chance to further collaborate with an outreach-minded public or school library.

Further Particulars on The Fatherhood Project

Name of Project: The Fatherhood Project® (sponsored by the Families and Work Institute)
Contact: James A. Levine, Ph.D., Director, or Edward W. Pitt, M.S.W., Associate Director
Address: The Fatherhood Project
Families and Work Institute
330 Seventh Avenue, 14th Floor
New York, NY 10001
Phone: (212) 465-2044
Fax: (212) 465-8637
E-mail: jlevine@familiesandwork.org
Mission/Goals: The Fatherhood Project is a national research and education project that is examining the future of fatherhood and developing ways to support men's involvement in child rearing. Its books, films, consultation, seminars, and training all present practical strategies to support fathers and mothers in their parenting roles. The institutional home of The Fatherhood Project is the Families and Work Institute, a nonprofit organization that addresses the changing nature of work and family life. FWI is committed to finding research-based strategies that foster mutually supportive connections among workplaces, families, and communities.
Background/History: The Fatherhood Project is the longest-running national initiative on fatherhood. It was founded in 1981 at the Bank Street College of Education in New York City by Dr. James A. Levine, and relocated in 1989 to the Families and Work Institute. In 1992, Ed Pitt, formerly director of health and social welfare programs at the National Urban League, joined the project as associate director.
Featured Component: The Male Involvement Project is a national training initiative that helps Head Start and early childhood programs get fathers and other significant men involved in their programs and in the lives of their children. Training is delivered by a national network of practitioners who have already been successful at increasing male involvement in their own programs. More than 2,000 practitioners have been trained in the last several years.
Target Population: The Fatherhood Project targets communities, businesses, and families for its many training components. The Male Involvement Project in particular focuses on early childhood programs and Head Start.
Comments: The Fatherhood Project publications and materials are among the best available in the United States. The longevity of the project may bring historical wisdom, but its administrators do not rest on their laurels—they seek current solutions to current problems and new strategies for ongoing problems.
Featured Publications:
Working Fathers: New Strategies for Balancing Work and Family by James Levine and Todd Pittinsky.
Parenting expert James A. Levine, director of the Fatherhood Project, and Todd L. Pittinsky of the Harvard Business School present a groundbreaking examination of the work-family dilemma and offer a proven and effective game plan to help fathers as well as mothers,

Further Particulars on The Fatherhood Project (continued)

employees as well as managers, succeed in managing the competing demands of home and work.

Working Fathers challenges conventional understanding of both the American workplace and the American family, showing:

- Why men's level of work-family conflict, although equal to women's, has remained an "invisible dilemma," something men don't talk about and the media has not picked up on.
- Why creating a father-friendly workplace is good for business productivity.
- Why creating a father-friendly workplace is a key to advancing women's equal opportunity.
- How media focus on paternity leave sidetracks the creation of the father-friendly workplace.
- Why fathers who want to improve their relationships with their children need to spend more time with their wives.
- Why addressing men's work-family conflict should be a key component of corporate diversity strategies.

New Expectations: Community Strategies for Responsible Fatherhood by James A. Levine, with Edward W. Pitt.

This release from the Fatherhood Project promotes a new way of thinking and acting to promote responsible fatherhood, including a jargon-free review of research, a state-of-the-art review of community-based strategies, tips from leading practitioners, and a guide to more than 300 programs nationwide and to the 100 most useful publications.

Getting Men Involved: Strategies for Early Childhood Programs by James A. Levine, Dennis T. Murphy, and Sherrill Wilson.

This is a hands-on guide for people working in early childhood programs who want to involve fathers and other significant males in children's lives. The first part outlines four "stages" of reaching and working with men and includes more than 100 practical strategies. The second part profiles 14 exemplary programs throughout the United States. A resource section includes an annotated bibliography of books for children that feature men in nurturing roles.

Fatherhood USA

This two-part documentary explores fatherhood beyond the stereotypes of deadbeat dads and Mr. Moms. It aired on PBS in June 1998 and was repeated after that by many stations. The first program, Dedicated, Not Deadbeat, looks at fathers in Baltimore and Boston who are finding community support in trying to be good fathers. The second program, Juggling Family and Work, focuses on three men in intact families who confront the daily dilemma of being a dad and handling the pressures of a workplace that isn't always "father-friendly."

Further Particulars on The Fatherhood Project (continued)

Fatherhood Workshop Kit

The Fatherhood Workshop kit, based on the two-part documentary Fatherhood USA, includes four video modules, a 24-page facilitator's guide, and a Fatherhood Tips handout. It is designed for community-based organizations and/or employers who want to be more effective in supporting the involvement of fathers in the lives of their children.

The four video workshop modules are:

- The Importance of Fathers
- Father-Mother Communication
- Juggling Work and Family
- Fathers and Social Support.

Note: Most of the information in this section was found on The Fatherhood Project Web site (www.fatherhoodproject.org/) and in Diane L. Carroad's interview of Jim Levine (1994).

CONCLUSION

We knew a public library director who believed wholeheartedly in quality library service inside the walls of "his" library, but heaven forbid one ever talked of outreach. It will always be simply "his" library if he refuses to look out the library's windows at the community's needs. Before another generation of children is sacrificed to a limited life without strong literacy skills, let's allow the library to be the strong advocate for words and books and information it was meant to be, both inside and outside its walls. Let's focus on reaching families and fathers to help children face the brightest future they can make for themselves in a community that cares for each one.

6 RESOURCES FOR FAMILIES AND LIBRARIES

This chapter provides resources that libraries might consider purchasing for their collections or bookmarking on their Web sites. These are good materials to support inspirational fathering or sound-father programs. Highlight them in displays or reading clubs. Shine a spotlight on the role of fathering in your community through the kinds of resources provided in this chapter. Read something that seems interesting to you; we all need to continue our educations to provide the best service possible.

RESOURCES ON FATHERING

FATHERING IN GENERAL

Abdullah, Omanii. 1993. *I Wanna Be the Kinda Father My Mother Was*. Syracuse, N.Y.: New Readers Press.
Easy-to-read poems directed toward young African American males. These thoughtful poems will be fine conversation starters for fathering groups. The reading level makes them appropriate for family literacy programs as well.

Blankenhorn, David. 1995. *Fatherless America*. New York: Basic Books.
Author Blankenhorn does not hesitate to state his strong opinions that fathers are critical to children's welfare and development at all levels, but especially on a day-to-day basis. A good push for getting fathers fully committed to their children's lives, but also a book to be cautious about regarding the message sent to single mothers.

Brott, Armin A. 1995. *The Expectant Father: Facts, Tips, and Advice for Dads-to-Be*. New York: Abbeyville Press.
This guide might attract men on its own, with its cover background design being a classic buttoned-down striped shirt. A quick review of the contents demonstrates that this is not the typical overview of prenatal and pregnancy development. It has a great deal of content particularly useful to fathers-to-be: ways to show your wife you care and what to do when left with a crying baby are two great sections. It also contains good information on the Family and Medical Leave Act of 1993.

———. 1997. *The New Father: A Dad's Guide to the First Year.* New York: Abbeyville Press.
A month-by-month guide to baby's development that includes items of particular concern to traditional fathers, such as how to get to know your baby as an individual even though you spend only a short time together daily. Brott emphasizes the importance of fathers reading to their children. This and all of Brott's books contain useful, up-to-date book lists recommended for reading aloud.

———. 1998. *The New Father: A Dad's Guide to the Toddler Years.* New York: Abbeyville Press.
Brott provides sound advice on topics relevant to parents of toddlers, such as helping baby deal with separation anxiety and what to do about TV, with accompanying book lists about reading to children. A display of the read-aloud titles recommended by Brott would probably be a successful library promotion for fathers.

Canfield, Ken R. 1992. *The 7 Secrets of Effective Fathers: Becoming the Father You Want to Be.* Wheaton, Ill.: Tyndale House.
This book presents guidelines for implementing the seven principles of effective fathering (commitment, knowing your child, consistency, protecting and providing, loving the child's mother, active listening, spiritual equipping) as developed through research conducted at the National Center for Fathering in Kansas City.

Dadmag.com. (www.dadmag.com)
This Web site/Web magazine offers a full spectrum of sound advice and resources for fathers, summed up well by this excerpted letter from the editor: "Why are we here? It's simple. Because in print or online, there's never been a real home for dads. We're members of the Great Ignored. Read the so-called parenting magazines and you'd think it was mom who single-handedly produced, raised and fretted over the kids. Our good friends in the men's magazine field like to pretend fathers don't exist. But life for guys doesn't stop when you're a dad. Fact is, it gets a lot richer and more exciting. Oh, yes—and complicated. So we're here to remind you of your fantastic accomplishment—and to guide you through the rough spots. Because, let's face it, nobody exactly prepared us for some of the sacrifice and compromise . . . We don't pretend to have all the answers. We don't even have all the questions. But we are here to help, to listen, even to entertain. Don't expect a lot of recycled sentiment. We promise to be responsible—but also provocative."

Dads Can: Building Father Involvement. (www.dadscan.org)
This Canadian site "promotes responsible and involved fathering by supporting men's personal development into fatherhood
and healthy fathering patterns in our society." The site includes
these sections: Fathering Tools, a chat room where many practical issues such as safety and managing car trips are discussed,
and a Fathering Information Network Directory (F.I.N.D.). The
site's "10 + 1 Tips for Father Involvement" would be very useful
for any fathering program or discussion. It includes encourage-
ment for fathers to "tell your story" to children and to promote
father-friendliness at work.

Families and Work Institute. (www.familiesandwork.org)
The Families and Work Institute was founded in 1989 by Dana
Friedman and Ellen Galinsky. Galinsky currently heads the project.
The institute is a "non-profit organization that addresses the
changing nature of work and family life . . . committed to finding
research-based strategies that foster mutually supportive connections among workplaces, families, and communities." This site is
a fine source of information on family research and policy as well
as technical assistance.

Fatherhood Initiative, Department of Health and Human Services.
(www.fatherhood.hhs.gov)
The Department of Health and Human Services has developed a
special initiative to support and strengthen the roles of fathers in
families. This initiative is guided by the following principles:

- All fathers can be important contributors to the well-being of their children.
- Parents are partners in raising their children, even when
  they do not live in the same household.
- The roles fathers play in families are diverse and related
  to cultural and community norms.
- Men should receive the education and support necessary
  to prepare them for the responsibility of parenthood.
- Government can encourage and promote father involvement through its programs and through its own workforce
  policies.

The Fatherhood Initiative notes, "The Department's activities account for those circumstances under which increased involvement
by a father or a mother may not be in the best interest of the
child. This is true for a small number of children, however. The
Department strongly supports family preservation and reunifica-

tion efforts when they do not risk the safety of the child." Components of the initiative include "Caring for Young Children," "Fathers and Children's Health," a "Toolkit for Fatherhood," "Research Reports," and "Program Evaluations."

Hass, Aaron. 1994. *The Gift of Fatherhood: How Men's Lives are Transformed by Their Children*. New York: Fireside.
Hass's work presents the social and emotional rewards of fatherhood, along with advice about how to develop more patience with children and how to find more time to enjoy them. His book also contains useful advice regarding the situations of divorced fathers and stepfathers.

Heinowitz, Jack. 1995. *Pregnant Fathers: Entering Parenthood Together*. San Diego: Parents as Partners Press.
Based on his own experiences, author Jack Heinowitz believes that to become a new kind of father, fatherhood must start at the beginning—pregnancy. His book contains advice to fathers at each phase of pregnancy, messages that are enhanced by many photographs of fathers and their children.

National Center for Fathering. (www.fathers.com)
A well-organized site that includes tips on fathering, a chat room, a bulletin board, humor, and research reviews. The site's mission is to "inspire and equip men to be better fathers," although most information is also very Christian in orientation. Founded in 1990 by Dr. Ken Canfield in response to a dramatic trend toward "fatherlessness" in America, the center conducts research on fathers and fathering and develops practical resources to prepare dads for nearly every fathering situation.

National Fatherhood Initiative. (www.fatherhood.org)
A nonsectarian, nonpartisan organization, the NFI was founded in 1994 to stimulate a society-wide movement to confront the growing problem of father absence. Its mission is to improve the well-being of children by increasing the number of children growing up with involved, committed, and responsible fathers in their lives. NFI organizes conferences and support programs, and provides resources to promote responsible fathering.

Pitts, Leonard, Jr. 1999. *Becoming Dad: Black Men and the Journey to Fatherhood*. Atlanta: Longstreet.
Leonard Pitts, the talented syndicated columnist, looks at fatherhood in the black family today through the lens of his own tense relationship as a son and his rewarding relationship as a dad.

Robbins, Elizabeth. 1996. *Fathers: A Loving Tribute*. New York: Random House.
This book of short writings about and by fathers celebrates and motivates fatherhood in its words and pictures, for example, this succinct English proverb: "One father is more than a hundred schoolmasters."

Roker, Al. 2000. *Don't Make Me Stop This Car! Adventures in Fatherhood*. New York: Scribner.
This humorous and sometimes touching view of parenting, especially in two-career families, might make a good first read for fathers. The vignettes presented in the short chapters might provide interesting discussion starters for a fathers' group.

Special Issue on Fathers and Sons. 2001. *Bookbird: A Journal of International Children's Literature, 39* (2).
This special issue of *Bookbird*, the Journal of the International Board on Books for Young People (IBBY), is devoted to fathers and sons and takes a broad, international view. "Masculinity in Australian Children's Literature," "Evolving Relationships of Fathers and Sons in Bengali Literature for Children," and "Affirmations of Fatherhood in Recent African American Picture Books" are just three of the articles included.

FATHERS AT WORK

Levine, James A., and Todd L. Pittinsky. 1997. *Working Fathers: New Strategies for Balancing Work and Family*. New York: Addison-Wesley.
Although this is a book for working fathers, working mothers will find it valuable as well. Its focus is on how the workplace impacts fatherhood, and confronts the stereotype of the father that can't or won't integrate work and family. The authors explain common stresses, but also suggest strategies for managing the "father self" at work and the "work self" at home.

Levine, Suzanne Braun. 2000. *Father Courage: What Happens When Men Put Family First*. New York: Harcourt.
This informative book will help those of us who are concerned about fatherhood to understand the culturally influenced difficulties many fathers experience when trying to be more involved in their families. We are reminded, for example, that the workplace is even less family-friendly for fathers than for mothers. Levine includes success stories as well, so readers can find models of successful "father courage" in this book.

FATHERS AT PLAY

Father's World. (www.fathersworld.com)
This Web site contains an amazing range of practical content (health, news, legal information) for all kinds of dads. It is rich with ideas for activities as well: games for fathers and children to play, recipes and suggestions for making the kitchen a classroom, and even suggestions for fathers interacting with one another (e.g., how to organize a weekly poker gathering).

Sullivan, S. Adams. 1992. *The Father's Almanac.* New York: Doubleday.
The real strength of this book is that it is full of activities for fathers to do with their children, throughout the year and across the years of childhood—games to play, toys to build, projects to work on together. This is a good companion for developing the playful role of fathering. The book also contains some advice on children's development and on managing work and fatherhood, but these areas are not as thoroughly or accurately covered here as in other sources listed.

SINGLE OR DIVORCED FATHERS

Biller, Henry B., and Robet J. Trotter. 1994. *The Father Factor: What You Need to Know to Make a Difference.* New York: Pocket Books.
Even though *The Father Factor*'s excellent content on how to be a good father is appropriate for all dads, the sections on single fathers and divorced fathers are especially useful.

Dolmetsch, Paul, and Alexa Shih, eds. 1985. *The Kids' Book About Single-Parent Families.* New York: Doubleday.
A rich resource for parents and children alike, as reflected in the authors' dedication: "To everyone who has lived, does live, and will live in a single-parent family." This book introduces children to the typical "stages" of development that single families go through, especially in the first few years. It provides guidelines for juggling two families and households. The chapter on the "ABCs of Single-Parent Families" covers a range of issues children confront, from reduced attention to a parent's depression. This book would be useful for a single fathers' support group, helping these fathers understand the challenges of their children's worlds.

Glennon, Will. 1995. *Fathering: Strengthening Connection with Your Children No Matter Where You Are.* Berkeley, Calif: Conari.
Advice for separated fathers is presented through interviews with more than 100 fathers representing a diverse population.

Gregg, Chuck. 1995. *Single Fatherhood: The Complete Guide.* New York: Sulzburger and Graham.
A lifelong guide for single fathers that includes good "how to do its" for daily tasks such as managing household duties, as well as for long-term planning such as preparing your child for college. Content helps fathers understand the unique and sometimes challenging aspects of their children's experiences as members of father-headed households.

Wallerstein, Judith S., and Joan Berlin Kelly. 1980. *Surviving the Breakup: How Children and Parents Cope with Divorce.* New York: Basic Books.
An older but quite helpful resource that examines the many effects of divorce on both children and parents.

See also sections on **Child Rearing in Divorced Families and Stepfamilies** (page 119) and **Resources on Child Rearing and Children's Development (Gender Related)**, especially Hope Edelman's *Motherless Daughters: The Legacy of Loss* (page 121).

STAY-AT-HOME DADS

At-Home Dad. (www.slowlane.com)
This on-line newsletter is edited by Peter Baylies. People who subscribe to the magazine are also provided with the *At-Home Dad Network* (www.slowlane.com) as a free service. The magazine is aimed at fathers who stay at home with their children, and is filled with tips for playing with and teaching children, handling problems, and even nurturing Dad, the caregiver. Sections include a "Feature Cover Story." "Spotlight On Dad" interviews and stories, "Home Business," "KidTips," and "Father Connections."

Daddys Home: An Online Resource for Primary Caregiver Fathers. (www.daddyshome.com)
Articles and resources on parenting for dads, with a section called The Kitchen, all from primary caregiving fathers.

Slowlane.com: The Online Resource for Stay at Home Dads. (www.slowlane.com)
Slowlane.com is a searchable on-line reference, resource, and network for stay-at-home dads (SAHD) and their families. The site provides dads with a searchable collection of articles and media clips written by, for, and about primary caregiving fathers. It also hosts multiple Web sites for at-home dads, including independent SAHD groups and several local Dad-to-Dad chapters, all of whose missions are to help dads connect with each other in their local

areas. Slowlane.com also contains an extensive collection of links to sites for all fathering issues, including local and international dad organizations, single dads, new dads, divorced dads, custody issues, personal stories, connecting with other dads, and much more.

TEEN FATHERS

Gravelle, Karen, and Leslie Peterson. 1992. *Teenage Fathers*. New York: Simon & Schuster.
The thoughts, feelings, and experiences of thirteen diverse teenage fathers are presented in short, easy-to-read chapters. A range of role models is presented, including a few teen dads who are uninvolved but most who are struggling to be or already are successfully involved with their children.

Lindsay, Jeanne W. 2000. *Teen Dads: Rights, Responsibilities and Joys*, 2d ed. Buena Park, Calif.: Morning Glory Press.
This book contains many sound recommendations for teen fathers, all the more valid because they are based on scores of interviews with teen dads. The book answers nearly every question one imagines a teen dad might have.

Lerman, Robert I., and Theodora J. Ooms, eds. 1993. *Young Unwed Fathers: Changing Roles & Emerging Policies*. Philadelphia: Temple University Press.
Lerman and Ooms present a broad spectrum of content regarding young unwed fathers, including statistical, sociological, legal, policy, and programmatic information.

FATHERS OF EXCEPTIONAL CHILDREN

Jacobs, Edward H. 1998. *Fathering the ADHD Child: A Book for Fathers, Mothers, and Professionals*. Northvale, N.J.: J. Aronson.
This book presents information on the challenges of parenting a child with ADHD that are unique to fathers. Its content is designed to help fathers understand diagnosis and assessment, and how children's learning needs are determined. Advice is included to help fathers work more effectively with their spouses, and to help them deal with their own emotional reactions.

Kilcarr, Patrick J., and Patricia O. Quinn. 1997. *Voices From Fatherhood: Fathers, Sons and ADHD*. New York: Brunner/Mazel.
Researchers and teachers often recommend that young males with Attention Deficit Hyperactivity Disorder spend more time with their fathers and that fathers should help mentor and provide

appropriate behavior models for their sons. This book, written by a father with two ADHD sons, provides an understanding and practical guide for fathers embarking on this journey.

May, James. 1992. *Circles of Care and Understanding: Support Programs for Fathers of Children with Special Needs.* Bethesda, Md.: Association for the Care of Children's Health.
This manual for motivating and guiding anyone wishing to establish a support group for fathers of exceptional children includes strategies and personal stories derived from James May's years of experience in working with these fathers. Useful appendices include, among other topics, recruitment techniques, sample activities, and evaluation strategies.

National Fathers' Network. (www.fathersnetwork.org)
The National Fathers' Network "assists men in overcoming the isolation and helplessness they often feel when their children are born with or develop special health care needs and developmental disabilities." The organization runs a demonstration program in Bellevue, Washington, and provides outreach support to individuals and organizations through its Web site. Support to organizations includes curricula and monographs on developing effective father support programs. The Web site contains articles by dads, photos, bulletin boards, information for providers, a calendar of events, and links to other resources. Information is available in Spanish as well as English.

See also the monthly column "Father's Voices" in *Exceptional Parent* magazine.

RESOURCES ON STRATEGIES FOR PROFESSIONALS WHO WORK WITH FATHERS

The Fatherhood Project Home Page. (www.fatherhoodproject.org)
The Fatherhood Project is a "national research and education project that is examining the future of fatherhood and developing ways to support men's involvement in child rearing." The project was begun in 1981 at the Bank Street College of Education and relocated in 1989 to the Families and Work Institute. Well-known researchers/practitioners James A. Levine, Ph.D., and

Edward W. Pitt, M.S.W., are the project director and associate director, respectively. The Web site contains descriptions of the project's various components, information about publications (including a Fatherhood Workshop Kit) and films produced by the project, and links to other fathering resources on the Web.

Father-to-Father/FatherNet. (www.cyfc.umn.edu/FatherNet)
Father-to-Father is a national effort to unite men in the task of being a strong and positive force in their children's lives. With assistance from central resource teams, local communities or agencies that choose to participate in Father-to-Father will develop their own plan to expand and enhance existing father support programs, to create new opportunities for men to come together one-on-one or in groups to support each other in their role as fathers, and to rally businesses, congregations, schools, and agencies to focus on the importance of fathers in children's lives.

Full-Time Dads Online. (www.fathering.com/ftd)
This site is host to the on-line newsletter *Full-Time Dads*. Current articles and selected print articles from past issues are archived. Archival articles cover a range of topics, and would provide interesting discussion starters.

Levine, James A., Dennis T. Murphy, and Sherrill Wilson. 1993. *Getting Men Involved: Strategies for Early Childhood Programs.* New York: Scholastic.
Although the title focuses on early childhood education, this accessible manual is an outstanding resource for anyone wishing to involve fathers in their programs. The strategies and information contained here are based on extensive examinations of successful programs, many of which primarily serve low-income families. The book also contains an appendix of children's books grouped by characters' race and ethnicity. Easily applied concepts and practices abound in this useful guide.

Levine, James A., with Edward W. Pitt. 1995. *New Expectations: Community Strategies for Responsible Fatherhood.* New York: Families and Work Institute.
Another practical manual for practitioners, *New Expectations* is based on The Fatherhood Project's approach to supporting fathers' involvement with children. It includes useful descriptions of many successful programs, a curriculum for dads, identification of more than 300 fathering programs listed by state, and national and state resources for those seeking to develop community programs.

May, James. 1992. *Circles of Care and Understanding: Support Programs for Fathers of Children with Special Needs.* (See page 115.)

Public/Private Ventures. 1995. *Fatherhood Development: A Curriculum for Young Fathers.* Philadelphia: Public/Private Ventures. This instructional guide was developed for use by the Public/Private Ventures model program for young fathers.

Reading Is Fundamental. 2001. *Fathers' Roles/Men's Voices.* Show 204. RIF Exchange. Videocassette.
This hour-long video program from the media wing of Reading Is Fundamental focuses on strategies for engaging men in children's literacy initiatives and features guests who are working directly with dads, including Christopher Barnes, the Family Services Coordinator of the St. Francis Xavier Head Start in Baltimore, and Robert Ortiz of Cal State, Fullerton. Steven Herb, coauthor of this book, also appears on the program, addressing the role of libraries in connecting fathers, books, and children. For further information, see www.rifnet.org/204/204_index.html.

RESOURCES ON GRANDPARENTING

AARP. *Grandparents Raising Grandchildren: Where to Find Help.* Washington, D.C.: www.aarp.org/confacts/programs/grandraising.html.
Founded in 1958 by retired California educator Dr. Ethel Percy Andrus, AARP (formerly known as the American Association of Retired Persons) today represents more than 34 million members. More than half of the members are working either full-time or part-time; the rest are fully retired. The role of AARP members in the lives of their grandchildren, especially those primarily responsible for their grandchildren's upbringing, is the focus of this portion of AARP's extensive (and helpful) Web site.

Cohen, Joan S. *Helping Your Grandchildren Through Their Parents' Divorce.* 1994. New York: Walker.
This thoroughly informative book for grandparents contains advice for dealing with a broad range of circumstances. Appendices contain resources for networking, statutes on grandparents' visitation, and helpful books and publications.

De Toledo, Sylvie, and Deborah Brown. 1995. *Grandparents as Parents: A Survival Guide for Raising a Second Family*. New York: Guilford Press.
The title describes the approach of this volume designed to help grandparents with a right to that feeling of déjà vu regarding child rearing.

Kornhaber, Arthur, 1994. *Grandparent Power!* New York: Crown.
This book, written by the founder of the Foundation for Grandparenting (www.grandparenting.org), is filled with wisdom and practices related to securing grandparents' important roles in their grandchildren's lives.

Zullo, Kathryn and Allan Zullo. 1998. *The Nanas and the Papas: A Boomer's Guide to Grandparenting*. Kansas City, Mo.: Andrews McMeel.
As the title suggests (remember the Mamas and the Papas?), this grandparent guide is perfect for baby boomers who have become grandparents. The Zullos' suggestions include boomer-specific ways to have fun with grandchildren (tell them about rotary phones, peashooters, and home milk delivery; sing them Sheb Wooley's "The Purple People Eater" for fun, Herman's Hermits "There's a Kind of Hush" for bedtime). But maybe more importantly, the authors have included specific ways to deal with the many family issues today's grandparents are coping with: being a good long-distance grandparent, helping grandchildren deal with their parents' or grandparents' divorce, and living in multigenerational households.

RESOURCES ON CHILD REARING AND CHILDREN'S DEVELOPMENT

GENERAL

Brazelton, T. Berry. 1984. *To Listen to a Child: Understanding the Normal Problems of Growing Up*. New York: Perseus.
The highly useful information and recommendations come from America's most popular pediatrician. Informed by years of research and practice, Dr. Brazelton presents practical and accessible suggestions about how to deal with common parenting difficulties, including dealing with fears, discipline, and emotional difficulties.

Cooper, Scott. 2000. *Sticks and Stones: Seven Ways Your Child Can Deal with Teasing, Conflict, and Other Hard Times.* New York: Random House.
Developmentally sound and accessible advice about the kinds of difficult situations that children experience during their school years and that are traditionally referred to Dad. The advice is presented using birds for analogies (e.g., teasing is dealt with in "the way of the hummingbird"), making the advice easy to picture and retrieve. This small, easily read, and easy-to-use resource might be especially helpful for fathers of children who have learning or behavior problems.

Mathews, Virginia H., and Susan Roman. 1999. *A Library Head Start to Literacy: The Resource Notebook for the Library-Museum-Head Start Partnership.* Washington, D.C.: Center for the Book/Library of Congress.
Developed under the auspices of the Center for the Book at the Library of Congress and in collaboration with the Association for Library Service to Children (a division of the American Library Association), this excellent manual is the complete guide to library-based literacy programming and literacy collaboration in the community. Order from your book jobber or from the Center for the Book: Library of Congress, The Center for the Book, 101 Independence Avenue SE, Washington, DC 20540-4920; call (202) 707-5221; fax (202) 707-0269; or e-mail cfbook@loc.gov. Additional literacy materials are available under the auspices of the Born to Read project developed by Dr. Roman and others at the Association for Library Service to Children, 50 East Huron Street, Chicago, IL 60611; (800) 545-2433.

CHILD REARING IN DIVORCED FAMILIES AND STEPFAMILIES

Ricci, Isolina. 1997. *Mom's House, Dad's House: Making Two Homes for Your Children.* New York: Fireside.
This is a wonderful reference for parents. The 20 chapters and several appendices will help families deal with a wide range of topics, from initially helping children develop feelings of security and continuity to helping plan family events such as weddings.

Visher, Emily B., and John S. Visher. 1991. *How to Win As a Step Family.* 2nd ed. New York: Brunner/Mazel.
This useful resource was written by the founders of The Step Family Association of America. It is easy to read and contains suggestions and guidelines for handling such issues as deceased parents, legal questions, and dealing with grandparents and ex-spouses.

Particular attention is given to what one might expect in terms of children's reactions to the situations discussed.

RESOURCES ON CHILD REARING AND CHILDREN'S DEVELOPMENT (GENDER RELATED)

BOYS

Boyd-Franklin, Nancy, and A. J. Franklin. 2000. *Boys into Men: Raising Our African American Teenage Sons.* New York: Dutton.
Boys into Men includes challenging topics such as black kids in white schools, peer and media pressures, and drug use. The book provides helpful suggestions of what parents should be aware of in their children and what they can do about problem situations. The resource lists contain information about supportive national and regional organizations and programs.

Elium, Don, and Jeanne Elium. 1996. *Raising a Son: Parents and the Making of a Healthy Man.* Berkeley, Calif.: Celestial Arts.
An easy-to-read-and-interpret guide to raising male children from birth through adulthood. The Eliums share developmental information related to nurturing sons, as well as approaches for dealing with the challenges presented by both biology and our culture.

Garbarino, James, and Claire Bedard. 2001. *Parents under Siege: Why You Are the Solution, Not the Problem in Your Child's Life.* New York: The Free Press.
A troubling yet ultimately hopeful look at teen violence, with a focus on the parents of Dylan Klebold of Columbine High School, and what parents can do to truly know their children. The spotlight shines on the early years and the development of communication patterns and trust that will prevent children from developing a toxic secret life.

Kindlon, Dan, and Michel Thompson. 1999. *Raising Cain: Protecting the Emotional Life of Boys.* New York: Random House.
Based on a review of the state of boys' development in today's world, the authors present their conclusions about what boys need to face the struggles they meet in our educational and cultural worlds. The book pays specific attention to the needs of males in terms of issues such as discipline, drinking and drugs, depression, and suicide.

Miedzian, Myriam. 1991. *Boys Will Be Boys: Breaking the Link Between Masculinity and Violence.* New York: Doubleday.
Miedzian challenges the notion that males are naturally more violent than females, and emphasizes that "father's nurturant involvement in rearing boys plays a major role in discouraging violence in them."

GIRLS

American Association of University Women. 1995. *How Schools Shortchange Girls: A Study of Major Findings on Girls and Education.* New York: Marlowe.
This study summarizes the 1992 AAUW's report on the scholastic achievements of girls vs. boys from preschool through high school. Data on classroom experiences, school grades, SAT scores, and other standardized tests are included. It concludes with suggestions for the kinds of experiences that girls need in order to fulfill their intellectual potential.

Edelman, Hope. 1994. *Motherless Daughters: The Legacy of Loss.* Reading, Mass.: Addison-Wesley.
Through personal stories of 92 motherless women who were interviewed and many more who submitted information through the mail, Edelman helps us understand the effects that the loss of a mother has on girls in early childhood, middle childhood, and adolescence. The chapter "Daddy's Little Girl" is especially helpful for fathers trying to discern and cope with a girl's many strong feelings.

Elium, Jeanne, and Don Elium. 1994. *Raising a Daughter: Parents and the Awakening of a Healthy Woman.* Berkeley, Calif.: Celestial Arts.
This focus on daughters is another helpful parenting guide from the prolific Eliums, whose other titles include *Raising a Teenager: Parents and the Nurturing of a Responsible Teen* and *Raising a Family: Living on Planet Parenthood.* See the **Boys** section for their *Raising a Son: Parents and the Making of a Healthy Man.*

Orenstein, Peggy. 1994. *School Girls: Young Women, Self-esteem, and the Confidence Gap.* New York: Doubleday.
This report on the experiences of schoolgirls from an urban and a suburban middle school during the 1992-1993 school year is based on observations and interviews. Implications are made concerning the roles parents and teachers can play in nurturing the social and intellectual development of girls.

ADDITIONAL WEB RESOURCES WITH A FOCUS ON FATHERS AND FATHERING

American Coalition for Fathers and Children. (www.acfc.org) The members of the American Coalition for Fathers and Children dedicate themselves and their efforts "to the creation of a family law system, legislative system, and public awareness which promotes equal rights for *ALL* parties affected by divorce, and the breakup of a family or establishment of paternity. It is our belief through our involvement and dedication, we can have a positive effect on the emotional and psychological well-being of children." The ACFC is one of a number of strong advocacy sites for fathers that are quite conservative in their approach to all aspects of fathering. It does not lessen the value of some of their resources, but the overall tone of such sites sometimes paints a negative picture of perceived roadblocks to fathers getting everything they want or need. These perceived roadblocks may be the courts, antifather/promother laws, or mothers themselves. Caveat emptor.

Center on Fathers, Families, and Public Policy. (www.cffpp.org) CFFPP is a nationally focused public policy organization conducting policy research, technical assistance, training, litigation, and public education in order to focus attention on the barriers faced by never-married low-income fathers and their families.

Dads and Daughters. (www.dadsanddaughters.org) DADS is a national nonprofit membership organization of fathers and daughters that provides tools to strengthen father-daughter relationships and to transform the pervasive cultural messages that value daughters more for how they look than for who they are.

Dads at a Distance. (www.daads.com) This resource for traveling or noncustodial fathers (from the National Long Distance Relationship Building Institute) seeks to maintain and strengthen the relationships fathers have with their children while they are away.

Families Like Ours, Inc. (www.familieslikeours.org)

This nonprofit organization's extensive Web site is devoted to the needs and support of gay, lesbian, bisexual, and transgender adoptive and preadoptive families.

Fathers Are Parents Too. (www.fapt.org)
FAPT is a Georgia-based coalition of fathers, mothers, grandparents, and others working to ensure the rights of children to have a loving, nurturing relationship with both of their parents and their families. The site tends toward the conservative on many issues.

Fathers Direct. (www.fathersdirect.com)
This site "for fathers, by fathers" offers a library of books on parenting (including children's books), activities, and advice.

FatherWork: Stories, Ideas and Activities to Encourage Generative Fathering. (http://fatherwork.byu.edu)
The two founders, associate professors of family sciences at Brigham Young University, believe that many fathers are pioneers in their efforts to care for their children today, and that they are blazing trails and exploring unmapped territory. They contend that most fathers want to do a good job, but that they often face significant barriers to achieving that goal. Their focus is on good fathering, not good fathers. They assume that most fathers want to improve and that all fathers make mistakes. Based on the concept that stories joined with ideas provide a helpful way to promote learning and change, FatherWork's interesting approach focuses on using stories to understand and encourage good fathering.

La Pa's Transformation of Fatherhood. (www.lapas.org)
La Pa's, a self-described "wink at Lamaze," tries to give expectant fathers a good idea of what to expect after the baby is born. Created by two good friends who happen to be dads as well as family therapists/counselors, the site includes a pop quiz about impending fatherhood, information about fatherhood, Today's Father (Myth of the Divorced Dad), an archive, and on-line resources.

Promoting Responsible Fatherhood. (www.vev.ch/en/index.htm)
International Web site based in Switzerland (available in English, German, and French) that promotes responsible fatherhood and motherhood whatever the status of the relationship of the parents. The goal is an equally good relationship for the children with the father and the mother.

Single and Custodial Fathers Network, Inc. (www.scfn.org)
SCFN is an international member-supported nonprofit organization dedicated to helping fathers meet the challenge of being parents. The organization provides informational and supportive services to fathers and their families, and supports fatherhood through research, publications, and interactive communications.

7 CHILDREN'S BOOKS ABOUT FATHERS AND FATHERING

This chapter provides annotations on more than 450 children's books designed for children birth through age eight; the books are divided into dozens of subject and format categories. Although many books appear only once or twice, others appear up to six times, depending on their suitability for multiple category listings. The subject lists were designed to support library programming for fathers and collection development in support of fathers and families.

INFORMATIONAL AND NONFICTION BOOKS

ANIMAL PARENTS

Collard, Sneed B., III. 2000. *Animal Dads*. Illustrated by Steve Jenkins. New York: Houghton Mifflin Company. From poison-arrow frog chauffeurs to desert isopod house cleaners, this book presents fun and interesting facts about dads from the animal kingdom. A perfect book for discussions on Father's Day.

Cutchins, Judy, and Ginny Johnston. 1994. *Parenting Papas: Unusual Animal Fathers*. New York: Morrow Junior Books. This highly informative book presents facts about animal dads that are involved in gestational or parental duties.

Dijs, Carla. 1990. *Are You My Daddy?* New York: Simon & Schuster. This simple pop-up book is a surefire hit with preschoolers, who will love the silliness of the concept that a polar bear, turtle, ostrich, or crocodile could be a baby tiger's daddy!

Heller, Ruth. 1981. *Chickens Aren't the Only Ones*. New York: Grosset & Dunlap. This factual book teaches about the many types of animals that lay eggs, including a group of animal fathers who play important paternal roles.

Marzollo, Jean. 2000. *Papa Papa*. Illustrated by Laura Regan. New York: HarperCollins Children's Book Group. This charming board book depicts in delicate rhymes animal babies with their fathers. Readers might wish to consider the companion book, *Mama Mama*.

Rockwell, Anne. 1994. *Ducklings and Pollywogs*. Illustrated by Lizzy Rockwell. New York: Macmillan Publishing Company. A father and daughter explore the many animals and plants at a pond through the four seasons.

Swinburne, Stephen R. 1999. *Safe, Warm, and Snug*. Illustrated by Jose Aruego and Ariane Dewey. San Diego: Gulliver Books. This factual book outlines the ways in which animal fathers and mothers protect their infant young.

Wood, Jakki. 1992. *Dads Are Such Fun*. Illustrated by Rog Bonner. New York: Simon & Schuster Books for Young Readers. This simple book shows through the use of human and animal fathers and their children that dads are wonderful for many different reasons.

FAMOUS DADS

Gutman, Bill. 1993. *Ken Griffey, Sr. and Ken Griffey, Jr., Father and Son Teammates*. Brookfield, Conn.: Millbrook Press, Inc. Although this book needs to be updated for those readers interested more in statistics and recent career information, it is a good biography for older readers and adults interested in this history-making father and son pair. Readers might be surprised to learn of the indirect nature of the influence Ken, Sr. had in shaping his young ball-playing son, and that for many years he was entirely absent from Ken, Jr.'s life.

Monjo, F. N. 1961. *The One Bad Thing about Father*. Illustrated by Rocco Negri. New York: Harper & Row. An I CAN READ History Book. Told through the voice of Quentin, Theodore Roosevelt's son, this story captures wonderful family moments shared in the White House.

Moutoussamy-Ashe, Jeanne. 1993. *Daddy and Me: A Photo Story of Arthur Ashe and His Daughter Camera*. New York: Alfred A. Knopf. This photo-essay featuring Arthur Ashe and his daughter, Camera, depicts the true love this famous father shared with his daughter. A wonderful book for discussions about AIDS, unconditional love, and living with illness.

Smith, Will. 1999. *Just the Two of Us*. Illustrated by Kadir Nelson. New York: Scholastic Press. This book uses the powerful and positive lyrics of Will Smith's song "Just the Two of Us" and beautifully crafted illustrations to depict the growing relationship between a father and his son.

FATHERS WHO ARE PHYSICALLY CHALLENGED

Abbott, Deborah, and Henry Kisor. 1994. *One TV Blasting and a Pig Outdoors*. Illustrated by Leslie Morrill. Morton Grove, Ill.: Albert Whitman & Company. Although this book is fictional, a boy's narrative account of life with his deaf father reads more like a biographical portrait. The narrative contains a good deal of information about deafness and many lighthearted anecdotes that portray parenting challenges.

Moutoussamy-Ashe, Jeanne. 1993. *Daddy and Me: A Photo Story of Arthur Ashe and His Daughter Camera*. New York: Alfred A. Knopf. This photo-essay featuring Arthur Ashe and his daughter, Camera, depicts the true love this famous father shared with his daughter. A wonderful book for discussions about AIDS, unconditional love, and living with illness.

POETRY

Hoberman, Mary Ann. 1991. *Fathers, Mothers, Sisters, Brothers: A Collection of Family Poems*. Illustrated by Marylin Hafner. Boston: Little, Brown & Company. This book of poetry highlights many types of families.

Lauture, Denizé. 1996. *Father and Son*. Illustrated by Jonathan Green. New York: Penguin Putnam Books for Young Readers. The author's dedication to this poem about a father and son is worth mentioning: "To all children who show great respect and love to every decent man they meet down the many roads of life. To all men who understand that they must love, adopt, and give a hand to all children of our poor planet."

Livingston, Myra Cohn. 1989. *Poems for Fathers*. Illustrated by Robert Casilla. New York: Holiday House. This is a simple collection of poems covering many topics related to fathers.

Manushkin, Fran. 1995. *The Matzah That Papa Brought Home*. Illustrated by Ned Bittinger. New York: Scholastic, Inc. The repetitious rhyming text and detailed illustrations of this book bring to life the culture of a Jewish family celebrating Passover.

Micklos, John. 2000. *Daddy Poems*. Illustrated by Robert Casilla. Foreword by Jim Trelease. Honesdale, Penn.: Boyds Mills Press. This poetic celebration of fathers depicts dads of many ethnicities.

Moss, Jeff. 1999. *The Dad of the Dad of the Dad of Your Dad: Stories about Kids and their Fathers*. Illustrated by Chris Demarest. New York: Ballantine Publishing Group. A collection of entertaining poetry about the relationships between fathers and children during various historic time periods, such as the Stone Age. Older children will appreciate this one.

Steptoe, Javaka, illustrator. 2001. *In Daddy's Arms I Am Tall: African Americans Celebrating Fathers*. New York: Lee & Low Books, Inc. A captivating picture-book anthology of poems that portray as many different feelings about fathers as there are authors. There is something here for all age groups.

Walters, Virginia. 1999. *Are We There Yet, Daddy?* Illustrated by S. D. Schindler. New York: Viking. This rhyming repetitive text counts down the miles on a 100-mile journey to Grandma's house as a patient father responds to that all-too-frequently asked question.

PHOTO-ESSAYS

Bailey, Debbie. 1991. *My Dad*. Photo-illustrated by Susan Huszar. Willowdale, Ontario: Annick Press. This simple board book highlights visually and through simple text the relationship toddlers and fathers have, and features fathers of many ethnicities.

Cone, Molly. 1983. *Paul David Silverman Is a Father*. Photo-illustrated by Harold Roth. New York: Dutton. This book outlines through simple text and photographs the story of teenage parents who decide to get married.

Greenspun, Adele Aron. 1991. *Daddies*. New York: Philomel Books. This simple book with touching black-and-white photographs captures the many ways fathers love their children.

Hausherr, Rosmarie. 1997. *Celebrating Families.* New York: Scholastic, Inc. Families with stepparents, incarcerated fathers, and biracial parents are among the many different families presented in this nonfiction book.

Miller, Margaret. 1998. *Big and Little.* New York: Greenwillow Books. The fun of relative size is emphasized in this book with colorful photographic images and simple text; many types of families and people are featured.

Morris, Ann. 1995. *The Daddy Book.* Photo-illustrated by Ken Heyman. Parsippany, N.J.: Silver Burdett Press. Many kinds of dads are depicted loving, playing, and working with their children in this multicultural photo-essay. Thumbnail photos and additional notes are in the "Index to Daddies."

———. 1993. *Puddle Jumper: How a Toy Is Made.* Photo-illustrated by Ken Heyman. New York: Lothrop, Lee & Shepard Books. Sarah helps her father build a rocking toy in his wood shop.

Moutoussamy-Ashe, Jeanne. 1993. *Daddy and Me: A Photo Story of Arthur Ashe and His Daughter Camera.* New York: Alfred A. Knopf. This photo-essay featuring Arthur Ashe and his daughter, Camera, depicts the true love this famous father shared with his daughter. A wonderful book for discussions about AIDS, unconditional love, and living with illness.

Rotner, Shelley, and Sheila M. Kelly. 2000. *Lots of Dads.* Photo-illustrated by Shelley Rotner. New York: Penguin Putnam Books for Young Readers. Babies and young children are shown with their fathers in a variety of positive nurturing situations.

Senisi, Ellen B. 1998. *For My Family, Love, Allie.* Morton Grove, Ill.: Albert Whitman & Company. In this extended family gathering, which is a celebration of Jamaican food and culture, grandfathers, uncles, and fathers all share cooking and parenting responsibilities with the women. Photographs depict Allie's biracial parents and the upbeat occasion.

BOOKS FOR SPECIFIC AGE GROUPS

BOARD BOOKS AND BOOKS FOR BABIES AND TODDLERS

Bailey, Debbie. 1991. *My Dad.* Photo-illustrated by Susan Huszar. Willowdale, Ontario: Annick Press. Visually and through simple text, this simple board book highlights the relationship toddlers and fathers have, and features fathers of many ethnicities.

Cabban, Vanessa. 1999. *Bertie and Small and the Brave Sea Journey.* Cambridge, Mass.: Candlewick Press. Daddy joins in the imaginative game with his toddler, a toy rabbit, a stuffed crocodile, and a real dog.

Dijs, Carla. 1990. *Are You My Daddy?* New York: Simon & Schuster. This simple pop-up book is a sure-fire hit with preschoolers, who will surely love the silliness of the concept that a polar bear, turtle, ostrich, or crocodile could be a baby tiger's daddy!

———. 1996. *Daddy, Would You Love Me If... ?* New York: Simon & Schuster. Daddy penguin eases a young penguin's concerns about growing up different from him, thus losing his love, in this pop-up story.

Falwell, Cathryn. 1992. *Nicky Loves Daddy.* New York: Clarion Books. This simple book for toddlers, with large text, expresses the tender love a young boy feels for his father as they go for a walk.

Greenfield, Eloise. 1991. *My Daddy and I.* Illustrated by Jan Spivey Gilchrist. New York: Black Butterfly Children's Books. Cooking, cleaning, reading—daddy and son do everything together in this board book best suited for preschoolers.

Johnson, Angela. 1994. *Joshua's Night Whispers.* Illustrated by Rhonda Mitchell. New York: Orchard Books. Joshua is awakened by night whispers and finds comfort in his father's arms in this board book.

Le Saux, Alain. *King Daddy, Daddy Scratches, Daddy Sleeps,* and *Daddy Shaves.* See **Series.**

Marzollo, Jean. 2000. *Papa Papa.* Illustrated by Laura Regan. New York: HarperCollins Children's Book Group. This charming board book depicts in delicate rhymes animal babies with their fathers. Readers might wish to consider the companion book, *Mama Mama.*

Ormerod, Jan. *Messy Baby.* See **Series.**

Oxenbury, Helen. 1991. *Good Night, Good Morning.* New York: Penguin Putnam Books for Young Readers. In this cheerful, textless board book, the reader finds a mischievous young child and his father engaging in many activities, including reading, bathing, and shaving.

———. 1998. *Tom and Pippo Read a Story.* New York: Simon & Schuster Children's Publishing. Tom is an excellent role model for his toddler peers who are becoming interested in books. When Daddy takes time out from his newspaper to read with Tom, he becomes a role model for fathers.

Reasoner, Charles. 1997. *Whose Daddy Does This?* New York: Penguin Putnam Books for Young Readers. Adults and toddlers will have fun sliding apart this board book to discover the animal answers to questions such as "Whose daddy baby-sits all day long?" and "Whose daddy leads the pack?"

Regan, Dian Curtis. 1996. *Daddies.* Illustrated by Mary Morgan. New York: Scholastic Inc. Babies' and toddlers' voices express, in gentle rhymes, the various activities enjoyed with their daddies.

Taylor, Ann. 1999. *Baby Dance*. Illustrated by Marjorie Van Heerden. New York: HarperCollins Children's Book Group. While Mama naps, Daddy magically transforms a baby's tears into smiles, thanks to a little song and dance therapy in this rhythmic board book.

Williams, Vera B. 1990. *"More More More," Said the Baby: Three Love Stories*. New York: Greenwillow Books. This wonderfully colorful book will either make you want to be a little baby again, being tossed and tickled and talked to tenderly, or make you want to emulate the loving daddy and other adults providing all the fun.

Wood, Jakki. 1992. *Dads Are Such Fun*. Illustrated by Rog Bonner. New York: Simon & Schuster Books for Young Readers. This simple book shows through the use of human and animal fathers and their children that dads are wonderful for many different reasons.

PICTURE BOOKS FOR PRESCHOOLERS

Anderson, Peggy Perry. 2001. *To the Tub*. New York: Houghton Mifflin Company. Parents will especially relate to the frustrated father frog's attempts to get junior to the bathtub, and both children and parents will enjoy the ending, in which father's playful side takes over.

Asch, Frank. 1984. *Just Like Daddy*. New York: Simon & Schuster Books for Young Readers. A young bear emulates Daddy Bear as they prepare for a fishing trip that ends with a surprise.

Brillhart, Julie. 1995. *When Daddy Came to School*. Morton Grove, Ill.: Albert Whitman & Company. On his son's third birthday, Daddy spends the day with him at preschool—a gift more precious than anything money could buy.

———. 1997. *When Daddy Took Us Camping*. Morton Grove, Ill.: Albert Whitman & Company. Dad has an amazing ability to create an authentic camping experience for his children under unusual circumstances.

Brown, Margaret Wise. 1998. *The Little Scarecrow Boy*. Illustrated by David Diaz. New York: HarperCollins Publishers. Although this scarecrow dad is mean, fierce, and scary, he also exhibits much sensitivity in dealing with his inexperienced, young scarecrow son.

Browne, Anthony. 2000. *My Dad*. New York: Farrar, Straus, & Giroux. Dad can do anything and do it well in this cleverly illustrated picture book.

Buckley, Helen E. 1999. *Where Did Josie Go?* Illustrated by Jan Ormerod. New York: Morrow/Avon. Readers can participate in the search for Josie, along with Mom and Dad, who indulge in this now classic game of hide-and-seek. Toddlers may ask questions regarding Mom's big stomach!

Butterworth, Nick. 1992. *My Dad Is Awesome*. Cambridge, Mass.: Candlewick Press. A young child idolizes his dad for such things as being able to cook three-layer cakes and running as fast as a cheetah. The illustrations depict Dad enthusiastically in this wondrous role.

Carle, Eric. 1986. *Papa, Please Get the Moon for Me*. Natick, Mass.: Picture Book Studio USA. Monica asks for the moon and, miraculously, this superdad delivers! But there's a catch: The moon continues to get smaller and smaller.

Carmichael, Clay. 1996. *Bear at the Beach*. New York: North-South Books. Bear longs for a father, and discovers him in the night sky.

Catalanotto, Peter. 1999. *The Painter*. New York: Scholastic, Inc. A father balances parenting responsibilities, including imaginative and silly playtime with his young daughter, and work responsibilities in his art studio.

Dunbar, Joyce. 1998. *Tell Me Something Happy Before I Go to Sleep*. Illustrated by Debi Gliori. San Diego: Harcourt Brace & Company. Big brother Willoughby soothes his little sister, Willa, who is too afraid of bad dreams to fall asleep, by reminding her of many happy things.

Fox, Mem. 1996. *Zoo-Looking*. Illustrated by Candace Whitman. Greenvale, N.Y.: Mondo Publishing. Flora and her dad explore the zoo in this simple rhyming book.

Graham, Bob. 2000. *Max*. Cambridge, Mass.: Candlewick Press. Max is the super son of superhero parents, but he cannot fly yet! Children will identify with Max's plight and agree that "Everyone's different in *some* way, aren't they?"

Grambling, Lois G. 1998. *Daddy Will Be There*. Illustrated by Walter Gaffney-Kessell. New York: Greenwillow Books. As a young girl becomes more independent—riding her bike all by herself, going to birthday parties, starting kindergarten—she comes to understand that no matter what she does, her father will always be there for her.

Greenfield, Eloise. 1993. *First Pink Light*. Illustrated by Jan Spivey Gilchrist. New York: Writers & Readers Publishing, Inc. A young boy awaits the return of his father, who is expected home in early morning. The illustrations especially convey the love and admiration felt between the boy and his father.

———. 1993. *Lisa's Daddy and Daughter Day*. Illustrated by Jan Spivey Gilchrist. Littleton, Mass.: Sundance Publishing. Spending the whole day with daddy, talking and taking it easy, is special for his daughter.

Heap, Sue. 1998. *Cowboy Baby*. Cambridge: Candlewick Press. The bedtime routine is extended a bit while Sheriff Pa allows Cowboy Baby to search for his stuffed animals and then continues his playful role in a game of hide-and-seek. Readers might wish to consider the continued story of this father and son in *Cowboy Kid* (2000).

Janovitz, Marilyn. 1998. *Can I Help?* New York: North-South Books, Inc. Father wolf exhibits much patience and love as his young cub eagerly "assists" with outdoor chores.

————. *Is it Time?* 1994. New York: North-South Books. In this cumulative rhyming story, father wolf lovingly helps his young cub prepare for bed.

Johnson, Angela. 2000. *Daddy Calls Me Man*. Illustrated by Rhonda Mitchell. New York: Scholastic, Inc. The secure and loving environment that his parents have provided are demonstrated in a young boy's poetic enthusiasm for life, and daddy's statement is like icing on a cake.

Lambert, Paulette Livers. 1995. *Evening: An Appalachian Lullaby*. Niwot, Colo.: Roberts Rinehart Publishers. It is bedtime on the farm; father patiently attends to the extended ritual with his young sons before relaxing on the porch with his fiddle.

London, Jonathan. 1994. *Let's Go, Froggy!* Illustrated by Frank Remkiewicz. New York: Viking. In this repetitious, fun text, Froggy awakes to a beautiful day and the promise of an extra-special picnic and bike ride with his dad; that is, if he gets ready in time.

Long, Earlene. 1987. *Gone Fishing*. Illustrated by Richard Brown. New York: Houghton Mifflin Company. Using the concepts of "big" and "little," a young boy describes preparations for a fishing trip with his father.

MacDonald, Margaret Read. 2001. *Mabela the Clever*. Illustrated by Tim Coffey. Morton Grove, Ill.: Albert Whitman & Company. Mabela was once the smallest mouse in the village, but thanks to a lesson in cleverness from her father, she just might save everyone from their worst enemy, the cat.

McBratney, Sam. 1999. *Guess How Much I Love You/Adivina Cuanto Te Quiero*. Illustrated by Anita Jeram. Nashville: Tommy Nelson. Big Nutbrown Hare and Little Nutbrown Hare try to outdo each other's measures of love while frolicking around in this popular bedtime book.

————. 2000. *Just You and Me*. Illustrated by Ivan Bates. Cambridge, Mass.: Candlewick Press. Big Gander Goose, whether intended to represent a father or other male caregiver, plays both protector and nurturer to Little Goosey in this warm story.

Miller, Margaret. 1998. *Big and Little*. New York: Greenwillow Books. The fun of relative size is emphasized in this book with colorful photographic images and simple text; many types of families and people are featured.

————. 1994. *Where's Jenna?* New York: Simon & Schuster Books for Young Readers. While Dad feeds the baby, Jenna plays hide-and-seek with Mom. An ideal depiction of shared parental responsibilities.

Miyamoto, Tadao. 1994. *Papa and Me*. Minneapolis: The Lerner Publishing Group. While papa bear and baby bear fish, father reassures his son that they are, in fact, father and son, because of special memories they share together. Adults will especially like the ending.

Morris, Ann. 1990. *Loving*. Photo-illustrated by Ken Heyman. New York: Lothrop, Lee & Shepard Books. Depicting families from all over the world, this book of photographs is perfect for younger children.

Sachar, Louis. 1992. *Monkey Soup*. New York: Alfred A. Knopf Books for Young Readers. Dad is sick in bed and at the mercy of Mom, who cooks him chicken soup; when his young daughter serves up her version of get-well "soup," his fathering abilities kick in. Preschoolers will love the surprise ending.

Sansone, Adele. 2001. *The Little Green Goose*. Illustrated by Alan Marks. New York: North-South Books, Inc. A perfect book for preschool story times. A male goose goes out of his way to demonstrate his nurturing abilities; his adopted offspring learns that dads can be every bit as warm and loving as moms.

Skofield, James. 1993. *'Round and Around*. Illustrated by James Graham Hale. New York: HarperCollins Publishers. While on a walk with his father and their dog, Sam, Dan observes many things in nature that move in circles. But as the sun sets and dad teaches Dan that even the Earth moves in a circle, Dan observes that the best circle of all is a hug.

Smith, Eddie. 1994. *A Lullaby for Daddy*. Illustrated by Susan Anderson. Lawrenceville, N.J.: Africa World Press. Daddy, a musician, and his young daughter compose a lullaby together, which they sing as part of their bedtime ritual.

Wallace, John. 1996. *Little Bean*. New York: HarperCollins Children's Book Group. This book highlights the conflicts between working and parenting demands, and is sure to help a young child envision Daddy's business trip. The warm resolution supports reading as an important activity shared by fathers and children.

Wild, Margaret. 1999. *Tom Goes to Kindergarten*. Illustrated by David Legge. Morton Grove, Ill.: Albert Whitman & Company. Tom likes kindergarten so much that soon the whole family wants to go too! The illustrations are great depictions of shared parental duties.

BEGINNING CHAPTER BOOKS

Brenner, Barbara. 1995. *Wagon Wheels*. Photo-illustrated by Don Bolognese. New York: HarperCollins Children's Book Group. In this 19th-century true story, a father must leave his sons behind on the prairie while he goes in search of land.

Christopher, Matt. 1992. *Centerfield Ballhawk*. Illustrated by Ellen Beier. Boston: Little, Brown & Company. José wants to excel at baseball in order to gain the respect and attention of his emotionally distant father, a widower who once played minor-league baseball.

Godwin, Laura. 1998. *Forest*. Illustrated by Stacey Schuett. New York: HarperCollins Publishers. The rescue of a fawn allows father to show his tender, caring qualities while sharing both work and parenting responsibilities with mother.

Greenwood, Pamela D. 1994. *I Found Mouse*. Illustrated by Jennifer Plecas. New York: Clarion Books. Tessie's mom, brother, and best friend are all gone for the summer, so she amuses herself by adopting a stray cat that she names Mouse, and develops a warm relationship with her father in the raising of the kitten.

Marks, Alan. 1993. *The Thief's Daughter*. New York: Farrar, Straus & Giroux. Magpie, whose poor father tells her magnificent stories about royal households, discovers the truth behind her father's life and learns an important lesson about honesty in this fairy-tale-like beginning chapter book.

McCreary, Laura and Mark Myers. 2001. *Angela Anaconda: The Best Dad*. Based on the scripts by Charlotte Fullerton and Mark Myers. Illustrated by Barry Goldberg. New York: Simon Spotlight. This short chapter book features two stories about Angela Anaconda, her dad, and her eternal enemy Nanette Manoir. The first story sees father and daughter entering a square-dancing competition; the second sees them going fishing.

Monjo, F. N. 1961. *The One Bad Thing about Father*. Illustrated by Rocco Negri. New York: Harper & Row. An I CAN READ History Book. Told through the voice of Quentin, Theodore Roosevelt's son, this story captures wonderful family moments shared in the White House.

Rylant, Cynthia. *Henry and Mudge*. See **Series**.

CHAPTER BOOKS FOR UP TO AGE 8

Bowdish, Lynea. 2000. *Brooklyn, Bugsy, and Me*. Illustrated by Nancy Carpenter. New York: Farrar, Straus and Giroux. It is 1953, and Sam and his mother move from West Virginia to Brooklyn after the death of Sam's father. There they live with grandfather Bugsy, who wants little to do with his hurting grandson.

———. 1996. *Living with My Stepfather Is Like Living with a Moose*. Illustrated by Blanche Sims. New York: Farrar, Straus and Giroux. Adjusting to a stepfather who does not share Sam's fifth grade sports prowess is difficult, but open-mindedness helps both of them to appreciate one another's abilities.

Cleary, Beverly. 1990. *Ramona and Her Father*. Illustrated by Alan Tiegreen. New York: Morrow/Avon. Ramona Quimby is in second grade when her father loses his job, requiring many family sacrifices, such as Whopperburgers. When Ramona mounts her antismoking campaign, Dad plays another kind of victim.

Duffey, Betsy. 1998. *Spotlight on Cody*. Illustrated by Ellen Thompson. New York: Viking Penguin. When third grader Cody deals with an identity crisis, he also helps his father out of a middle-aged slump in this fourth book in the contemporary, humorous series.

Galbraith, Kathryn O. 1995. *Holding onto Sunday*. Illustrated by Michael Hays. New York: Margaret K. McElderry Books. In this short chapter book, a single-parent father sets aside Sundays from his busy work schedule to spend time with his daughter in a variety of activities.

Hesse, Karen. 1998. *Sable*. Illustrated by Marcia Sewall. Madison, Wisc.: Turtleback Books. The conflicts between ten-year-old Tate Marshall and her sensitive but conservative father, regarding a stray dog and other issues, provide insight into parenting dilemmas and decision-making challenges.

Howe, James. 1995. *Pinky and Rex and the Double-Dad Weekend*. Illustrated by Melissa Sweet. New York: Atheneum Books. Rather than cancel a camping trip when it rains, two dads exhibit much resourcefulness and create extra-special quality time with their daughters in this installment of the series starring Pinky and Rex.

King-Smith, Dick. 2000. *The Water Horse*. Illustrated by David Parkins. New York: Alfred A. Knopf Books for Young Readers. Set during the 1930s in Scotland, both father and grandfather bring much wisdom and assistance to the children who rescue a water horse, or sea monster, in this fantasy.

Koller, Jackie French. 1995. *The Dragonling*. Illustrated by Judith Mitchell. New York: Pocket Books. This first book in a fantasy series that includes *A Dragon in the Family* (1993) through *Dragons and Kings* (1998), introduces the aggressive, authoritative father in a major conflict with his approval-seeking nine-year-old son.

Koss, Amy Goldman. 2000. *How I Saved Hanukkah*. Illustrated by Diane Degroat. New York: Penguin Putnam Books for Young Readers. The traditional father role is depicted in this story about a family celebrating Hanukkah while father has to be away on business.

MacLachlan, Patricia. 1985. *Sarah, Plain and Tall*. New York: Harper & Row Publishers. When Papa invited a mail-order bride to live with his family on the prairie, he could not have known the joy she would bring back to the mourning household. See also the sequel, *Skylark*.

Sherman, Charlotte Watson. 1996. *Eli and the Swamp Man*. Illustrated by James E. Ransome. New York: HarperCollins Children's Books. A homeless man offers eight-year old Eli some sage advice and friendship, filling a void left in Eli's life by his divorced father and from the alienation he feels toward his stepfather.

Willner-Pardo, Gina. 1994. *What I'll Remember When I Am a Grownup*. Illustrated by Walter Lyon Krudop. Boston: Houghton Mifflin Company. The experience of one divorce causes Daniel to worry, unnecessarily, that his father's second marriage might end the same way. The adults in this short book are especially supportive and respectful.

GREAT READ-ALOUDS FOR FAMILIES AND CLASSROOMS

Browne, Anthony. 1998. *Voices in the Park*. New York: DK. When pet dogs Victoria and Albert romp at the park, two worlds collide. This unique tale allows readers to experience a moment through the very different perspectives of an upper-class mother and her son, Charles, and of a lower-class father and his daughter, Smudge.

Degen, Bruce. 2000. *Daddy Is a Doodlebug*. New York: HarperCollins Publishers. This book captures the magic of everyday activities in the lives of a father and son doodlebug. The funny rhymes will make this a read-aloud favorite.

Gugler, Laurel Dee. 1997. *Muddle Cuddle*. Iillustrated by Vlasta van Kampen. Toronto: Annick Press. A young boy and his twin sisters crowd daddy's lap with themselves and their sundry toys.

King-Smith, Dick. 2000. *The Water Horse*. Illustrated by David Parkins. New York: Alfred A. Knopf Books for Young Readers. Set during the 1930s in Scotland, both father and grandfather bring much wisdom and assistance to the children who rescue a water horse, or sea monster, in this fantasy.

Manushkin, Fran. 1995. *The Matzah That Papa Brought Home*. Illustrated by Ned Bittinger. New York: Scholastic, Inc. The repetitious rhyming text and detailed illustrations of this book bring to life the culture of a Jewish family celebrating Passover.

Martin, Bill, Jr. 1993. *Old Devil Wind*. Illustrated by Barry Root. San Diego: Harcourt Brace & Company. In this scary, compounding story, various everyday objects assume more spooky demeanors and are forbidden to act so until Halloween.

McKenzie, Ellen Kindt. 1993. *The King, the Princess, and the Tinker*. Illustrated by William Low. New York: Henry Holt Books for Young Readers. A king's fathering role consists only of annual inspections of the children to see that they are growing, and at no time are the children or the queen allowed to look at him, which tends to create strained relationships. This fun chapter book will appeal to all ages.

Moss, Jeff. 1999. *The Dad of the Dad of the Dad of Your Dad: Stories about Kids and Their Fathers*. Illustrated by Chris Demarest. New York: Ballantine Publishing Group. A collection of entertaining poetry about the relationships between fathers and children during various historic time periods, such as the Stone Age. Older children will appreciate this one.

Patron, Susan. 1994. *Dark Cloud Strong Breeze*. Illustrated by Peter Catalanotto. New York: Orchard Books. In this fun, rhyming text a father locks his keys in the car right before a storm breaks, but his daughter saves the day.

Paxton, Tom. 1996. *The Marvelous Toy*. Illustrated by Elizabeth Sayles. New York: Morrow Junior Books. A father gives his son an extraordinary and unique new toy; later in life the son goes on to give a similar toy to his son. This clever book would be great for reading aloud, and includes a song to sing in the repeating text.

Sansone, Adele. 2001. *The Little Green Goose*. Illustrated by Alan Marks. New York: North-South Books, Inc. A perfect book for preschool story times. A male goose goes out of his way to demonstrate his nurturing abilities; his adopted offspring learns that dads can be every bit as warm and loving as moms.

Van Laan, Nancy. 1995. *Mama Rocks, Papa Sings*. Illustrated by Roberta Smith. New York: Alfred A. Knopf Books for Young Readers. Based on a true story about Haitian missionaries who adopted 28 children, this book depicts, in Creole and English, parents who welcome children with loving, open arms and who support each other. The rhythmic, repetitive text makes a fun read-aloud and would be a good selection for classroom participation.

Walters, Virginia. 1999. *Are We There Yet, Daddy?* Illustrated by S. D. Schindler. New York: Viking. This rhyming repetitive text counts down the miles on a 100-mile journey to Grandma's house as a patient father responds to that all-too-frequently asked question.

PICTURE BOOKS

ABSENT FATHERS

Ballard, Robin. 1992. *My Father Is Far Away*. New York: Greenwillow Books. While taking part in mundane, everyday activities, a young girl daydreams of all the exciting things her father must be doing while he is away.

Boelts, Maribeth. 2000. *Big Daddy, Frog Wrestler*. Illustrated by Benrei Huang. Morton Grove, Ill.: Albert Whitman & Company. Big Daddy and his son, Curtis, love wrestling, but when Big Daddy gets a chance to wrestle all over the world, he must choose between wrestling and his son.

Carmichael, Clay. 1996. *Bear at the Beach*. New York: North-South Books. Bear longs for a father, and discovers him in the night sky.

Eyvindsom, Peter. 1991. *Old Enough*. Illustrated by Wendy Wolsak. Winnipeg: Pemmican Publications, Inc. A father who neglected his growing son learns from his mistakes and appreciates his newborn grandchild—a bad dad turned good.

Lindsay, Jeanne Warren. 1991. *Do I Have a Daddy?: A Story About a Single-Parent Child*. Illustrated by Cheryl Boeller. Buena Park, Calif.: Morning Glory Press. In this timely book, young Erik seeks to understand where his daddy is. Mother explains that not all mommies and daddies get married, and encourages him to spend time with his Uncle Bob and grandfather. A resources section at the back of this book might assist in discussions about single-parenthood, absent fathers, or the importance of male role models.

Schindel, John. 1995. *Dear Daddy*. Illustrated by Dorothy Donohue. Morton Grove, Ill.: Albert Whitman & Company. Jesse writes letters to his father on the other side of the country, and thinks he will never get one in return.

Smalls, Irene. 1995. *Father's Day Blues: What Do You Do About Father's Day When All You Have Are Mothers?* Illustrated by Kevin McGovern. Stamford, Conn.: Longmeadow Press. When Cheryl discusses her writing assignment about Father's Day with her adult female relatives, she realizes that her love for Daddy will never cease, despite his absence from her life.

Valentine, Johnny. 1992. *The Daddy Machine.* Illustrated by Lynette Schmidt. Boston: Alyson Wonderland. The children of lesbian parents wish for a dad and, after building a contraption that "manufactures" dads, get more than they bargained for. This is a positive look at what dads are like and what they do.

Vigna, Judith. 1991. *Saying Goodbye to Daddy.* Morton Grove, Ill.: Albert Whitman & Company. When Clare's father dies unexpectedly in a car accident, his young daughter must learn how to say goodbye to him.

Williams, Vera B. 2001. *Amber Was Brave, Essie Was Smart.* New York: Greenwillow Books. Amber and Essie are loving/fighting/making-up/wonderful sisters in this story made of poems and pictures. The main theme is the extraordinariness of everyday life punctuated by the pining for an absent father—jailed for forging a check when he lost his job. A joyous reunion awaits his release at the end of the story.

Winthrop, Elizabeth. 1998. *As the Crow Flies.* Illustrated by Joan Sandin. New York: Clarion Books. Mikey's parents are divorced; he lives with his mother in Arizona and his father lives in Delaware, "seven states away as the crow flies." Dad's annual visit brings lots of special memories and a wonderful surprise.

Wyeth, Sharon Dennis. 1995. *Always My Dad.* Illustrated by Raúl Colón. New York: Knopf. Dad is having problems "getting his life together"; his constant shifting from job to job and his lack of presence in his children's lives have them all upset.

Ziefert, Harriet. 1991. *When Daddy Had the Chicken Pox.* Illustrated by Lionel Kalish. New York: HarperCollins Publishers. Dad, who has everyone greatly concerned after contracting chicken pox from his children, cannot attend his daughter's ballet recital, but makes up for it when he is well.

Zolotow, Charlotte. 1971. *A Father Like That.* Illustrated by Ben Shecter. New York: Harper & Row, Publishers. A boy tells his mother about all of the wonderful things he would like to be doing with his absent father; she reminds him that when he is older he can be the kind of father he always wanted.

ABSENT FATHERS, AWAY AT WAR

Anaya, Rudolfo. 1998. *The Farolitos of Christmas.* Illustrated by Edward Gonzalez. New York: Hyperion Paperbacks for Children. In this warm World War II-era story, father is wounded and hospitalized, and Grandfather (Abuelo) is too ill to create the traditional luminarias, which forces Luz, her friends, and her family to prepare for Christmas on their own.

Mellecker, Judith. 1992. *Randolph's Dream.* Illustrated by Robert Andrew Parker. New York: Random House Value Publishing, Inc. Through very realistic dreams, seven-year-old Randolph is able to deal with the helplessness and loneliness he feels as a result of his father being stationed in North Africa, and his own displacement from his home and mother in London during World War II.

Ray, Deborah Kogan. 1990. *My Daddy Was a Soldier: A World War II Story.* New York: Holiday House. This touching story outlines major events in America during World War II through the eyes of Jeannie, whose father is away fighting the war.

Wetzel, JoAnne Stewart. 1995. *The Christmas Box.* Illustrated by Barry Root. New York: Random House Value Publishing, Inc. While Dad is stationed in Japan during the Korean War, he sends home a box full of very special Christmas gifts, which bridges the distance between his family and him.

Yolen, Jane. 1991. *All Those Secrets of the World.* Illustrated by Leslie Baker. Boston: Little, Brown & Company. Janie's father goes away to war, but before he returns she learns a valuable lesson about perspective that can be applied to human emotions.

ABSENT FATHERS, HOMECOMINGS

Clifton, Lucille. 1977. *Amifika.* Illustrated by Thomas DiGrazia. New York: E. P. Dutton. Amifika hears his mother discussing his father's homecoming and the lack of room in their small apartment and becomes afraid that he will be one of the things thrown out to make room for daddy.

Lewin, Hugh. 1994. *Jafta: The Homecoming.* Illustrated by Lisa Kopper. New York: Knopf. Things are changing in South Africa; soon Jafta's father will be able to come home from the city where he has been working. See also *Jafta's Father.*

McKinley, Robin. 1992. *My Father Is in the Navy.* Illustrated by Martine Gourbault. New York: Greenwillow Books. Sara cannot remember her daddy, and is not very excited about his return from sea.

Riecken, Nancy. 1996. *Today Is the Day.* Illustrated by Catherine Stock. Boston: Houghton Mifflin Company. Yesenia, a young Mexican girl, awaits the return of her father, who has been working away from home, in the hopes that he will have brought enough money for her to attend school.

Roy, Ron. 1980. *Breakfast with My Father.* Illustrated by Troy Howell. Boston: Houghton Mifflin Company. During a period of marital separation that ultimately ends in reunion, a father and his son meet to have breakfast every Saturday morning.

Williams, Vera B. 2001. *Amber Was Brave, Essie Was Smart.* New York: Greenwillow Books. Amber and Essie are loving/fighting/making-up/wonderful sisters in this story made of poems and pictures. The main theme is the extraordinariness of everyday life punctuated by the pining for an absent father—jailed for forging a check when he lost his job. A joyous reunion awaits his release at the end of the story.

Yolen, Jane. 1991. *All Those Secrets of the World.* Illustrated by Leslie Baker. Boston: Little, Brown & Company. Janie's father goes away to war, but before he returns she learns a valuable lesson about perspective that can be applied to human emotions.Absent Fathers, Incarcerated

ABSENT FATHERS, INCARCERATED

Butterworth, Oliver. 1993. *A Visit to the Big House.* Illustrated by Susan Avishai. Boston: Houghton Mifflin Company. A range of emotions is gently presented in this story about a family's visit to the prison where dad is serving time for theft.

Hickman, Martha Whitmore. 1990. *When Andy's Father Went to Prison.* Illustrated by Larry Raymond. Niles, Ill.: Albert Whitman & Company. Originally published as *When Can Daddy Come Home?*, this book captures the anxiety, stress, and heartache one young boy feels when his father goes to jail and the family moves to be closer to the prison.

Williams, Vera B. 2001. *Amber Was Brave, Essie Was Smart.* New York: Greenwillow Books. Amber and Essie are loving/fighting/making-up/wonderful sisters in this story made of poems and pictures. The main theme is the extraordinariness of everyday life punctuated by the pining for an absent father—jailed for forging a check when he lost his job. A joyous reunion awaits his release at the end of the story.

ABSENT FATHERS, WORKING AWAY FROM HOME

Carter, Dorothy. 1999. *Wilhe'mina Miles after the Stork Night.* Illustrated by Harvey Stevenson. New York: Farrar, Straus and Giroux. While working in New York City, Daddy regularly sends home letters and money, which are appreciated, but his presence cannot be replaced so easily, especially the night that Wilhe'mina becomes a big sister.

Conway, Celeste. 1994. *Where Is Papa Now?* Honesdale, Penn.: Boyds Mills Press, In this Victorian-era story, Papa is far away from home, at work trading goods in exotic lands, and his young daughter, who continuously asks Mother for information about his travels, sorely misses him.

Fowler, Susi Gregg. 1994. *I'll See You When the Moon Is Full.* Illustrated by Jim Fowler. New York: Greenwillow Books. When dad goes out of town on business trips, his young son misses him very much. Dad assures his son that he will be home by the time the moon is full, and delivers an impromptu astronomy lesson at the same time!

Greenfield, Eloise. 1993. *First Pink Light.* Illustrated by Jan Spivey Gilchrist. New York: Writers & Readers Publishing, Inc. A young boy awaits the return of his father, who is expected home in early morning. The illustrations especially convey the love and admiration felt between the boy and his father.

Grifalconi, Ann. 1999. *Tiny's Hat.* New York: HarperCollins Children's Book Group. Tiny's father is a blues musician who travels a lot, and when he is away for long periods, Tiny gets the blues herself.

Hanson, Regina. 1995. *The Tangerine Tree.* Illustrated by Harvey Stevenson. New York: Houghton Mifflin Company. Papa must leave his impoverished Jamaican family for work in New York, but a book given to his young daughter, along with reading goals, will help to shorten the time that he is away.

Isadora, Rachel. 2000. *At the Crossroads.* New York: Morrow/Avon. The emotions that Zolani, his siblings, and his friends feel for their fathers, who have been away for 10 months working in the South African mines, are strongly indicative of the importance of fathers in children's lives.

Lewin, Hugh. 1994. *Jafta: The Homecoming.* Illustrated by Lisa Kopper. New York: Knopf. Things are changing in South Africa; soon Jafta's father will be able to come home from the city where he has been working. See also *Jafta's Father.*

McCormick, Wendy. 1999. *Daddy, Will You Miss Me?* Illustrated by Jennifer Eachus. New York: Simon & Schuster Children's Publishing. Before he leaves for a month long trip to Africa, a father sensitively and poetically reassures his young son that he will be loved and missed.

McKinley, Robin. 1992. *My Father Is in the Navy.* Illustrated by Martine Gourbault. New York: Greenwillow Books. Sara cannot remember her daddy, and is not very excited about his return from sea.

Riecken, Nancy. 1996. *Today Is the Day.* Illustrated by Catherine Stock. Boston: Houghton Mifflin Company. Yesenia, a young Mexican girl, awaits the return of her father who has been working away from home, in the hopes that he will have brought enough money for her to attend school.

Wallace, John. 1996. *Little Bean.* New York: HarperCollins Children's Book Group. This book highlights the conflicts between working and parenting demands, and is sure to help a young child envision Daddy's business trip. The warm resolution supports reading as an important activity between fathers and children.

ADJUSTING TO STEPPARENT

Best, Cari. 1996. *Getting Used to Harry.* Illustrated by Diane Palmisciano. New York: Scholastic, Inc. In this lively, upbeat story, Cynthia, feeling a bit alienated, bonds with her new stepfather after he takes her on a special nighttime flashlight walk.

Brown, Laurene Krasny, and Marc Brown. 1986. *Dinosaurs Divorce: A Guide for Changing Families.* Boston: Little, Brown & Company. Using illustrations of dinosaurs for comfort, this guide for children seeks to validate the feelings children of divorcing parents might be having, and to prepare them for changes that might ensue.

Cook, Jean Thor. 1995. *Room for a Stepdaddy*. Illustrated by Martine Gourbault. Morton Grove, Ill.: Albert Whitman & Company. Joey has a very hard time adjusting to a life with three parents—Mom, Dad, and his new stepdaddy, Bill—but ultimately he comes to believe the wisdom his father imparted to him: love is like the sand on the beach; there is always enough to go around.

Gibbons, Faye. 1996. *Mountain Wedding*. Illustrated by Ted Rand. New York: Morrow Junior Books. The children from two large rural families are antagonistic toward the impending marriage of their widowed parents, until a series of humorous mishaps occurs during the ceremony.

Jukes, Mavis. 1984. *Like Jake and Me*. Illustrated by Lloyd Bloom. New York: Dragonfly Books. Alex, who loves ballet, does not have much in common with his stepfather, Jake, a cowboy. A funny misunderstanding about a spider helps them bond.

MacLachlan, Patricia. 1985. *Sarah, Plain and Tall*. New York: Harper & Row, Publishers. When Papa invited a mail-order bride to live with his family on the prairie, he could not have known the joy she would bring back to the mourning household. See also the sequel, *Skylark*.

Ransom, Candice F. 1993. *We're Growing Together*. Illustrated by Virginia Wright-Frierson. New York: Simon & Schuster Children's Publishing. A new house in the country and a new stepfather with little parenting experience are both big adjustments for a five-year-old girl, but a warm friendship between the two evolves.

Rogers, Fred. 1997. *Let's Talk About It: Stepfamilies*. Photo-illustrated by Jim Judkis. New York: G. P. Putnam's Sons. From Mister Rogers "Let's Talk About It" series, this book walks through many common scenarios associated with remarriage and stepfamilies.

ADOPTION AND FOSTER PARENTS

Hoberman, Mary Ann. 1991. *Fathers, Mothers, Sisters, Brothers: A Collection of Family Poems*. Illustrated by Marylin Hafner. Boston: Little, Brown & Company. This book of poetry highlights many types of families.

Munsch, Robert. 1983. *David's Father*. Illustrated by Michael Martchenko. Toronto: Annick Press. David and his father do not look much alike because David was adopted, but David's new friend soon discovers that even giant fathers are fun.

Sansone, Adele. 2001. *The Little Green Goose*. Illustrated by Alan Marks. New York: North-South Books, Inc. A perfect book for preschool story times. A male goose goes out of his way to demonstrate his nurturing abilities; his adopted offspring learns that dads can be every bit as warm and loving as moms.

Shepard, Steve. 1991. *Elvis Hornbill: International Business Bird*. New York: Holt & Company. A human couple adopts a young bird they name Elvis who, despite his father's efforts to persuade him to become a musician, is interested only in finance, business, and computer science.

Stanley, Diane. 1996, 1999. *Saving Sweetness* and *Raising Sweetness*. Illustrated by G. Brian Karas. New York: The Putnam Publishing Group. In these two zany books, a caring and sensitive but inept sheriff adopts a runaway from an orphanage, Sweetness, and eight other orphans. No other author handles adoption in such a light manner; these books show how love can be found in the most unusual circumstances.

Turner, Ann. 1990. *Through Moon and Stars and Night Skies*. Illustrated by James Graham Hale. New York: Harper & Row. A young boy enjoys retelling the story of his mother's adoption and fearful journey to live with his new parents.

Van Laan, Nancy. 1995. *Mama Rocks, Papa Sings*. Illustrated by Roberta Smith. New York: Alfred A. Knopf Books for Young Readers. Based on a true story about Haitian missionaries who adopted 28 children, this book depicts, in Creole and English, parents who welcome children with loving, open arms and who support each other. The rhythmic, repetitive text makes a fun read-aloud and would be a good selection for classroom participation.

BEDTIME AND FEARS

Appelt, Kathi. 1999. *Cowboy Dreams: Sleep Tight, Little Buckaroo*. Illustrated by Barry Root. New York: HarperCollins Publishers. This whimsical look at bedtime follows a little buckaroo as he mimics the other cowboys and settles in for a refreshing sleep under the stars; includes some Spanish words.

Bunting, Eve. 1987. *Ghost's Hour, Spook's Hour*. Illustrated by Donald Carrick. New York: Clarion Books. A young boy and his dog are frightened by nighttime sounds, and are further distressed by a ghost sighting.

Cazet, Denys. 1992. *"I'm Not Sleepy."* New York: Orchard Books. Alex is not tired, so dad tells him a story guaranteed to put him to sleep.

Corentin, Philippe. 1997. *Papa!* San Francisco: Chronicle Books. "There's a monster in my bed!" is familiar to many parents, and this book humorously begs the question *just who is a monster?*

Curtis, Munzee. 1997. *When the Big Dog Barks*. Illustrated by Susan Avishai. New York: HarperCollins Children's Books Group. Dogs, storms, and strangers are just some of the fears father (and mother) help to dispel in their young daughter by being accessible, understanding, and patient.

Donovan, Mary Lee. 1993. *Papa's Bedtime Story*. Illustrated by Kimberly Bulcken Root. New York: Alfred A. Knopf Books for Young Readers. Fathers throughout the animal world comfort their babies with bedtime stories, while a log cabin family does the same.

Dunbar, Joyce. 1998. *Tell Me Something Happy Before I Go to Sleep*. Illustrated by Debi Gliori. San Diego: Harcourt Brace & Company. Big brother Willoughby soothes his little sister, Willa, who is too afraid of bad dreams to fall asleep, by reminding her of many happy things.

Heap, Sue. *Cowboy Baby*. 1998. Cambridge, Mass.: Candlewick Press. The bedtime routine is extended a bit while Sheriff Pa allows Cowboy Baby to search for his stuffed animals and then continues his playful role in a game of hide-and-seek.

Horn, Peter. 1999. *When I Grow Up ...*. Illustrated by Christina Kadmon. New York: North-South Books, Inc. A turtle father gently supports his young son's late-night thoughts about growing up.

Janovitz, Marilyn. 1994. *Is It Time?* New York: North-South Books. In this cumulative rhyming story, father wolf lovingly helps his young cub prepare for bed.

Johnson, Angela. 1994. *Joshua's Night Whispers*. Illustrated by Rhonda Mitchell. New York: Orchard Books. Joshua is awakened by night whispers and finds comfort in his father's arms in this board book.

Lambert, Paulette Livers. 1995. *Evening: An Appalachian Lullaby*. Niwot, Colo.: Roberts Rinehart Publishers. It is bedtime on the farm; father patiently attends to the extended ritual with his young sons before relaxing on the porch with his fiddle.

Lemieux, Margo. 1996. *Paul and the Wolf*. Illustrated by Bill Nelson. Parsippany, N.J.: Silver Burdett Press. Having been exposed to *Peter and the Wolf* at school, a boy fears wolves at bedtime, until Dad alleviates his fears with a Native American wolf tale and personal commentary.

Manushkin, Fran. 1994. *Peeping and Sleeping*. Illustrated by Jennifer Plecas. New York: Clarion Books. When Barry cannot sleep because of a mysterious and scary "PEEP-peep" he hears outside his window, Daddy promises to stay close as they go exploring outside at night.

Martin, David. 2001. *Piggy and Dad*. Illustrated by Frank Remkiewicz. Cambridge, Mass.: Candlewick Press. Candlewick Press's Brand New Readers. This set of four books designed to help beginning readers captures a truly loving relationship between Piggy and his dad. Titles included are *Piggy's Bath*, *Piggy's Bedtime*, *Piggy's Sandwich*, and *Piggy's Pictures*.

McBratney, Sam. 1999. *Guess How Much I Love You/Adivina Cuanto Te Quiero*. Illustrated by Anita Jeram. Nashville: Tommy Nelson. Big Nutbrown Hare and Little Nutbrown Hare try to outdo each other's measures of love while frolicking around in this popular bedtime book.

McMullan, Kate. 1994. *Good Night, Stella*. Illustrated by Emma Chichester Clark. Cambridge, Mass.: Candlewick Press. Young Stella's imagination overflows at bedtime, making sleep impossible, but Dad, who is the caretaker for the evening, exercises much patience and cleverness in this humorous story.

———. 2000. *Papa's Song*. Illustrated by Jim McMullan. New York: Farrar, Straus and Giroux. After Granny Bear, Grandpa Bear, and Mama Bear all give it a try, Papa Bear finds the perfect melody to put Baby Bear to sleep.

Pettigrew, Eileen. 1992. *Night-Time*. Illustrated by William Kimber. Toronto: Annick Press. Michael's dad takes him on a very special nighttime walk around the neighborhood, recounting his own fond memories of his father.

Rabe, Berniece. 1988. *Where's Chimpy?* Photo-illustrated by Diane Schmidt. Niles, Ill.: Albert Whitman & Company. Daddy helps his daughter Misty, who has Down Syndrome, find her cherished toy monkey in this book that focuses on bedtime rituals and counting, not on disability.

Rathmann, Peggy. 1998. *10 Minutes Till Bedtime*. New York: Penguin Putnam Books for Young Readers. Father is totally immersed in his newspaper and has very little interaction during the bedtime ritual; this clever story about a "10-minute hamster tour" is perfect for sharing at bedtime. (Fathers should consult other titles in this section for better bedtime parenting techniques!)

Smith, Eddie. 1994. *A Lullaby for Daddy*. Illustrated by Susan Anderson. Lawrenceville, N.J.: Africa World Press. Daddy, a musician, and his young daughter compose a lullaby together which they sing as part of their bedtime ritual.

Spinelli, Eileen. 2000. *Night Shift Daddy*. Illustrated by Melissa Iwai. New York: Hyperion Books for Children. Daddy reads a story to his daughter and tenderly tucks her into bed before going to work the night shift as a janitor; when he returns she happily reciprocates.

Stevenson, Harvey. 1997. *Big, Scary Wolf*. New York: Houghton Mifflin Company. Dad uses a bit of psychology, a lump of creativity, and a hunk of loving patience to ease Rose's fears about a wolf in her bedroom.

Turner, Ann. 1990. *Through Moon and Stars and Night Skies*. Illustrated by James Graham Hale. New York: Harper & Row. A young boy enjoys retelling his mother the story of his adoption and fearful journey to live with his new parents.

BIRTHDAYS

Brillhart, Julie. 1995. *When Daddy Came to School*. Morton Grove, Ill.: Albert Whitman & Company. On his son's third birthday, Daddy spends the day with him at preschool—a gift more precious than anything money could buy.

Cummings, Pat. 1994. *Carousel*. New York: Simon & Schuster Children's Publishing. Not even a toy carousel, a special gift from Daddy, can dull the anger that a young girl feels when he accidentally misses her birthday.

Demas, Corinne. 2000. *Nina's Waltz*. Illustrated by Deborah Lanino. New York: Orchard Books. Nina's father is a championship fiddler, but when wasps sting him his daughter has to step in and compete in his place.

Estes, Kristyn Rehling. 1999. *Manuela's Gift*. Illustrated by Claire B. Cotts. San Francisco: Chronicle Books. Times are hard for Manuela's Mama, Papa, and Abuela, but on her birthday she realizes there is still much to celebrate. This book contains many Spanish words.

Hermes, Patricia. 1996. *When Snow Lay Soft on the Mountains*. Illustrated by Leslie Baker. New York: Little, Brown & Company. Financial hardships, the death of Mama, and father's influenza cause Hallie to keep many wishes to herself while helping to nurse her father back to health in this quiet 1800s story. One special wish comes true on her birthday.

Hughes, Shirley. 1997. *Alfie and the Birthday Surprise*. New York: Lothrop, Lee & Shepard Books. After Bob's cherished cat dies, his daughter, Maureen, enlists the help of Alfie and his family to plan a birthday party with one very special surprise. A good book for discussions about death.

Ketteman, Helen. 1992. *Not Yet, Yvette*. Illustrated by Irene Trivas. Morton Grove, Ill.: Albert Whitman & Company. Yvette and her father clean the house, go shopping, and bake a cake for her mom's birthday. Mom is a veterinarian and dad appears to stay at home with Yvette.

Polacco, Patricia. 1991. *Some Birthday!* New York: Simon & Schuster Books for Young Readers. It is Patricia's birthday and her father, who is divorced from her mother, seems to have forgotten entirely. Little does she know, this birthday will turn into her best ever, complete with monster hunt, camping trip, and the perfect gifts.

Roberts, Bethany. 1993. *The Two O'Clock Secret*. Illustrated by Robin Kramer. Morton Grove, Ill.: Albert Whitman & Company. The family has the perfect surprise for daddy's birthday—his twin brother home from the Navy—but it is hard to keep a secret!

Wadsworth, Ginger. 1994. *Tomorrow Is Daddy's Birthday*. Illustrated by Maxie Chambliss. Honesdale, Penn.: Boyds Mills Press. Rachel is so excited about the gift she will be giving her father for his birthday that she cannot help but share her secret with those around her.

CHILDREN WITH DISABILITIES

Lakin, Patricia. 1994. *Dad and Me in the Morning*. Illustrated by Robert G. Steele. Morton Grove, Ill.: Albert Whitman & Company. A hearing-impaired child wakes his father before dawn to enjoy the sunrise and other sensuous moments at the seashore.

O'Shaughnessy, Ellen. 1992. *Somebody Called Me a Retard Today . . . and My Heart Felt Sad*. Illustrated by David Garner. New York: Walker & Company. A young girl is called a "retard" at school; her father comforts her and reminds her of her unique and special abilities instead of focusing on her disabilities.

Rabe, Berniece. 1988. *Where's Chimpy?* Photo-illustrated by Diane Schmidt. Niles, Ill.: Albert Whitman & Company. Daddy helps his daughter Misty, who has Down Syndrome, find her cherished toy monkey in this book that focuses on bedtime rituals and counting, not on disability.

DEATH

Carson, Jo. 1992. *You Hold Me and I'll Hold You*. Illustrated by Annie Cannon. New York: Orchard Books. Dad, who is a single parent, tenderly comforts his daughter at a family funeral.

Clifton, Lucille. 1983. *Everett Anderson's Goodbye*. Illustrated by Ann Grifalconi. New York: Henry Holt & Company. This book outlines the five stages of grief—denial, anger, bargaining, depression, and acceptance—through the use of a child whose father has just died.

Cooke, Trish. 2000. *The Grandad Tree*. Illustrated by Sharon Wilson. Cambridge, Mass.: Candlewick Press. Focusing on life cycles, this book depicts growth and remembrance through the symbol of the family apple tree. After their Grandad dies, Leigh and Vin cherish even more dearly the apple tree and the wonderful times they had there with him.

Haseley, Dennis. 1986. *Kite Flier*. Illustrated by David Wiesner. New York: Four Winds Press. A husband and wife share a special relationship flying kites, and when she dies giving birth he shares his kite-making gift with his son.

Heide, Florence Parry, and Roxanne Heide Pierce. 1998. *Tío Armando*. Illustrated by Ann Grifalconi. New York: Lothrop, Lee & Shepard Books. A young girl develops a very special relationship with her philosophical great-uncle in this story featuring Spanish words.

Hughes, Shirley. 1997. *Alfie and the Birthday Surprise*. New York: Lothrop, Lee & Shepard Books. After Bob's cherished cat dies, his daughter, Maureen, enlists the help of Alfie and his family to plan a birthday party with one very special surprise. The loss of a cherished pet softens the harsh death theme and make this is a good book for discussions about passages in life.

Madenski, Melissa. 1991. *Some of the Pieces*. Illustrated by Deborah Kogan Ray. Boston: Little, Brown & Company. On the one-year anniversary of his father's death, a young boy recalls many fond memories and the pain of the sudden loss.

Powell, E. Sandy. 1980. *Geranium Morning*. Illustrated by Renée Graef. Minneapolis: CarolRhoda Books. In this now classic story, a boy is plagued by guilt after his father dies, but finds solace in a friend whose mother is also dying.

Spelman, Cornelia. 1996. *After Charlotte's Mom Died*. Illustrated by Judith Friedman. Morton Grove, Ill.: Albert Whitman & Company. With the help of a therapist, Dad's parenting abilities improve, including communication with his six-year-old daughter, and the grief shared as the result of mother's fatal car accident becomes more manageable.

Spohn, David. *Nate's Treasure*. See **Series**.

Vigna, Judith. 1991. *Saying Goodbye to Daddy*. Morton Grove, Ill.: Albert Whitman & Company, When Clare's father dies unexpectedly in a car accident, his young daughter must learn how to say goodbye to him.

DISCUSSIONS

Browne, Anthony. 1986. *Piggybook*. New York: Alfred A. Knopf. Mr. Piggott and his two sons, Simon and Patrick, are of no help to Mrs. Piggott, who decides to leave and teach them a lesson about helping out. The house goes to ruin and the male Piggotts turn into pigs by the time she returns. Wonderful for discussions about household chores.

_____. 1998. *Voices in the Park*. New York: DK. When pet dogs Victoria and Albert romp at the park, two worlds collide. This unique tale allows readers to experience a moment through the very different perspectives of an upper-class mother and her son, Charles, and of a lower-class father and his daughter, Smudge. A great book for discussions of kindness and prejudice.

Bunting, Eve. 1998. *Your Move*. Illustrated by James Ransome. San Diego: Harcourt Brace & Company. James always stays home to take care of his little brother, Isaac, at night when his mom goes to work, but tonight the two will experience something much more terrifying. This riveting book offers a glimpse into an extremely positive and responsible brotherly relationship, and would be great for discussions about gangs, violence, or guns.

Campbell, Ann-Jeanette. 1998. *Dora's Box*. Illustrated by Fabian Negrin. New York: Alfred A. Knopf Inc. In this tale based on the Greek mythological character Pandora, a girl grows up without compassion because her parents have prevented her from experiencing evil and sadness. This would certainly spark some good classroom discussions.

Clifton, Lucille. 1983. *Everett Anderson's Goodbye*. Illustrated by Ann Grifalconi. New York: Henry Holt & Company. This book outlines the five stages of grief—denial, anger, bargaining, depression, and acceptance—through the use of a child whose father has just died.

Cole, Kenneth. 2001. *No Bad News*. Photo-illustrated by John Ruebartsch. Morton Grove, Ill.: Albert Whitman & Company. A walk alone through the urban streets of his neighborhood to get a haircut causes young Marcus to reflect only on the negatives in his environment; a community of positive male role models at the barbershop changes his mind. The retouching of the photography in this book is beautiful.

Collard, Sneed B., III. 2000. *Animal Dads*. Illustrated by Steve Jenkins. New York: Houghton Mifflin Company. From poison-arrow frog chauffeurs to desert isopod house cleaners, this book presents fun and interesting facts about dads from the animal kingdom. A perfect book for discussions on Father's Day.

de Paola, Tomie. 1980. *Now One Foot, Now the Other*. New York: G. P. Putnam's Sons. Bob, little Bobby's grandfather, namesake, and best friend, suffers a physically and mentally debilitating stroke. The student becomes the teacher as young Bobby returns the favor Bob long ago taught him, and helps his grandfather relearn how to walk. Great for discussions about aging, sickness, and memory loss.

DiSalvo-Ryan, DyAnne. 2000. *Grandpa's Corner Store*. New York: HarperCollins Publishers. Lucy must come up with a solution when a brand-new supermarket being built down the street threatens her grandpa's cozy and landmark grocery store. Good for discussions about change and community.

Graham, Bob. 2000. *Max*. Cambridge, Mass.: Candlewick Press. Max is the super son of superhero parents, but he cannot fly yet! Children will identify with Max's plight and agree that "Everyone's different in *some* way, aren't they?" This book is an excellent segue into discussions about differences in growth and maturation.

Heo, Yumi. 1996. *Father's Rubber Shoes*. New York: Scholastic, Inc. Yungsu's father works long hours so that he can provide his son with a better life than he had growing up in Korea. Immigration, the importance of work, and parental responsibilities are all topics presented here and good for starting discussions.

Hughes, Shirley. 1997. *Alfie and the Birthday Surprise*. New York: Lothrop, Lee & Shepard Books. After Bob's cherished cat dies, his daughter, Maureen, enlists the help of Alfie and his family to plan a birthday party with one very special surprise. A good book for discussions about death.

King, Stephen Michael. 1996. *A Special Kind of Love*. New York: Scholastic, Inc. A father shows his love for his son by creating castles, airplanes, and kites out of boxes. This would be a good book to begin discussions about the different ways in which parents show and communicate love.

Lindsay, Jeanne Warren. 1991. *Do I Have a Daddy?: A Story About a Single-Parent Child*. Illustrated by Cheryl Boeller. Buena Park, Calif.: Morning Glory Press. In this timely book, young Erik seeks to understand where his daddy is. Mother explains that not all mommies and daddies get married, and encourages him to spend time with his Uncle Bob and grandfather. A resources section at the back of this book might assist in discussions about single-parenthood, absent fathers, or the importance of male role models.

Mandelbaum, Pili. 1990. *You Be Me, I'll Be You*. New York: Kane/Miller Book Publishers. When Anna complains that she does not like her dark skin and curly hair, dad gets creative. This depiction of a biracial family is a beautiful one, marked by one very special child. Great for discussions about race and beauty.

Manushkin, Fran. 1995. *The Matzah That Papa Brought Home.* Illustrated by Ned Bittinger. New York: Scholastic Inc. The repetitious rhyming text and detailed illustrations of this book bring to life the culture of a Jewish family celebrating Passover. An information supplement might help with discussions and questions about this celebration.

Moutoussamy-Ashe, Jeanne. 1993. *Daddy and Me: A Photo Story of Arthur Ashe and His Daughter Camera.* New York: Alfred A. Knopf. This photo-essay featuring Arthur Ashe and his daughter, Camera, depicts the true love this famous father shared with his daughter. A wonderful book for discussions about AIDS, unconditional love, and living with illness.

Munson, Derek. 2000. *Enemy Pie.* Illustrated by Tara Calahan King. San Francisco: Chronicle Books. Dad has just the recipe to take care of his son's new enemy: enemy pie! This book is sure to spark discussions about acceptance and the difficulty of making new friends.

O'Shaughnessy, Ellen. 1992. *Somebody Called Me a Retard Today . . . and My Heart Felt Sad.* Illustrated by David Garner. New York: Walker & Company. A young girl is called a "retard" at school; her father comforts her and reminds her of her unique and special abilities instead of focusing on her disabilities.

Rabe, Berniece. 1988. *Where's Chimpy?* Photo-illustrated by Diane Schmidt. Niles, Ill.: Albert Whitman & Company. Daddy helps his daughter Misty, who has Down Syndrome, find her cherished toy monkey in this book that focuses on bedtime rituals and counting, not on disability. An informational section might help better answer questions regarding Down Syndrome and disability.

Stevenson, James. 1996. *I Meant to Tell You.* New York: HarperCollins Children's Book Group. Parents of older children can especially relate to Stevenson's own memories of his daughter's youth, typical things like the day she learned to ride a bike, the beach vacation, the dance classes, and more intimate occasions that he has chosen to share.

Vigna, Judith. 1988. *I Wish Daddy Didn't Drink So Much.* Niles, Ill.: Albert Whitman & Company. When a young daughter gets upset about daddy ruining Christmas, mommy must explain that daddy's moods and hurtful behavior are because of alcoholism, a disease with which they can help him. An informational section at the back addresses issues about alcoholism.

———. 1991. *Saying Goodbye to Daddy.* Morton Grove, Ill.: Albert Whitman & Company. When Clare's father dies unexpectedly in a car accident, his young daughter must learn how to say goodbye to him.

Weninger, Brigitte. 1995. *Good-Bye, Daddy!* Illustrated by Alan Marks. New York: North-South Books. When Tom's dad leaves after his visit, Tom is inconsolable; only a story from his teddy bear can make things all right. This book deals with familial separation in a softer way by duplicating the theme with a bear family.

Zolotow, Charlotte. 1972. *William's Doll.* Illustrated by William Pène Du Bois. New York: HarperCollins Children's Book Group. Parents who cringe at the thought of giving a doll to a boy must read this classic story in which a grandmother's wisdom triumphs over a father's stubborn insensitivity.

DIVORCE AND SEPARATION

Brown, Laurene Krasny, and Marc Brown. 1986. *Dinosaurs Divorce: A Guide for Changing Families.* Boston: Little, Brown & Company. Using illustrations of dinosaurs for comfort, this guide for children seeks to validate the feelings children of divorcing parents might be having, and to prepare them for changes that might ensue.

Masurel, Claire. 2001. *Two Homes.* Illustrated by Kady MacDonald Denton. Cambridge, Mass.: Candlewick Press. Alex has two homes, two favorite chairs, and two parents to love.

DIVORCE AND SEPARATION, FATHERS IN A CUSTODIAL ROLE

Gauthier, Bertrand. 1993. *Zachary in I'm Zachary!* Illustrated by Daniel Sylvestre. Milwaukee: Gareth Stevens, Inc. This first book in a French-Canadian series introduces the divorced, custodial father, David, and his exuberant son, Zach, in a very warm and positive but realistic relationship that frequently tests the father's patience. The comic-book-style illustrations and humorous scenarios make for an upbeat series. Other titles include, *Zachary in the Championship, Zachary in Camping Out, Zachary in the Winner,* and *Zachary in the Present.*

McBratney, Sam. 2000. *Just You and Me.* Illustrated by Ivan Bates. Cambridge, Mass.: Candlewick Press. Big Gander Goose, whether intended to represent a father or other male caregiver, plays both protector and nurturer to Little Goosey in this warm story.

Polacco, Patricia. 1991. *Some Birthday!* New York: Simon & Schuster Books for Young Readers. It is Patricia's birthday and her father, who is divorced from her mother, seems to have forgotten entirely. Little does she know, this birthday will turn into her best ever, complete with monster hunt, camping trip, and the perfect gifts.

Vigna, Judith. 1997. *I Live With Daddy.* Morton Grove, Ill.: Albert Whitman & Company. A school-aged girl narrates this portrait of life with Dad, who is a strong role model for custodial fathers, and her relationship with her distant, celebrity mother.

DIVORCE AND SEPARATION, FATHERS IN A NONCUSTODIAL ROLE

Best, Cari. 1997. *Taxi! Taxi!* Illustrated by Dale Gottlieb. New York: Scholastic, Inc. Although Tina wishes that Papi lived with Mama and her, he demonstrates his love every Sunday when they spend the day together.

Binch, Caroline. 1998. *Since Dad Left*. Brookfield, Conn.: Millbrook Press, Inc. When Sid visits his dad for the first time after his parents' separation, Dad gives him just enough breathing space to allow for adjustment to the unusual residence and lifestyle.

Caines, Jeannette. 1977. *Daddy*. Illustrated by Ronald Himler. New York: Harper & Row. This is a simple, charming story of a noncustodial father and the time he shares with his daughter, Windy, on Saturdays.

Caseley, Judith. 1995. *Priscilla Twice*. New York: HarperCollins Children's Book Group. Priscilla's initial difficulty adjusting to her parents' divorce is handled in an upbeat manner.

Girard, Linda Walvoord. *At Daddy's on Saturdays*. Illustrated by Judith Friedman. Morton Grove, Ill.: Albert Whitman & Company. Katie has a hard time adjusting to her parents' divorce, but spending time with her father in his new apartment helps her realize that she can have *two* homes full of love.

Hoffman, Mary. 2000. *Boundless Grace*. Illustrated by Caroline Binch. New York: Penguin Putnam Books for Young Readers. When Grace visits her remarried father in Africa, he and his family help to dispel Grace's limited notions about families, fathers, and stepmothers, culled from reading fairytales. This is the sequel to *Amazing Grace* (1998).

Roy, Ron. 1980. *Breakfast with My Father*. Illustrated by Troy Howell. New York: Houghton Mifflin Company. During a period of marital separation that ultimately ends in reunion, a father and son meet to have breakfast every Saturday morning.

Rush, Ken. 1994. *Friday's Journey*. New York: Orchard Books. While riding the subway to spend the weekend at his dad's place, a young boy remembers fondly places he and his parents used to go together, and asks his father to return to them.

Schindel, John. 1995. *Dear Daddy*. Illustrated by Dorothy Donohue. Morton Grove, Ill.: Albert Whitman & Company. Jesse writes letters to his father on the other side of the country, and thinks he will never get one in return.

Spelman, Cornelia M. 2001. *Mama and Daddy Bear's Divorce*. Illustrated by Kathy Parkinson. Morton Grove, Ill.: Albert Whitman & Company. Four-year-old Dinah learns that divorce does not mean the end of parental love and involvement. The bear characters will especially allow for younger children to relate to the message.

Weninger, Brigitte. 1995. *Good-Bye, Daddy!* Illustrated by Alan Marks. New York: North-South Books. When Tom's dad leaves after his visit, Tom is inconsolable; only a story from his teddy bear can make things all right. This book deals with familial separation in a softer way by duplicating the theme with a bear family.

Winthrop, Elizabeth. 1998. *As the Crow Flies*. Illustrated by Joan Sandin. New York: Clarion Books. Mikey's parents are divorced; he lives with his mother in Arizona, and his father lives in Delaware, "seven states away as the crow flies." Dad's annual visit brings lots of special memories and a wonderful surprise.

ILLNESS

de Paola, Tomie. 1980. *Now One Foot, Now the Other*. New York: G. P. Putnam's Sons. Bob, little Bobby's grandfather, namesake, and best friend, suffers a physically and mentally debilitating stroke. The student becomes the teacher as young Bobby returns the favor Bob long ago taught him, and helps his grandfather relearn how to walk. Great for discussions about aging, sickness, and memory loss.

———. 1997. *The Days of the Blackbird: A Tale of Northern Italy*. New York: Penguin Putnam Books for Young Readers. In this Italian fable, a widowed duke shares many simple pleasures with his daughter until he becomes ill.

Hermes, Patricia. 1996. *When Snow Lay Soft on the Mountains*. Illustrated by Leslie Baker. New York: Little, Brown & Company. Financial hardships, the death of Mama, and father's influenza cause Hallie to keep many wishes to herself, while helping to nurse her father back to health in this quiet 1800s story. One special wish comes true on her birthday.

Lasky, Kathryn. 1997. *Marven of the Great North Woods*. Illustrated by Kevin Hawkes. San Diego: Harcourt Brace & Company. When an influenza epidemic spread across American in 1918, Marven Lasky was sent to live with French Canadian lumberjacks in the great north woods of Minnesota to be kept safe from the disease. This is the true story of the author's father.

McAllister, Angela. 1994. *The Ice Palace*. Illustrated by Angela Barrett. New York: G. P. Putnam's Sons. When Anna falls sick during the hottest, driest season of the year, her father goes to work entertaining her with stories of the north wind and of ice palaces. With the presentation of Anna's special gift at the end of the book, many young readers might have questions regarding cooling methods before the invention of refrigerators.

Moutoussamy-Ashe, Jeanne. 1993. *Daddy and Me: A Photo Story of Arthur Ashe and His Daughter Camera*. New York: Alfred A. Knopf. This photo-essay featuring Arthur Ashe and his daughter, Camera, depicts the true love this famous father shared with his daughter. A wonderful book for discussions about AIDS, unconditional love, and living with illness.

Powell, E. Sandy. 1980. *Geranium Morning*. Illustrated by Renée Graef. Minneapolis: CarolRhoda Books. In this now classic story, a boy is plagued by guilt after his father dies, but finds solace in a friend whose mother is also dying.

Sachar, Louis. 1992. *Monkey Soup*. New York: Alfred A. Knopf Books for Young Readers. Dad is sick in bed and at the mercy of Mom, who cooks him chicken soup; when his young daughter serves up her version of get-well "soup," his fathering abilities kick in. Preschoolers will love the surprise ending.

Vigna, Judith. 1988. *I Wish Daddy Didn't Drink So Much*. Niles, Ill.: Albert Whitman & Company. When a young daughter gets upset about daddy ruining Christmas, mommy must explain that daddy's moods and hurtful behavior are because of alcoholism, a disease with which they can help him. An informational section at the back addresses issues about alcoholism.

Ziefert, Harriet. 1991. *When Daddy Had the Chicken Pox*. Illustrated by Lionel Kalish. New York: HarperCollins Publishers. Dad, who has everyone greatly concerned after contracting chicken pox from his children, cannot attend his daughter's ballet recital, but makes up for it when he is well.

NEW BABY

Agell, Charlotte. 1994. *I Wear Long Green Hair in Summer* and *Mud Makes Me Dance in the Spring*. Gardiner, Maine: Tilbury House Publishers. Dad supports Mom, who is busy with the new baby brother, by spending quality time with his young daughter in these two hand-size books, part of a series that celebrates family life with simple text and illustrations. See also *I Slide into the White of Winter* and *Wind Spins Me around in Fall* (1994).

Cazet, Denys. 1995. *Dancing*. Music by Craig Bond. New York: Orchard Books. Dad spends some valuable one-on-one time singing and dancing with his son Alex, who wants only to send his new baby brother back to the hospital.

Gliori, Debi. 1999. *Mr. Bear's New Baby*. New York: Scholastic, Inc. Both Mr. and Mrs. Bear share nighttime baby duty, along with many sleepy neighbors, in this latest addition to the Bear family saga.

Hiatt, Fred. 1999. *Baby Talk*. Illustrated by Mark Graham. New York: Margaret K. McElderry Books. Young Joey learns to love his new baby brother when they develop a special language and become inseparable. Although not in a custodial role, Joey is a wonderful brotherly caregiver.

Mennen, Ingrid. 1994. *One Round Moon and a Star for Me*. Illustrated by Niki Daly. New York: Orchard Books. When a new baby is born into the family, Papa must reassure his son of his love. This story is set in a Lesotho village and features many words from Lesotho, South Africa.

SUBSTANCE ABUSE AND ALCOHOLISM

Carrick, Carol. 1994. *Banana Beer*. Illustrated by Margot Apple. Morton Grove, Ill.: Albert Whitman & Company. By using monkey characters rather than humans, and banana beer, the author creates a comfortable distance for children in this bibliotherapeutic story about an alcoholic father.

Cole, Kenneth. 2001. *No Bad News*. Photo-illustrated by John Ruebartsch. Morton Grove, Ill.: Albert Whitman & Company. A walk alone through the urban streets of his neighborhood to get a haircut causes young Marcus to reflect only on the negatives in his environment; a community of positive male role models at the barbershop changes his mind. The retouching of the photography in this book is beautiful.

Daly, Niki. 1995. *My Dad*. New York: Margaret K. McElderry Books. This is a very sensitive and emotional portrayal of an alcoholic father whose embarrassing behavior alienates and frustrates his family.

Thomas, Jane Resh. 1996. *Daddy Doesn't Have to Be a Giant Anymore*. Illustrated by Marcia Sewall. New York: Clarion Books. A young girl is confused and terrified by her father's erratic and violent alcohol-induced behavior. Family and friends come together to address the issue, which prompts him to seek treatment.

Vigna, Judith. 1988. *I Wish Daddy Didn't Drink So Much*. Niles, Ill.: Albert Whitman & Company. When a young daughter gets upset about daddy ruining Christmas, mommy must explain that daddy's moods and hurtful behavior are because of alcoholism, a disease with which they can help him. An informational section at the back addresses issues about alcoholism.

UNEMPLOYMENT AND FINANCIAL HARDSHIPS

Adler, David A. 1999. *The Babe and I*. Illustrated by Terry Widener. San Diego: Harcourt Trade Publishers. Set during the Depression, a boy turns his birthday disappointment, caused by dad's unannounced unemployment, into a newspaper-selling venture; in so doing, he gains an understanding of his father's situation as well as tickets to a Yankees game.

Browne, Anthony. 1998. *Voices in the Park*. New York: DK. When pet dogs Victoria and Albert romp at the park, two worlds collide. This unique tale allows readers to experience a moment through the very different perspectives of an upper-class mother and her son, Charles, and of a lower-class father and his daughter, Smudge.

Bunting, Eve. 1993. *Fly Away Home*. Illustrated by Ronald Himler. Boston: Houghton Mifflin Company. With rents unaffordable for his widowed father, a part-time janitor, Andrew and he survive in an airport terminal with other homeless people.

———. 1996. *Going Home*. Illustrated by David Diaz. New York: HarperCollins. Joanna Cotler Books. Carlos and his family are going home to Mexico for Christmas, but how can home be in America and in Mexico? This book features extremely self-sacrificing parents who would do anything to provide better opportunities for their children.

Demas, Corinne. 2000. *Nina's Waltz*. Illustrated by Deborah Lanino. New York: Orchard Books. Nina's father is a championship fiddler, but when wasps sting him his daughter has to step in and compete in his place.

Dumbleton, Mike, and Tom Jellett. 1999. *Downsized*. Sydney: Random House Australia. A very shrewd young daughter finds a creative way to get her father out of the slump he has been in since unemployment took over their lives. This upbeat Australian story would be especially therapeutic for families in similar situations.

Egielski, Richard. 1998. *Jazper*. New York: HarperCollins. A Laura Geringer Book. When Jazper comes home to find his father in bandages, he realizes he must go make a living for the two of them and ends up getting mixed up with some magical moths. This is a very cute story with funny illustrations of the bug town.

Estes, Kristyn Rehling. 1999. *Manuela's Gift*. Illustrated by Claire B. Cotts. San Francisco: Chronicle Books. Times are hard for Manuela's Mama, Papa, and Abuela, but on her birthday she realizes there is still much to celebrate. This book contains many Spanish words.

Eversole, Robyn H. 1998. *The Gift Stone*. Illustrated by Allen Garns. New York: Alfred A. Knopf Books for Young Readers. Dad has found work in an opal mine, which means living underground, and Jean misses her old house with real windows and grass outside, or wishes she could live with Grandma and Granddad, who are unable to support her. This Australian story blends hardships with hope.

Figueredo, D. H. 1999. *When This World Was New*. Illustrated by Enrique O. Sanchez. New York: Lee & Low Books, Inc. A Latino father, new to the United States and facing many uncertainties, takes time to enjoy a snowfall with his son, which ends up being therapeutic as well as fun.

Hanson, Regina. 1995. *The Tangerine Tree*. Illustrated by Harvey Stevenson. Boston: Houghton Mifflin Company. Papa must leave his impoverished Jamaican family for work in New York, but a book given to his young daughter, along with reading goals, will help to shorten the time that he is away.

Hartley, Deborah. 1986. *Up North in Winter*. Illustrated by Lydia Dabcovich. New York: E. P. Dutton. This book about the author's great-grandfather recounts tough times during a very cold winter when Grandpa Ole had to walk for miles through the snow to work for his family.

Hazen, Barbara Shook. 1983. *Tight Times*. Illustrated by Trina Schart Hyman. New York: Penguin Putnam Books for Young Readers. In this now classic family story, father remains loving and sensitive to his small son despite the stress of unemployment and financial difficulties.

Marks, Alan. 1993. *The Thief's Daughter*. New York: Farrar, Straus & Giroux. Magpie, whose poor father tells her magnificent stories about royal households, discovers the truth behind her father's life and learns an important lesson about honesty in this fairy-tale-like beginning chapter book.

Maslac, Evelyn Hughes. 1996. *Finding a Job for Daddy*. Illustrated by Kay Life. Morton Grove, Ill.: Albert Whitman & Company. Readers for whom this bibliotherapeutic title is geared may find reassurance in the warm portrayal of a family stressed by dad's unemployment.

Myers, Bernice. 1991. *The Gold Watch*. New York: Lothrop, Lee & Shepard Books. Although Dad loses his job and the family suffers financial hardships, this story remains upbeat and presents a warm relationship between father and son.

Quinlan, Patricia. 1987. *My Dad Takes Care of Me*. Illustrated by Vlasta van Kampen. Toronto: Annick Press. Luke's father lost his job and takes cares of him at home now. Although he continues to look for jobs, this book presents a stay-at-home dad.

Riecken, Nancy. 1996. *Today Is the Day*. Illustrated by Catherine Stock. Boston: Houghton Mifflin Company. Yesenia, a young Mexican girl, awaits the return of her father who has been working away from home in the hopes that he will have brought enough money for her to attend school.

Sawyer, Ruth. 1997. *The Remarkable Christmas of the Cobbler's Sons*. Illustrated by Barbara Cooney. New York: Viking Penguin. In this Austrian tale, a poor, widowed cobbler demonstrates a playful manner in raising his three sons despite their poverty. They experience Christmastime prosperity thanks to a surprise visit from an eccentric goblin king.

Vigna, Judith. 1988. *I Wish Daddy Didn't Drink So Much*. Niles, Ill.: Albert Whitman & Company. When a young daughter gets upset about daddy ruining Christmas, mommy must explain that daddy's moods and hurtful behavior are because of alcoholism, a disease with which they can help him. An informational section at the back addresses issues about alcoholism.

Wyeth, Sharon Dennis. 1995. *Always My Dad*. Illustrated by Raúl Colón. New York: Knopf. Dad is having problems "getting his life together"; his constant shifting from job to job and his lack of presence in his children's lives have them all upset.

BOOKS FOR HOLIDAYS AND SEASONS

AUTUMN

Agell, Charlotte. 1994. *Wind Spins Me Around in Fall* and *Mud Makes Me Dance in the Spring*. Gardiner, Maine: Tilbury House Publishers. Dad supports Mom, who is busy with the new baby brother, by spending quality time with his young daughter in these two hand-size books, part of a series that celebrates family life with simple text and illustrations. See also *I Slide into the White of Winter* and *I Wear Long Green Hair in Summer* (1994).

Jukes, Mavis. 1984. *Like Jake and Me*. Illustrated by Lloyd Bloom. New York: Dragonfly Books. Alex, who loves ballet, does not have much in common with his stepfather, Jake, a cowboy. A funny misunderstanding about a spider helps them bond.

Rockwell, Anne. 1994. *Ducklings and Pollywogs*. Illustrated by Lizzy Rockwell. New York: Macmillan Publishing Company. A father and daughter explore the many animals and plants at a pond through the four seasons.

CHRISTMAS

Anaya, Rudolfo. 1998. *The Farolitos of Christmas*. Illustrated by Edward Gonzalez. New York: Hyperion Paperbacks for Children. In this warm World War II-era story, father is wounded and hospitalized, and Grandfather (Abuelo) is too ill to create the traditional luminarias, which forces Luz, her friends, and her family to prepare for Christmas on their own.

Bunting, Eve. 1996. *Going Home*. Illustrated by David Diaz. New York: HarperCollins. Joanna Cotler Books. Carlos and his family are going home to Mexico for Christmas, but how can home be in America *and* in Mexico? This book features extremely self-sacrificing parents who would do anything to provide better opportunities for their children.

George, William T. 1992. *Christmas at Long Pond*. Illustrated by Lindsay Barrett George. New York: Greenwillow. A search for a Christmas tree allows Dad and son to enjoy the woods and Dad to play the role of naturalist.

Houston, Gloria. 1998. *Littlejim's Gift: An Appalachian Christmas Story*. Illustrated by Thomas B. Allen. New York: Penguin Putnam Books for Young Readers. Littlejim is a scholar with a heart of gold. He yearns more than anything to please Papa, which is practically impossible, but they both find solace during this World War I Christmastime.

Ransom, Candice F. 1997. *One Christmas Dawn*. Illustrated by Peter Fiore. Mahwah, N.J.: Troll Communications. The winter of 1917 is one of the coldest ever, so cold that Father must leave home to work in the city, and his ten-year-old daughter wonders if he will make it home for Christmas.

Ray, Deborah Kogan. 1990. *My Daddy Was a Soldier: A World War II Story*. New York: Holiday House. This touching story outlines major events in America during World War II through the eyes of Jeannie, whose father is away fighting the war.

Sawyer, Ruth. 1997. *The Remarkable Christmas of the Cobbler's Sons*. Illustrated by Barbara Cooney. New York: Viking Penguin. In this Austrian tale, a poor, widowed cobbler demonstrates a playful manner in raising his three sons despite their poverty. They experience Christmastime prosperity thanks to a surprise visit from an eccentric goblin king.

Wetzel, JoAnne Stewart. 1995. *The Christmas Box*. Illustrated by Barry Root. New York: Random House Value Publishing, Inc. While Dad is stationed in Japan during the Korean War, he sends home a box full of very special Christmas gifts, which bridges the distance between his family and him.

Wojciechowski, Susan. 1995. *The Christmas Miracle of Jonathan Toomey*. Illustrated by P. J. Lynch. Cambridge, Mass.: Candlewick Press. Jonathan Toomey, a woodcarver known as Mr. Gloomy to the village children, experiences the miracle of love when carving a special nativity for widow McDowell and her son.

FATHER'S DAY

Bunting, Eve. 2000. *A Perfect Father's Day*. Illustrated by Susan Meddaugh. Boston: Houghton Mifflin Company. This tongue-in-cheek celebration, managed by a four-year-old daughter, includes visits to her favorite fast-food restaurant and a park.

Collard, Sneed B. III. 2000. *Animal Dads*. Illustrated by Steve Jenkins. New York: Houghton Mifflin Company. From poison-arrow frog chauffeurs to desert isopod house cleaners, this book presents fun and interesting facts about dads from the animal kingdom. A perfect book for discussions on Father's Day.

Guettier, Benedicte. 1999. *The Father Who Had 10 Children*. New York: Penguin Putnam Books for Young Readers. In this humorous glimpse at parental burnout, Dad does it all—cooks, dresses, chauffeurs, bathes, and reads bedtime stories to 10 children—plus goes to work and, in his spare time, builds a boat in which he intends to sail on a solo journey. A surefire hit for fathers.

Kroll, Steven. 1988. *Happy Father's Day*. Illustrated by Marylin Hafner. New York: Holiday House, Inc. Reading this story before Father's Day might inspire children to plan their own special celebrations, but a reading on Father's Day could prove advantageous for dads as well.

Sansone, Adele. 2001. *The Little Green Goose*. Illustrated by Alan Marks. New York: North-South Books, Inc. A perfect book for preschool story times. A male goose goes out of his way to demonstrate his nurturing abilities; his adopted offspring learns that dads can be every bit as warm and loving as moms.

HANUKKAH

Koss, Amy Goldman. 2000. *How I Saved Hanukkah*. Illustrated by Diane Degroat. New York: Penguin Putnam Books for Young Readers. The traditional father role is depicted in this story about a family celebrating Hanukkah while father has to be away on business.

Oberman, Sheldon. 1997. *By the Hanukkah Light*. Illustrated by Neil Waldman. Honesdale, Penn.: Boyds Mills Press. Grandfather tells two stories of Hanukkah to his expectant grandchildren: the miraculous first Hanukkah with the Macabees, and the fearful, secretive Hanukkahs of his youth in Nazi Europe.

Zalben, Jane Breskin. 1994. *Papa's Latkes*. New York: Henry Holt. When Mama Bear tires of making latkes, and the cubs' attempts fail, Papa salvages the holiday tradition with delicious results.

PASSOVER

Manushkin, Fran. 1995. *The Matzah That Papa Brought Home*. Illustrated by Ned Bittinger. New York: Scholastic, Inc. The repetitious rhyming text and detailed illustrations of this book bring to life the culture of a Jewish family celebrating Passover.

SPRING

Agell, Charlotte. 1994. *Mud Makes Me Dance in the Spring*. Gardiner, Maine: Tilbury House Publishers. Dad supports Mom, who is busy with the new baby brother, by spending quality time with his young daughter in this hand-size book, part of a series that celebrates family life with simple text and illustrations. See also *I Wear Long Green Hair in Summer, I Slide into the White of Winter*, and *Wind Spins Me Around in Fall* (1994).

Rockwell, Anne. 1994. *Ducklings and Pollywogs*. Illustrated by Lizzy Rockwell. New York: Macmillan Publishing Company. A father and daughter explore the many animals and plants at a pond through the four seasons.

San Souci, Daniel. 1993. *Country Road*. New York: Doubleday Books for Young Readers. Dad and his generally disinterested son go walking along an old road, coming to appreciate the wildlife and one another along the way.

SUMMER

Agell, Charlotte. 1994. *I Wear Long Green Hair in Summer*. Gardiner, Maine: Tilbury House Publishers. Dad supports Mom, who is busy with the new baby brother, by spending quality time with his young daughter in this hand-size book, part of a series that celebrates family life with simple text and illustrations. See also *Mud Makes Me Dance in the Spring, I Slide into the White of Winter*, and *Wind Spins Me Around in Fall* (1994).

Greenwood, Pamela D. 1994. *I Found Mouse*. Illustrated by Jennifer Plecas. New York: Clarion Books. Since Tessie's mom, brother, and best friend are all gone for the summer, she amuses herself by adopting a stray cat that she names Mouse, and develops a warm relationship with her father in the raising of the kitten.

Monfried, Lucia. 1993. *The Daddies Boat*. Illustrated by Michele Chessare. New York: Penguin Putnam Books for Young Readers. An island resort is the setting for this story about summer's simple pleasures, enhanced by warm family interactions and a surprise ending.

Munson, Derek. 2000. *Enemy Pie*. Illustrated by Tara Calahan King. San Francisco: Chronicle Books. It was shaping up to be the best summer ever for a young boy, when Jeremy Ross moved to the neighborhood, becoming his first enemy. Fortunately, dad had enemies growing up too, and he has just the recipe to take care of them: enemy pie!

Rockwell, Anne. 1994. *Ducklings and Pollywogs*. Illustrated by Lizzy Rockwell. New York: Macmillan Publishing Company. A father and daughter explore the many animals and plants at a pond through the four seasons.

Sanders, Scott Russell. 1997. *Meeting Trees*. Illustrated by Robert Hynes. Washington, D.C.: National Geographic Society. A father's passions for woodworking, trees, and nature are shared with his son in this story based on the author's life.

Shannon, George. 1993. *Climbing Kansas Mountains*. Illustrated by Thomas B. Allen. New York: Bradbury Press. A creative father helps alleviate his son's summertime boredom as they seek out mountains to climb in Kansas.

Spohn, David. *Starry Night*. See **Series**.

WINTER

Agell, Charlotte. 1994. *I Slide into the White of Winter*. Gardiner, Maine: Tilbury House Publishers. Dad supports Mom, who is busy with the new baby brother, by spending quality time with his young daughter in this hand-size book, part of a series that celebrates family life with simple text and illustrations. See also *I Wear Long Green Hair in Summer, Mud Makes Me Dance in the Spring*, and *Wind Spins Me Around in Fall* (1994).

Bradby, Marie. 1995. *The Longest Wait*. Illustrated by Peter Catalanotto. New York: Scholastic, Inc. Daddy must deliver mail by horseback in a snowstorm, which creates anxiety in a son awaiting his safe return, and delays snow playing time.

Figueredo, D. H. 1999. *When This World Was New*. Illustrated by Enrique O. Sanchez. New York: Lee & Low Books, Inc. A Latino father, new to the United States and facing many uncertainties, takes time to enjoy a snowfall with his son, which ends up being therapeutic as well as fun.

Hartley, Deborah. 1986. *Up North in Winter*. Illustrated by Lydia Dabcovich. New York: E. P. Dutton. This book about the author's great-grandfather recounts tough times during a very cold winter when Grandpa Ole had to walk for miles through the snow to work for his family.

Lasky, Kathryn. 1997. *Marven of the Great North Woods*. Illustrated by Kevin Hawkes. San Diego: Harcourt Brace & Company. When an influenza epidemic spread across American in 1918, Marven Lasky was sent to live with French Canadian lumberjacks in the great north woods of Minnesota to be kept safe from the disease. This is the true story of the author's father.

Rockwell, Anne. 1994. *Ducklings and Pollywogs*. Illustrated by Lizzy Rockwell. New York: Macmillan Publishing Company. A father and daughter explore the many animals and plants at a pond through the four seasons.

Spohn, David. *Winter Wood*. See **Series**.

Yolen, Jane. 1987. *Owl Moon*. Illustrated by John Schoenherr. New York: Philomel Books. This story depicts masterfully a father-daughter outing in search of great horned owls. The text and illustrations shine with lyrical beauty.

FATHERS IN HISTORICAL SETTINGS

THE DEPRESSION AND THE 20TH CENTURY

Adler, David A. 1999. *The Babe and I.* Illustrated by Terry Widener. San Diego: Harcourt Trade Publishers. Set during the Depression, a boy turns his birthday disappointment, caused by dad's unannounced unemployment, into a newspaper-selling venture; in so doing, he gains an understanding of his father's situation as well as tickets to a Yankees game.

Anaya, Rudolfo. 1998. *The Farolitos of Christmas.* Illustrated by Edward Gonzalez. New York: Hyperion Paperbacks for Children. In this warm World War II-era story, father is wounded and hospitalized, and Grandfather (Abuelo) is too ill to create the traditional luminarias, which forces Luz, her friends, and her family to prepare for Christmas on their own.

Coy, John. 2001. *Night Driving.* Illustrated by Peter McCarty. New York: Henry Holt & Company. On their way to a camping trip, a father and son drive late into the night, enjoying conversation, rest stops, and the magic of the night. The black-and-white illustrations depict the 1950s.

Hendershot, Judith. 1987. *In Coal Country.* Illustrated by Thomas B. Allen. New York: Alfred A. Knopf. In this vivid account of life in a small 1930s coal town, Papa is a coal miner who works hard for his family.

Houston, Gloria. 1998. *Littlejim's Gift: An Appalachian Christmas Story.* Illustrated by Thomas B. Allen. New York: Penguin Putnam Books for Young Readers. Littlejim is a scholar with a heart of gold. He yearns more than anything to please Papa, which is practically impossible, but they both find solace during this World War I Christmastime.

Lasky, Kathryn. 1997. *Marven of the Great North Woods.* Illustrated by Kevin Hawkes. New York: Harcourt Brace & Company. When an influenza epidemic spread across American in 1918, Marven Lasky was sent to live with French Canadian lumberjacks in the great north woods of Minnesota to be kept safe from the disease. This is the true story of the author's father.

Mellecker, Judith. 1992. *Randolph's Dream.* Illustrated by Robert Andrew Parker. New York: Random House Value Publishing, Inc. Through very realistic dreams, seven-year-old Randolph is able to deal with the helplessness and loneliness he feels as a result of his father being stationed in North Africa, and his own displacement from his home and mother in London during World War II.

Mochizuki, Ken. 1995. *Heroes.* Illustrated by Dom Lee. New York: Lee & Low Books, Inc. Donnie, who is Asian American, always has to be the "bad guy" when he and his friends play war because his friends will not believe that his father and uncle are decorated military heroes. This book is dedicated to the many people of Asian and Pacific Islander descent who have defended America with little or no recognition.

Monjo, F. N. 1961. *The One Bad Thing about Father.* Illustrated by Rocco Negri. New York: Harper & Row. An I CAN READ History Book. Told through the voice of Quentin, Theodore Roosevelt's son, this story captures wonderful family moments shared in the White House.

Ransom, Candice F. 1997. *One Christmas Dawn.* Illustrated by Peter Fiore. Mahwah, N.J.: Troll Communications, LLC. The winter of 1917 is one of the coldest ever, so cold that Father must leave home to work in the city, and his ten-year-old daughter wonders if he will make it home for Christmas.

Ray, Deborah Kogan. 1990. *My Daddy Was a Soldier: A World War II Story.* New York: Holiday House. This touching story outlines major events in America during World War II through the eyes of Jeannie, whose father is away fighting the war.

Tunnell, Michael O. 2000. *Mailing May.* Illustrated by Ted Rand. New York: Morrow/Avon. Based on a true story that took place in the early 1900s, a father finds a clever way to circumvent the train fare that otherwise would have prohibited his daughter from visiting Grandma.

Wallace, Ian. 1999. *Boy of the Deeps.* New York: DK. In this recounting of the author's grandfather's hard childhood, James accompanies his father down into "the deeps" of a coal mine for his first day on the job.

Wetzel, JoAnne Stewart. 1995. *The Christmas Box.* Illustrated by Barry Root. New York: Random House Value Publishing, Inc. While Dad is stationed in Japan during the Korean War, he sends home a box full of very special Christmas gifts, which bridges the distance between his family and he.

THE CIVIL WAR AND THE 19TH CENTURY

Conway, Celeste. 1994. *Where Is Papa Now?* Honesdale, Penn: Boyds Mills Press. In this Victorian-era story, Papa is far away from home, at work trading goods in exotic lands, and his young daughter, who continuously asks Mother for information about his travels, sorely misses him.

Crist-Evans, Craig. 1999. *Moon Over Tennessee: A Boy's Civil War Journal.* Illustrated by Bonnie Christensen. Boston: Houghton Mifflin Company. Written in a poetic journal style, this book acts as documentation of one 13-year-old boy's experiences with the Confederate Army during the Civil War, climaxing at the Battle of Gettysburg.

Donovan, Mary Lee. 1993. *Papa's Bedtime Story.* Illustrated by Kimberly Bulcken Root. New York: Alfred A. Knopf Books for Young Readers. Fathers throughout the animal world comfort their babies with bedtime stories, while a log cabin family does the same.

Hermes, Patricia. 1996. *When Snow Lay Soft on the Mountains*. Illustrated by Leslie Baker. Boston: Little, Brown & Company. Financial hardships, the death of Mama, and father's influenza cause Hallie to keep many wishes to herself while helping to nurse her father back to health in this quiet 1800s story. One special wish comes true on her birthday.

Howard, Elizabeth Fitzgerald. 1995. *Papa Tells Chita a Story*. Illustrated by Floyd Cooper. New York: Simon & Schuster Books for Young Readers. Father and Chita share quality time together after dinner as he recounts his days as a soldier in Cuba during the Spanish-American War.

Howard, Ellen. 1997. *The Log Cabin Quilt*. Illustrated by Ronald Himler. New York: Holiday House, Inc. After Mam dies, Pap hustles the family by covered wagon to Michigan, leaving behind all of her possessions and memories, except for some fabric scraps rescued by Granny. These become the chink to the emotional side of this traditional, hard-working, unemotional man.

Johnston, Tony. 1999. *The Wagon*. Illustrated by James E. Ransome. New York: Morrow/Avon. Papa is not just physically strong, he has a sound mind as well, which helps this slave family stay intact and alive with hope.

Joosse, Barbara. 1998. *Lewis & Papa, Adventure on the Santa Fe Trail*. Illustrated by Jon Van Zyle. San Francisco: Chronicle Books. The special nature of father-son relationships is detailed both in this story, which takes place in the American West, and in the author's personal note to the reader.

McClintock, Barbara. 1996. *The Fantastic Drawings of Danielle*. Boston: Houghton Mifflin Company. Father, a French photographer in the late 1800s, is unable to support his daughter's fantastical approach to art, until her artwork ends up supporting both of them.

Van Leeuwen, Jean. 1998. *Nothing Here but Trees*. Illustrated by Phil Boatwright. New York: Penguin Putnam Books for Young Readers. Father is depicted very traditionally as the strong provider and protector in this story of a pioneer family settling in the Ohio Northwest.

OTHER TIME PERIODS

Bradman, Tony. 1990. *The Sandal*. Illustrated by Philippe Dupasquier. New York: Penguin Putnam Books for Young Readers. A child's lost sandal provides the bridge to connect past, present, and future dads enjoying a day in the city with the children.

FATHERS AND CHILDREN ENGAGED IN SPORTS

BASEBALL

Adler, David A. 1999. *The Babe and I*. Illustrated by Terry Widener. San Diego: Harcourt Trade Publishers. Set during the Depression, a boy turns his birthday disappointment, caused by dad's unannounced unemployment, into a newspaper-selling venture. In so doing, he gains an understanding of his father's situation as well as tickets to a Yankees game.

Burleigh, Robert. 1998. *Home Run*. Illustrated by Mike Wimmer. New York: Silver Whistle. This lyrical book about George Herman Ruth Jr. is a great introduction to the man and the magic that was Babe Ruth.

Christopher, Matt. 1992. *Centerfield Ballhawk*. Illustrated by Ellen Beier. Boston: Little, Brown & Company. José wants to excel at baseball in order to gain the respect and attention of his emotionally distant father, a widower who once played minor-league baseball.

Curtis, Gavin. 2001. *The Bat Boy & His Violin*. Illustrated by E. B. Lewis. New York: Aladdin Paperbacks. Papa manages a Negro National League team, the Dukes, and is suffering from the worst season ever, until his son becomes "bat boy."

Friend, David. 1990. *Baseball, Football, Daddy and Me*. Illustrated by Rick Brown. New York: Viking. Father and son are the ultimate sports enthusiasts.

Greenspun, Adele Aron. 1991. *Daddies*. New York: Philomel Books. This simple book with touching black-and-white photographs captures the many ways fathers love their children.

Ketteman, Helen. 1998. *I Remember Papa*. Illustrated by Greg Shed. New York: Penguin Putnam Books for Young Readers. The lessons a father taught his son, such as the importance of saving money, of forgiveness, and of parental sacrifices, are remembered for a lifetime in this story about a father and son's passion for baseball.

Spohn, David. *Home Field*. See **Series**.

BASKETBALL

Barber, Barbara E. 1996. *Allie's Basketball Dream*. Illustrated by Darryl Ligasan. New York: Lee & Low Books, Inc. When Allie gets a new basketball from her father, she has hopes of one day becoming a professional basketball player, but first she must combat her peers and their very solidly placed gender ideas that insist basketball is for boys and jumping rope is for girls.

Smith, Will. 1999. *Just the Two of Us*. Illustrated by Kadir Nelson. New York: Scholastic Press. This book uses the powerful and positive lyrics of Will Smith's song "Just the Two of Us" and beautifully crafted illustrations to depict the growing relationship between a father and his son.

CAR RACING

Jennings, Dana A. 1997. *Me, Dad, & Number Six*. Illustrated by Goro Sasaki. New York: Harcourt Children's Books. Dad's passions for a '37 Pontiac coupe and car racing are imparted to his six-year-old son, allowing for bonding and quality time together.

FISHING

Asch, Frank. 1984. *Just Like Daddy*. New York: Simon & Schuster Books for Young Readers. A young bear emulates Daddy bear as they prepare for a fishing trip that ends with a surprise.

Creech, Sharon. 2000. *Fishing in the Air*. Illustrated by Chris Raschka. New York: Joanna Cotler Books. Father and son embark on a fishing excursion and share many imaginative moments, including a conversation about the father's days as a young boy learning to fish with his father.

London, Jonathan. 1996. *Old Salt, Young Salt*. Illustrated by Todd L. W. Doney. New York: HarperCollins Children's Book Group. A day spent fishing in the ocean allows Aaron to prove his seaworthiness to Dad.

Long, Earlene. 1987. *Gone Fishing*. Illustrated by Richard Brown. New York: Houghton Mifflin Company. Using the concepts of "big" and "little," a young boy describes preparations for a fishing trip with his father.

McCreary, Laura, and Mark Myers. 2001. *Angela Anaconda: The Best Dad*. Based on the scripts by Charlotte Fullerton and Mark Myers. Illustrated by Barry Goldberg. New York: Simon Spotlight. This short chapter book features two stories about Angela Anaconda, her dad, and her eternal enemy Nanette Manoir. The first story sees father and daughter entering a square-dancing competition; the second sees them going fishing.

Miyamoto, Tadao. 1994. *Papa and Me*. Minneapolis: The Lerner Publishing Group. While papa bear and baby bear fish, father reassures his son that they are, in fact, father and son, because of special memories they share together. Adults will especially like the ending.

Sharp, N. L. 2001. *Today I'm Going Fishing with My Dad*. Illustrated by Chris L. Demarest. Honesdale, N.J.: Boyds Mills Press. The son, whose honesty and maturity make this an extra-special story, describes the first father-son fishing trip of the season. This is "quality time" with a twist.

FOOTBALL

Friend, David. 1990. *Baseball, Football, Daddy and Me*. Illustrated by Rick Brown. New York: Viking. Father and son are the ultimate sports enthusiasts.

Kuskin, Karla. 1986. *The Dallas Titans Get Ready for Bed*. Illustrated by Marc Simont. New York: Harper & Row, Publishers. Although not about fathers, this book about the Dallas Titans' post-victory rituals might prove to be an interesting read for fathers and children interested in football.

Mochizuki, Ken. 1995. *Heroes*. Illustrated by Dom Lee. New York: Lee & Low Books, Inc. Donnie, who is Asian American, always has to be the "bad guy" when he and his friends play war because his friends will not believe that his father and uncle are decorated military heroes. This book is dedicated to the many people of Asian and Pacific Islander descent who have defended America with little or no recognition.

Sampson, Michael. 1996. *The Football That Won* . . . . Illustrated by Ted Rand. New York: Henry Holt and Company. A Bill Martin Book. Although this book featuring the Dallas Cowboys is not about fathers per se, it is a fun capturing of the excitement of a football game in a gridiron tribute to the traditional "house that Jack built."

SWIMMING

Greenspun, Adele Aron. *Daddies*. 1991. New York: Philomel Books. This simple book with touching black-and-white photographs captures the many ways fathers love their children.

Otey, Mimi. 1990. *Daddy Has a Pair of Striped Shorts*. New York: Farrar, Straus & Giroux. Daddy, a preacher, has a bright, colorful wardrobe full of patterns, which often embarrasses his children at swim class, the movies, and at school, but soon they learn to love him and his unique look.

Rice, Eve. 1996. *Swim!* Illustrated by Marisabina Russo. New York: HarperCollins Children's Book Group. Dad and his young daughter spend Saturday mornings at the indoor swimming pool in this simplistic story for preschoolers.

WRESTLING

Boelts, Maribeth. 2000. *Big Daddy, Frog Wrestler*. Illustrated by Benrei Huang. Morton Grove, Ill.: Albert Whitman & Company. Big Daddy and his son, Curtis, love wrestling, but when Big Daddy gets a chance to wrestle all over the world, he must choose between wrestling and his son.

Madenski, Melissa. 1991. *Some of the Pieces*. Illustrated by Deborah Kogan Ray. Boston: Little, Brown & Company. On the one-year anniversary of his father's death, a young boy recalls many fond memories and the pain of the sudden loss.

FATHERS AND CHILDREN ENGAGED IN ACTIVITIES TOGETHER

CAMPING

Brillhart, Julie. 1997. *When Daddy Took Us Camping*. Morton Grove, Ill.: Albert Whitman & Company. Dad has an amazing ability to create an authentic camping experience for his children under unusual circumstances.

Polacco, Patricia. 1991. *Some Birthday!* New York: Simon & Schuster Books for Young Readers. It is Patricia's birthday and her father, who is divorced from her mother, seems to have forgotten entirely. Little does she know, this birthday will turn into her best ever, complete with monster hunt, camping trip, and the perfect gifts.

Spohn, David. *Starry Night*. See **Series**.

CREATIVE ENDEAVORS

Caines, Jeannette. 1977. *Daddy*. Illustrated by Ronald Himler. New York: Harper & Row. This is a simple, charming story of a noncustodial father and the time he shares with his daughter, Windy, on Saturdays.

Catalanotto, Peter. 1999. *The Painter*. New York: Scholastic, Inc. A father balances parenting responsibilities, including imaginative and silly playtime with his young daughter, and work responsibilities in his art studio.

Cole, Babette. 1985.*The Trouble with Dad*. New York: G. P. Putnam's Sons. Dad has a rather boring job, so when he comes home he constructs robots that accidentally wreak havoc on the town.

Dumbleton, Mike, and Tom Jellett. 1999. *Downsized*. Sydney: Random House Australia. A very shrewd young daughter finds a creative way to get her father out of the slump he has been in since unemployment took over their lives. This upbeat Australian story would be especially therapeutic for families in similar situations.

Egielski, Richard. 1998. *Jazper*. New York: HarperCollins. A Laura Geringer Book. When Jazper comes home to find his father in bandages he realizes he must go make a living for the two of them and ends up getting mixed up with some magical moths. This is a very cute story with funny illustrations of the bug town.

Ehlert, Lois. 1997. *Hands*. San Diego: Harcourt Brace & Company. Cutout shapes such as father's work gloves, along with illustrations of collages and tools, provide a tactile portrait of a young child's creative parents and their influence on the child's developing artistic ambitions.

Friedman, Aileen. 1995. *A Cloak for the Dreamer*. Illustrated by Kim Howard. New York: Scholastic, Inc. A task assigned by a tailor father to his three sons results in very different garments and tests the father's ability to appreciate his sons' individuality.

Grifalconi, Ann. 1999. *Tiny's Hat*. New York: HarperCollins Children's Book Group. Tiny's father is a blues musician who travels a lot; when he is away for long periods, she gets the blues herself.

Haseley, Dennis. 1986. *Kite Flier*. Illustrated by David Wiesner. New York: Four Winds Press. A husband and wife share a special relationship flying kites; when she dies giving birth, he shares his kite-making gift with his son.

King, Stephen Michael. 1996. *A Special Kind of Love*. New York: Scholastic, Inc. A father shows his love for his son by creating castles, airplanes, and kites out of boxes.

Mandelbaum, Pili. 1990. *You Be Me, I'll Be You*. New York: Kane/Miller Book Publishers. When Anna complains that she does not like her dark skin and curly hair, dad gets creative. This depiction of a biracial family is a beautiful one, marked by one very special child.

Martin, David. 2001. *Piggy and Dad*. Illustrated by Frank Remkiewicz. Cambridge, Mass.: Candlewick Press. This set of four books designed to help beginning readers captures a truly loving relationship between Piggy and his dad. Titles included are *Piggy's Bath*, *Piggy's Bedtime*, *Piggy's Sandwich*, and *Piggy's Pictures*.

McClintock, Barbara. 1996. *The Fantastic Drawings of Danielle*. Boston: Houghton Mifflin Company. Father, a French photographer in the late 1800s, is unable to support his daughter's fantastical approach to art, until her artwork ends up supporting both of them.

Morris, Ann. 1993. *Puddle Jumper: How a Toy Is Made*. Photo-illustrated by Ken Heyman. New York: Lothrop, Lee & Shepard Books. Sarah helps her father build a rocking toy in his wood shop.

Seeger, Pete. 1986. *Abiyoyo: Based on a South African Lullaby and Folk Story*. Illustrated by Michael Hays. New York: Macmillan Publishing Company. The townsfolk ostracize a magician and his musician son until the day the pair defeats Abiyoyo the giant. The illustrations depict a town of incredibly diverse people.

Smith, Eddie. 1994. *A Lullaby for Daddy*. Illustrated by Susan Anderson. Lawrenceville, N.J.: Africa World Press. Daddy, a musician, and his young daughter compose a lullaby together, which they sing as part of their bedtime ritual.

Wild, Margaret. 1999. *Tom Goes to Kindergarten*. Illustrated by David Legge. Morton Grove, Ill.: Albert Whitman & Company. Tom likes kindergarten so much that soon the whole family wants to go too! The illustrations are great depictions of shared parental duties.

ENJOYING NATURE

Blake, Robert. 1997. *The Perfect Spot*. New York: Penguin Putnam Books for Young Readers. A father and his son have different but compatible reasons for a woodsy outing, allowing for a day of individual fulfillment and mutual fun.

Creech, Sharon. 2000. *Fishing in the Air*. Illustrated by Chris Raschka. New York: Joanna Cotler Books. Father and son embark on a fishing excursion and share many imaginative moments, including a conversation about the father's days as a young boy learning to fish with his father.

de Paola, Tomie. 1997. *The Days of the Blackbird: A Tale of Northern Italy*. New York: Penguin Putnam Books for Young Readers. In this Italian fable, a widowed duke shares many simple pleasures with his daughter until he becomes ill.

Figueredo, D. H. 1999. *When This World Was New*. Illustrated by Enrique O. Sanchez. New York: Lee & Low Books, Inc. A Latino father, new to the United States and facing many uncertainties, takes time to enjoy a snowfall with his son, which ends up being therapeutic as well as fun.

George, William T. 1992. *Christmas at Long Pond*. Illustrated by Lindsay Barrett George. New York: Greenwillow. A search for a Christmas tree allows Dad and son to enjoy the woods and Dad to play the role of naturalist.

Jukes, Mavis. 1984. *Like Jake and Me*. Illustrated by Lloyd Bloom. New York: Dragonfly Books. Alex, who loves ballet, does not have much in common with his stepfather, Jake, a cowboy. A funny misunderstanding about a spider helps them bond.

Lakin, Patricia. 1994. *Dad and Me in the Morning*. Illustrated by Robert G. Steele. Morton Grove, Ill.: Albert Whitman & Company. A hearing-impaired child wakes his father before dawn to enjoy the sunrise and other sensuous moments at the seashore.

London, Jonathan. 1994. *Let's Go, Froggy!* Illustrated by Frank Remkiewicz. New York: Viking. In this repetitious, fun text, Froggy awakes to a beautiful day and the promise of an extra-special picnic and bike ride with his dad; that is, if he gets ready in time.

Manushkin, Fran. 1994. *Peeping and Sleeping*. Illustrated by Jennifer Plecas. New York: Clarion Books. When Barry cannot sleep because of a mysterious and scary "PEEP-peep" he hears outside his window, Daddy promises to stay close as they go exploring outside at night.

McPhail, David M. 1990. *Ed and Me*. San Diego: Harcourt Brace Jovanovich, Publishers. This telling of a special father-daughter relationship is told with respect to Ed, the cherished old pickup truck in which the two share many happy memories.

Monfried, Lucia. 1993. *The Daddies Boat*. Illustrated by Michele Chessare. New York: Penguin Putnam Books for Young Readers. An island resort is the setting for this story about summer's simple pleasures, enhanced by warm family interactions and a surprise ending.

Peters, Lisa Westberg. 1995. *Meg and Dad Discover Treasure in the Air*. Illustrated by Deborah Durland DeSaix. New York: Henry Holt & Company. Meg is hunting for rubies but only finds "plain, old" rocks, which sparks an impromptu biology lesson from her father about the very first oxygen-producing organisms on earth.

Rockwell, Anne. 1994. *Ducklings and Pollywogs*. Illustrated by Lizzy Rockwell. New York: Macmillan Publishing Company. A father and daughter explore the many animals and plants at a pond through the four seasons.

Rush, Ken. 1994. *Friday's Journey*. New York: Orchard Books. While riding the subway to spend the weekend at his dad's place, a young boy remembers fondly places he and his parents used to go together, and asks his father to return to them.

Ryder, Joanne. 1994. *My Father's Hands*. Illustrated by Mark Graham. New York: Morrow Junior Books. A girl planting a garden with her father need not fear the creatures he discovers; she knows nothing in her father's hands will harm her.

San Souci, Daniel. 1993. *Country Road*. New York: Doubleday Books for Young Readers. Dad and his generally disinterested son go walking along an old road, coming to appreciate the wildlife and one another along the way.

Sanders, Scott Russell. 1997. *Meeting Trees*. Illustrated by Robert Hynes. Washington, D.C.: National Geographic Society. A father's passions for woodworking, trees, and nature are shared with his son in this story based on the author's life.

Skofield, James. 1993. *Round and Around*. Illustrated by James Graham Hale. New York: HarperCollins Publishers. While on a walk with his father and their dog, Sam, Dan observes many things in nature that move in circles. But as the sun sets and dad teaches Dan that even the Earth moves in a circle, Dan observes that the best circle of all is a hug.

Spohn, David. *Starry Night* and *Winter Wood*. See **Series**.

Stolz, Mary. 1993. *Say Something*. Illustrated by Alexander Koshkin. New York: HarperCollins Publishers. A young child asks his father to "say something about . . . " many things, revealing his father's spiritual and almost poetic view of the world.

Yolen, Jane. 1987. *Owl Moon*. Illustrated by John Schoenherr. New York: Philomel Books. This story depicts masterfully a father-daughter outing in search of great horned owls. The text and illustrations shine with lyrical beauty.

IMAGINATIVE PLAY

Bittner, Wolfgang. 1999. *Wake Up, Grizzly!* Translated by J. Alison James. Illustrated by Gustavo Rosemffet. New York: North-South Books, Inc. When awakened by his son on a Sunday morning, dad turns into a real bear—a warm, loving, fun kind of bear who indulges his son in an imaginative game under the covers.

Hearn, Dawson Diane. 1999. *Dad's Dinosaur Day.* New York: Aladdin Paperbacks. Dad's transformation into a dinosaur yields a day of fantastical fun for father and son.

Manushkin, Fran. 1994. *Peeping and Sleeping.* Illustrated by Jennifer Plecas. New York: Clarion Books. When Barry cannot sleep because of a mysterious and scary "PEEP-peep" he hears outside his window, Daddy promises to stay close as they go exploring outside at night.

Medearis, Angela S. 1994. *Our People.* Illustrated by Michael Bryant. New York: Atheneum Books for Young Readers. Father's history lessons are intertwined with play activities, such as building blocks and piggyback riding, providing inspiration for his daughter to imagine and dream.

Polacco, Patricia. 1991. *Some Birthday!* New York: Simon & Schuster Books for Young Readers. It is Patricia's birthday and her father, who is divorced from her mother, seems to have forgotten entirely. Little does she know, this birthday will turn into her best ever, complete with monster hunt, camping trip, and the perfect gifts.

Shannon, George. 1993. *Climbing Kansas Mountains.* Illustrated by Thomas B. Allen. New York: Bradbury Press. A creative father helps alleviate his son's summertime boredom as they seek out mountains to climb in Kansas.

Steig, William. 1998. *Pete's a Pizza.* New York: HarperCollins Publishers. When rain puts Pete in a bad mood, Dad saves the day by transforming his son into a pizza.

Wild, Margaret. 1999. *Tom Goes to Kindergarten.* Illustrated by David Legge. Morton Grove, Ill.: Albert Whitman & Company. Tom likes kindergarten so much that soon the whole family wants to go too! The illustrations are great depictions of shared parental duties.

Winthrop, Elizabeth. 1998. *As the Crow Flies.* Illustrated by Joan Sandin. New York: Clarion Books. Mikey's parents are divorced; he lives with his mother in Arizona, and his father lives in Delaware, "seven states away as the crow flies." Dad's annual visit brings lots of special memories and a wonderful surprise.

Wyeth, Sharon Dennis. 1995. *Always My Dad.* Illustrated by Raúl Colón. New York: Knopf. Dad is having problems "getting his life together"; his constant shifting from job to job and his lack of presence in his children's lives has them all upset.

MUSIC

Campbell, Louisa. 1996. *Phoebe's Fabulous Father.* Illustrated by Bridget Starr Taylor. San Diego: Harcourt Brace & Company. As Phoebe and her mother make their way around town, completing errands before their concert that evening, Phoebe wonders why her dad is not more like other dads. Includes a very surprising ending.

Cazet, Denys. 1995. *Dancing.* Music by Craig Bond. New York: Orchard Books. Dad spends some valuable one-on-one time singing and dancing with his son Alex, who wants only to send his new baby brother back to the hospital.

Demas, Corinne. 2000. *Nina's Waltz.* Illustrated by Deborah Lanino. New York: Orchard Books. Nina's father is a championship fiddler, but when wasps sting him, his daughter has to step in and compete in his place.

Grifalconi, Ann. 1999. *Tiny's Hat.* New York: HarperCollins Children's Book Group. Tiny's father is a blues musician who travels a lot; when he is away for long periods, she gets the blues herself.

McMullan, Kate. 2000. *Papa's Song.* Illustrated by Jim McMullan. New York: Farrar, Straus & Giroux. After Granny Bear, Grandpa Bear, and Mama Bear all give it a try, Papa Bear finds the perfect melody to put Baby Bear to sleep.

Paxton, Tom. 1996. *The Marvelous Toy.* Illustrated by Elizabeth Sayles. New York: Morrow Junior Books. A father gives his son an extraordinary and unique new toy; later in life the son goes on to give a similar toy to his son. This clever book would be great for reading aloud, and includes a song to sing the repeating text.

Sebastian, John. 1993. *J.B.'s Harmonica.* Illustrated by Garth Williams. San Diego: Harcourt Brace Jovanovich. J.B. plays harmonica well, but constant comparisons to his father, a professional harmonicist, have him considering quitting.

Seeger, Pete. 1986. *Abiyoyo: Based on a South African Lullaby and Folk Story.* Illustrated by Michael Hays. New York: Macmillian Publishing Company. The townsfolk ostracize a magician and his musician son until the day the pair defeats Abiyoyo the giant. The illustrations depict a town of incredibly diverse people.

Shepard, Steve. 1991. *Elvis Hornbill: International Business Bird.* New York: Holt & Company. A human couple adopts a young bird they name Elvis who, despite his father's efforts to persuade him to become a musician, is interested only in finance, business, and computer science.

Smith, Eddie. 1994. *A Lullaby for Daddy.* Illustrated by Susan Anderson. Lawrenceville, N.J.: Africa World Press. Daddy, a musician, and his young daughter compose a lullaby together, which they sing as part of their bedtime ritual.

Smith, Will. 1999. *Just the Two of Us.* Illustrated by Kadir Nelson. New York: Scholastic Press. This book uses the powerful and positive lyrics of Will Smith's song "Just the Two of Us" and beautifully crafted illustrations to depict the growing relationship between a father and his son.

Taylor, Ann. 1999. *Baby Dance*. Illustrated by Marjorie Van Heerden. New York: HarperCollins Children's Book Group. While Mama naps, Daddy magically transforms a baby's tears into smiles, thanks to a little song and dance therapy in this rhythmic board book.

Welch, Willy. 1999. *Dancing with Daddy*. Illustrated by Liza Woodruff. Dallas: Whispering Coyote Press. Dad cannot resist when his daughter pleads, "Dance with me, Daddy!" Before they know it, the world around them is dancing along.

Weidt, Maryann. 1995. *Daddy Played Music for the Cows*. Illustrated by Henri Sorensen. New York: Morrow/Avon. While Daddy milks the cows and tends to other chores, he and his daughter enjoy playful interaction and a love for country music.

READING TOGETHER

Degen, Bruce. 2000. *Daddy Is a Doodlebug*. New York: HarperCollins Publishers. This book captures the magic of everyday activities in the lives of a father and son doodlebug. The funny rhymes will make this a read-aloud favorite.

Egielski, Richard. 1998. *Jazper*. New York: HarperCollins. When Jazper comes home to find his father in bandages, he realizes he must go make a living for the two of them and ends up getting mixed up with some magical moths. This is a very cute story with funny illustrations of the bug town.

Greenspun, Adele Aron. 1991. *Daddies*. New York: Philomel Books. This simple book with touching black-and-white photographs captures the many ways fathers love their children.

Johnson, Dolores. 1994. *Papa's Stories*. New York: Macmillan Publishing Company. An illiterate father realizes that he needs to learn to read when his daughter goes to first grade and discovers that he has been making up the stories in her books all along.

Little, Jean, and Maggie De Vries. 1994. *Once Upon A Golden Apple*. Illustrated by Phoebe Gilman. New York: Penguin Putnam Books for Young Readers. While Mom tends to the crying baby, Dad creates zany, fractured fairy tales that entertain and spark the imagination of the other children.

Lindenbaum, Pija. 1991. *Else-Marie and Her Seven Little Daddies*. New York: Henry Holt & Company. Else-Marie is embarrassed about her seven small fathers, but when it is their turn to pick her up from playgroup, no one seems to notice that they are small or that there are seven of them! The quirky illustrations help tell the story of how Else-Marie learns to appreciate her fathers' uniqueness.

Martin, David. 2001. *Piggy and Dad*. Illustrated by Frank Remkiewicz. Cambridge, Mass.: Candlewick Press. This set of four books designed to help beginning readers captures a truly loving relationship between Piggy and his dad. Titles included are *Piggy's Bath*, *Piggy's Bedtime*, *Piggy's Sandwich*, and *Piggy's Pictures*.

Moutoussamy-Ashe, Jeanne. 1993. *Daddy and Me: A Photo Story of Arthur Ashe and His Daughter Camera*. New York: Alfred A. Knopf. This photo-essay featuring Arthur Ashe and his daughter, Camera, depicts the true love this famous father shared with his daughter. A wonderful book for discussions about AIDS, unconditional love, and living with illness.

Oxenbury, Helen. *Good Night, Good Morning*. 1991. New York: Penguin Putnam Books for Young Readers. In this cheerful, textless board book, the reader finds a mischievous young child and his father engaging in many activities, including reading, bathing, and shaving.

———. 1998. *Tom and Pippo Read a Story*. New York: Simon & Schuster Children's Publishing. Tom is an excellent role model for his toddler peers who are becoming interested in books, and when Daddy takes time out from his newspaper to read with Tom, he becomes a role model for fathers.

Rabe, Berniece. 1988. *Where's Chimpy?* Photo-illustrated by Diane Schmidt. Niles, Ill.: Albert Whitman & Company. Daddy helps his daughter Misty, who has Down Syndrome, find her cherished toy monkey in this book that focuses on bedtime rituals and counting, not on disability.

Spinelli, Eileen. 2000. *Night Shift Daddy*. Illustrated by Melissa Iwai. New York: Hyperion Books for Children. Daddy reads a story to his daughter and tenderly tucks her into bed before going to work the night shift as a janitor; when he returns, she happily reciprocates.

Wallace, John. 1996. *Little Bean*. New York: HarperCollins Children's Book Group. This book highlights the conflicts between working and parenting demands, and is sure to help a young child envision Daddy's business trip. The warm resolution supports reading as an important activity between fathers and children.

Winthrop, Elizabeth. 1998. *As the Crow Flies*. Illustrated by Joan Sandin. New York: Clarion Books. Mikey's parents are divorced; he lives with his mother in Arizona and his father lives in Delaware, "seven states away as the crow flies." Dad's annual visit brings lots of special memories and a wonderful surprise.

STARGAZING AND ENJOYING NIGHTTIME

Carle, Eric. 1986. *Papa, Please Get the Moon for Me*. Natick, Mass.: Picture Book Studio USA. Monica asks dad for the moon and, miraculously, this superdad delivers! But there's a catch: the moon continues to get smaller and smaller.

Carmichael, Clay. 1996. *Bear at the Beach*. New York: North-South Books. Bear longs for a father, and discovers him in the night sky.

Cazet, Denys. 1995. *Dancing*. Music by Craig Bond. New York: Orchard Books. Dad spends some valuable one-on-one time singing and dancing with his son Alex, who wants only to send his new baby brother back to the hospital.

Coy, John. 2001. *Night Driving*. Illustrated by Peter McCarty. New York: Henry Holt & Company. On their way to a camping trip, a father and son drive late into the night, enjoying conversation, rest stops, and the magic of the night. The black-and-white illustrations depict the 1950s.

Degen, Bruce. 2000. *Daddy Is a Doodlebug*. New York: HarperCollins Publishers. This book captures the magic of everyday activities in the lives of a father and son doodlebug. The funny rhymes will make this a read-aloud favorite.

Fowler, Susi Gregg. 1994. *I'll See You When the Moon Is Full*. Illustrated by Jim Fowler. New York: Greenwillow Books. When dad goes out of town on business trips, his young son misses him very much. Dad assures his son that he will be home by the time the moon is full, and delivers an impromptu astronomy lesson at the same time!

Hort, Lenny. 1997. *How Many Stars in the Sky*. Illustrated by James E. Ransome. New York: Morrow/Avon. Daddy's sense of adventure combines with his son's restlessness to portray a nurturing relationship and an overnight encounter with nature.

Johnson, Angela. 1994. *Joshua's Night Whispers*. Illustrated by Rhonda Mitchell. New York: Orchard Books. Joshua is awakened by night whispers and finds comfort in his father's arms in this board book.

Kinsey-Warnock, Natalie. 1994. *On a Starry Night*. Illustrated by David M. McPhail. New York: Scholastic, Inc. Papa joins his daughter and wife on the hillside above their farm for stargazing; when Papa tosses his daughter up into the sky, she pretends that she is interacting with the constellations.

Manushkin, Fran. 1994. *Peeping and Sleeping*. Illustrated by Jennifer Plecas. New York: Clarion Books. When Barry cannot sleep because of a mysterious and scary "PEEP-peep" he hears outside his window, Daddy promises to stay close as they go exploring outside at night.

McMullan, Kate. 2000. *Papa's Song*. Illustrated by Jim McMullan. New York: Farrar, Straus & Giroux. After Granny Bear, Grandpa Bear, and Mama Bear all give it a try, Papa Bear finds the perfect melody to put Baby Bear to sleep.

Mennen, Ingrid. 1994. *One Round Moon and a Star for Me*. Illustrated by Niki Daly. New York: Orchard Books. When a new baby is born into the family, Papa must reassure his son of his love. This story is set in a Lesotho village and features many words from Lesotho, South Africa.

Pettigrew, Eileen. 1992. *Night-Time*. Illustrated by William Kimber. Toronto: Annick Press. Michael's dad takes him on a very special nighttime walk around the neighborhood, recounting his own fond memories of his father.

Spohn, David. *Starry Night*. See **Series**.

Welch, Willy. 1999. *Dancing with Daddy*. Illustrated by Liza Woodruff. Dallas: Whispering Coyote Press. Dad cannot resist when his daughter pleads, "Dance with me, Daddy!" Before they know it, the world around them is dancing along.

STORYTELLING

Cazet, Denys. 1992. *"I'm Not Sleepy."* New York: Orchard Books. Alex is not tired, so dad tells him a story guaranteed to put him to sleep.

Davol, Marguerite W. 1995. *Papa Alonzo Leatherby: A Collection of Tall Tales from the Best Storyteller in Carroll County*. New York: Simon & Schuster Books for Young Readers. Papa Alonzo Leatherby is renowned in his county for being the best storyteller around, but when an especially vicious winter freeze comes along, he will need to find a way to thaw out his freezing stories.

Degen, Bruce. 2000. *Daddy Is a Doodlebug*. New York: HarperCollins Publishers. This book captures the magic of everyday activities in the lives of a father and son doodlebug. The funny rhymes will make this a read-aloud favorite.

Howard, Elizabeth Fitzgerald. 1995. *Papa Tells Chita a Story*. Illustrated by Floyd Cooper. New York: Simon & Schuster Books for Young Readers. Father and Chita share quality time together after dinner as he recounts his days as a soldier in Cuba during the Spanish-American War.

Johnson, Dolores. 1994. *Papa's Stories*. New York: Macmillan Publishing Company. An illiterate father realizes that he needs to learn to read when his daughter goes to first grade and discovers that he has been making up the stories in her books all along.

Kroll, Virginia. 1993. *Africa Brothers and Sisters*. Illustrated by Vanessa French. New York: Four Winds Press. In this highly informational text, Jesse and his father spend time recalling the many brother and sister tribes they have in Africa.

Lambert, Paulette Livers. 1995. *Evening: An Appalachian Lullaby*. Niwot, Colo.: Roberts Rinehart Publishers. It is bedtime on the farm; father patiently attends to the extended ritual with his young sons before relaxing on the porch with his fiddle.

Lemieux, Margo. 1996. *Paul and the Wolf*. Illustrated by Bill Nelson. Parsippany, N.J.: Silver Burdett Press. Having been exposed to *Peter and the Wolf* at school, a boy fears wolves at bedtime, until Dad alleviates his fears with a Native American wolf tale and personal commentary.

Madenski, Melissa. 1991. *Some of the Pieces*. Illustrated by Deborah Kogan Ray. Boston: Little, Brown & Company. On the one-year anniversary of his father's death, a young boy recalls many fond memories and the pain of the sudden loss.

McAllister, Angela. 1994. *The Ice Palace*. Illustrated by Angela Barrett. New York: G. P. Putnam's Sons. When Anna falls sick during the hottest, driest season of the year, her father goes to work entertaining her with stories of the north wind and of ice palaces. With the presentation of Anna's special gift at the end of the book, many young readers might have questions regarding cooling methods before the invention of refrigerators.

McCleary, William. 1988. *Wolf Story*. Illustrated by Warren Chappell. North Haven, Conn.: Linnet Books. In this now classic book, a father tells his young son stories about Waldo the wolf and the hen named Rainbow that always gets away.

Pettigrew, Eileen. 1992. *Night-Time*. Illustrated by William Kimber. Toronto: Annick Press. Michael's dad takes him on a very special nighttime walk around the neighborhood, recounting his own fond memories of his father.

Polacco, Patricia. 1999. *My Ol' Man*. New York: Penguin Putnam Books for Young Readers. A nostalgic portrait of a traveling salesman who entertains his children and ends up supporting them with his magical storytelling abilities when he becomes unemployed.

———. 1991. *Some Birthday!* New York: Simon & Schuster Books for Young Readers. It is Patricia's birthday and her father, who is divorced from her mother, seems to have forgotten entirely. Little does she know, this birthday will turn into her best ever, complete with monster hunt, camping trip, and the perfect gifts.

Seeger, Pete. 1986. *Abiyoyo: Based on a South African Lullaby and Folk Story*. Illustrated by Michael Hays. New York: Macmillian Publishing Company. The townsfolk ostracize a magician and his musician son until the day the pair defeats Abiyoyo the giant. The illustrations depict a town of incredibly diverse people.

Tompert, Ann. 1990. *Grandfather Tang's Story: A Tale Told with Tangrams*. Illustrated by Robert Andrew Parker. New York: Crown Publishers, Inc. Grandfather Tang and his granddaughter, Little Soo, construct a story together using tangrams.

Winthrop, Elizabeth. 1998. *As the Crow Flies*. Illustrated by Joan Sandin. New York: Clarion Books. Mikey's parents are divorced; he lives with his mother in Arizona and his father lives in Delaware, "seven states away as the crow flies." Dad's annual visit brings lots of special memories and a wonderful surprise.

VACATIONING

Layton, Neal. 1999. *Smile If You're Human*. New York: Penguin Putnam Books for Young Readers. Enjoying a vacation of sorts is what this family from outer space is doing here on Earth, with Dad more or less filling the traditional role of chauffeur, tour guide, and wearer of striped ties.

Monfried, Lucia. 1993. *The Daddies Boat*. Illustrated by Michele Chessare. New York: Penguin Putnam Books for Young Readers. An island resort is the setting for this story about summer's simple pleasures, enhanced by warm family interactions and a surprise ending.

Walters, Virginia. 1999. *Are We There Yet, Daddy?* Illustrated by S. D. Schindler. New York: Viking. This rhyming, repetitive text counts down the miles on a 100-mile journey to Grandma's house as a patient father responds to that all-too-frequently asked question.

VISITING MUSEUMS

Bradman, Tony. 1990. *The Sandal*. Illustrated by Philippe Dupasquier. New York: Penguin Putnam Books for Young Readers. A child's lost sandal provides the bridge to connect past, present, and future dads enjoying a day in the city with the children.

Hamanaka, Sheila. 1995. *Bebop-A-Do-Walk!* New York: Simon & Schuster Books for Young Readers. Emi, her friend, Martha, and her father take one very long walk all over the city of New York.

Rush, Ken. 1994. *Friday's Journey*. New York: Orchard Books. While riding the subway to spend the weekend at his dad's place, a young boy remembers fondly places he and his parents used to go together, and asks his father to return to them.

WORKING TOGETHER

Banks, Kate. 2000. *The Night Worker*. Illustrated by Georg Hallensleben. New York: Farrar, Straus & Giroux. Alex is surprised and thrilled when his Papa, who is a night worker at a construction site, takes him along to work while the rest of the city sleeps.

Cole, Babette. 1985. *The Trouble with Dad*. New York: G. P. Putnam's Sons. Dad has a rather boring job, so when he comes home he constructs robots that accidentally wreak havoc on the town.

Gardella, Tricia. 1997. *Casey's New Hat*. Illustrated by Margot Apple. Boston: Houghton Mifflin Company. Casey's growing out of the cowgirl hat from her toddler days, so on their next trip in to town, she and dad seek out the "right" hat. Grandpa joins in on the search and ends up helping his granddaughter find the perfect hat for a growing cowgirl.

———. 1996. *Just Like My Dad*. Illustrated by Margot Apple. New York: HarperCollins Children's Book Group. Dad and his young cowhand work together from morning to night on the ranch.

Greenberg, Melanie Hope. 1991. *My Father's Luncheonette*. New York: Dutton Children's Books. A young girl enjoys helping out at her father's luncheonette.

High, Linda Oatman. 2001. *Barn Savers*. Illustrated by Ted Lewin. Honesdale, Penn.: Boyds Mills Press. A father allows his son to feel mature and responsible as they work from dawn to dusk salvaging a barn.

Hines, Anna Grossnickle. 1986. *Daddy Makes the Best Spaghetti*. New York: Clarion Books. Corey's Dad creatively shares many domestic and parenting duties with Mom, including making dinner, becoming Bathman at bath time, and tucking in one very loved boy.

Janovitz, Marilyn. 1998. *Can I Help?* New York: North-South Books, Inc. Father wolf exhibits much patience and love as his young cub eagerly "assists" with outdoor chores.

————. 2001. *Good Morning, Little Fox*. New York: North-South Books. Little Fox and his father always spend the weekend together—sleeping late, making breakfast, and doing chores.

Ketteman, Helen. 1992. *Not Yet, Yvette*. Illustrated by Irene Trivas. Morton Grove, Ill.: Albert Whitman & Company. Yvette and her father clean the house, go shopping, and bake a cake for her mom's birthday. Mom is a veterinarian and dad appears to stay at home with Yvette.

Lindbergh, Reeve. 1994. *If I'd Known Then What I Know Now*. Illustrated by Kimberly Bulcken Root. New York: Viking. This humorous story tells of the various failed home improvement projects on which dad worked over the years. His family assures the reader at the end, however, that they would have him no other way.

McKay, Lawrence Jr. 1995. *Caravan*. Illustrated by Darryl Ligasan. New York: Lee & Low Books, Inc. Based on the lifestyle of Kirghiz caravaneers in Afghanistan, this story is about a ten-year-old son who assists his father in leading a caravan through rugged terrain and into the city where they will trade goods.

McPhail, David M. 1990. *Ed and Me*. San Diego: Harcourt Brace Jovanovich. This telling of a special father-daughter relationship is told with respect to Ed, the cherished old pickup truck in which the two share many happy memories.

Monjo, F. N. 1961. *The One Bad Thing about Father*. Illustrated by Rocco Negri. New York: Harper & Row. An I CAN READ History Book. Told through the voice of Quentin, Theodore Roosevelt's son, this story captures wonderful family moments shared in the White House.

Morris, Ann. 1993. *Puddle Jumper: How a Toy Is Made*. Photo-illustrated by Ken Heyman. New York: Lothrop, Lee & Shepard Books. Sarah helps her father build a rocking toy in his wood shop.

Munsch, Robert. 1990. *Something Good*. Illustrated by Michael Martchenko. Toronto: Annick Press. Dad and the kids are grocery shopping, but one very motivated and vocal daughter wants him to buy some "good" food: ice cream and candy.

Spinelli, Eileen. 1993. *Boy, Can He Dance!* Illustrated by Paul Yalowitz. New York: Four Winds Press. Tony loves to dance, and seeks nothing more than approval from his father and grandfather, both chefs who encourage him to continue the family business.

Spohn, David. *Winter Wood*. See **Series**.

Wallace, Ian. 1999. *Boy of the Deeps*. New York: DK. In this recounting of the author's grandfather's hard childhood, James accompanies his father down into "the deeps" of a coal mine for his first day on the job.

Williams, Sherley Anne. 1992. *Working Cotton*. Illustrated by Carole Byard. San Diego: Harcourt Brace Jovanovich. This story about migrant workers features a family working hard together and a father whose children are proud of his speed and skill at cotton-picking.

DADS AND DAUGHTERS ALONE—QUALITY TIME

Best, Cari. 1997. *Taxi! Taxi!* Illustrated by Dale Gottlieb. New York: Scholastic, Inc. Although Tina wishes that Papi lived with Mama and her, he demonstrates his love every Sunday when they spend the day together.

Caines, Jeannette. 1977. *Daddy*. Illustrated by Ronald Himler. New York: Harper & Row. This is a simple, charming story of a noncustodial father and the time he shares with his daughter, Windy, on Saturdays.

Carle, Eric. 1986. *Papa, Please Get the Moon for Me*. Natick, Mass.: Picture Book Studio USA. Monica asks dad for the moon and, miraculously, this superdad delivers! But there's a catch: the moon continues to get smaller and smaller.

Catalanotto, Peter. 1999. New York: *The Painter*. Scholastic, Inc. A father balances parenting responsibilities, including imaginative and silly playtime with his young daughter, and work responsibilities in his art studio.

Cazet, Denys. 1993. *Born in the Gravy*. New York: Orchard Books. Margarita tells her papa all about her first day of kindergarten. Features many Spanish words, the meanings of which are translated or implied.

Demas, Corinne. 2000. *Nina's Waltz*. Illustrated by Deborah Lanino. New York: Orchard Books. Nina's father is a championship fiddler, but when wasps sting him, his daughter has to step in and compete in his place.

de Paola, Tomie. 1997. *The Days of the Blackbird: A Tale of Northern Italy*. New York: Penguin Putnam Books for Young Readers. In this Italian fable, a widowed duke shares many simple pleasures with his daughter until he becomes ill.

Fox, Mem. 1996. *Zoo-Looking*. Illustrated by Candace Whitman. Greenvale, N.Y.: Mondo Publishing. Flora and her dad explore the zoo in this simple rhyming book.

Galbraith, Kathryn O. 1995. *Holding onto Sunday*. Illustrated by Michael Hays. New York: Margaret K. McElderry Books. In this short chapter book, a single-parent father sets aside Sundays from his busy work schedule to spend time with his daughter in a variety of activities.

Greenberg, Melanie Hope. 1991. *My Father's Luncheonette*. New York: Dutton Children's Books. A young girl enjoys helping out at her father's luncheonette.

Greenfield, Eloise. 1993. *Lisa's Daddy and Daughter Day*. Illustrated by Jan Spivey Gilchrist. Littleton, Mass.: Sundance Publishing. Spending the whole day with daddy, talking and taking it easy, is special for his daughter.

Greenwood, Pamela D. 1994. *I Found Mouse*. Illustrated by Jennifer Plecas. New York: Clarion Books. Since Tessie's mom, brother, and best friend are all gone for the summer, she amuses herself by adopting a stray cat that she names Mouse, and develops a warm relationship with her father in the raising of the kitten.

Howard, Elizabeth Fitzgerald. 1995. *Papa Tells Chita a Story*. Illustrated by Floyd Cooper. New York: Simon & Schuster Books for Young Readers. Father and daughter Chita share quality time together after dinner as he recounts his days as a soldier in Cuba during the Spanish-American War.

Johnson, Dolores. 1994. *Papa's Stories*. New York: Macmillan Publishing Company. An illiterate father realizes that he needs to learn to read when his daughter goes to first grade and discovers that he has been making up the stories in her books all along.

Ketteman, Helen. 1992. *Not Yet, Yvette*. Illustrated by Irene Trivas. Morton Grove, Ill.: Albert Whitman & Company. Yvette and her father clean the house, go shopping, and bake a cake for her mom's birthday. Mom is a veterinarian and dad appears to stay at home with Yvette.

Komaiko, Leah. 1999. *Just My Dad & Me*. Illustrated by Jeffrey Greene. New York: HarperCollins Children's Book Group. A daughter wishes just she and her dad could spend time at the beach alone, rather than with the extended family, but manages to find a special moment with him when she returns from an underwater adventure.

Lindenbaum, Pija. 1991. *Else-Marie and Her Seven Little Daddies*. New York: Henry Holt & Company. Else-Marie is embarrassed about her seven small fathers, but when it is their turn to pick her up from playgroup, no one seems to notice that they are small or that there are seven of them! The quirky illustrations help tell the story of how Else-Marie learns to appreciate her fathers' uniqueness.

Mandelbaum, Pili. 1990. *You Be Me, I'll Be You*. New York: Kane/Miller Book Publishers. When Anna complains that she does not like her dark skin and curly hair, dad gets creative. This depiction of a biracial family is a beautiful one, marked by one very special child.

McAllister, Angela. 1994. *The Ice Palace*. Illustrated by Angela Barrett. New York: G. P. Putnam's Sons. When Anna falls sick during the hottest, driest season of the year, her father goes to work entertaining her with stories of the north wind and of ice palaces. With the presentation of Anna's special gift at the end of the book, many young readers might have questions regarding cooling methods before the invention of refrigerators.

McCreary, Laura, and Mark Myers. 2001. *Angela Anaconda: The Best Dad*. Based on the scripts by Charlotte Fullerton and Mark Myers. Illustrated by Barry Goldberg. New York: Simon Spotlight. This short chapter book features two stories about Angela Anaconda, her dad, and her eternal enemy Nanette Manoir. The first story sees father and daughter entering a square-dancing competition and the second sees them going fishing.

McPhail, David M. 1990. *Ed and Me*. San Diego: Harcourt Brace Jovanovich. This telling of a special father-daughter relationship is told with respect to Ed, the cherished old pickup truck in which the two share many happy memories.

Morris, Ann. 1993. *Puddle Jumper: How a Toy Is Made*. Photo-illustrated by Ken Heyman. New York: Lothrop, Lee & Shepard Books. Sarah helps her father build a rocking toy in his wood shop.

Moutoussamy-Ashe, Jeanne. 1993. *Daddy and Me: A Photo Story of Arthur Ashe and His Daughter Camera*. New York: Alfred A. Knopf. This photo-essay featuring Arthur Ashe and his daughter, Camera, depicts the true love this famous father shared with his daughter. A wonderful book for discussions about AIDS, unconditional love, and living with illness.

Peters, Lisa Westberg. 1995. *Meg and Dad Discover Treasure in the Air*. Illustrated by Deborah Durland DeSaix. New York: Henry Holt & Company. Meg is hunting for rubies but only finds "plain, old" rocks, which sparks an impromptu biology lesson from her father about the very first oxygen-producing organisms on earth.

Rabe, Berniece. 1988. *Where's Chimpy?* Photo-illustrated by Diane Schmidt. Niles, Ill.: Albert Whitman & Company. Daddy helps his daughter Misty, who has Down Syndrome, find her cherished toy monkey in this book that focuses on bedtime rituals and counting, not on disability.

Rice, Eve. 1996. *Swim!* Illustrated by Marisabina Russo. New York: HarperCollins Children's Book Group. Dad and his young daughter spend Saturday mornings at the indoor swimming pool in this simplistic story for preschoolers.

Rockwell, Anne. 1994. *Ducklings and Pollywogs*. Illustrated by Lizzy Rockwell. New York: Macmillan Publishing Company. A father and daughter explore the many animals and plants at a pond through the four seasons.

Ryder, Joanne. 1994. *My Father's Hands*. Illustrated by Mark Graham. New York: Morrow Junior Books. A girl planting a garden with her father need not fear the creatures he discovers; she knows nothing in her father's hands will harm her.

Spinelli, Eileen. 2000. *Night Shift Daddy*. Illustrated by Melissa Iwai. New York: Hyperion Books for Children. Daddy reads a story to his daughter and tenderly tucks her into bed before going to work the night shift as a janitor. When he returns, she happily reciprocates.

Welch, Willy. 1999. *Dancing with Daddy*. Illustrated by Liza Woodruff. Dallas: Whispering Coyote Press. Dad cannot resist when his daughter pleads, "Dance with me, Daddy!" Before they know it, the world around them is dancing along.

Yolen, Jane. 1987. *Owl Moon*. Illustrated by John Schoenherr. New York: Philomel Books. This story depicts masterfully a father-daughter outing in search of great horned owls; the text and illustrations shine with lyrical beauty.

DADS AND SONS ALONE—QUALITY TIME

Banks, Kate. 2000. *The Night Worker*. Illustrated by Georg Hallensleben. New York: Farrar, Straus & Giroux. Alex is surprised and thrilled when his Papa, who is a night worker at a construction site, takes him along to work while the rest of the city sleeps.

Bittner, Wolfgang. 1999. *Wake Up, Grizzly!* Translated by J. Alison James. Illustrated by Gustavo Rosemffet. New York: North-South Books. Inc., When awoken by his son on a Sunday morning, dad turns into a real bear—a warm, loving, fun kind of bear who indulges his son in an imaginative game under the covers.

Boelts, Maribeth. 2000. *Big Daddy, Frog Wrestler*. Illustrated by Benrei Huang. Morton Grove, Ill.: Albert Whitman & Company. Big Daddy and his son, Curtis, love wrestling, but when Big Daddy gets a chance to wrestle all over the world, he must choose between wrestling and his son.

Bridges, Margaret P. 1999. *If I Were Your Father*. Illustrated by Kady M. Denton. New York: Morrow/Avon. While a father spends the day entertaining and taking care of his young son, they converse about what the son would do if he were the father. See also *If I Were Your Mother* (1999).

Cazet, Denys. 1995. *Dancing*. Music by Craig Bond. New York: Orchard Books. A Richard Jackson Book. Dad spends some valuable one-on-one time singing and dancing with his son Alex, who wants only to send his new baby brother back to the hospital.

———. 1992. *"I'm Not Sleepy."* New York: Orchard Books. Alex is not tired, so dad tells him a story guaranteed to put him to sleep.

Coy, John. 2001. *Night Driving*. Illustrated by Peter McCarty. New York: Henry Holt & Company. On their way to a camping trip, a father and son drive late into the night, enjoying conversation, rest stops, and the magic of the night. The black-and-white illustrations depict the 1950s.

Creech, Sharon. 2000. *Fishing in the Air*. Illustrated by Chris Raschka. New York: Joanna Cotler Books. Father and son embark on a fishing excursion and share many imaginative moments, including a conversation about the father's days as a young boy learning to fish with his father.

Degen, Bruce. 2000. *Daddy Is a Doodlebug*. New York: HarperCollins Publishers. This book captures the magic of everyday activities in the lives of a father and son doodlebug. The funny rhymes will make this a read-aloud favorite.

Falwell, Cathryn. 1992. *Nicky Loves Daddy*. New York: Clarion Books. This simple book for toddlers has large text, and expresses the tender love a young boy feels for his father as they go for a walk.

Friend, David. 1990. *Baseball, Football, Daddy and Me*. Illustrated by Rick Brown. New York: Viking. Father and son are the ultimate sports enthusiasts.

Garland, Sherry. 1998. *My Father's Boat*. Illustrated by Ted Rand. New York: Scholastic, Inc. A Vietnamese American shrimper teaches his son the tricks of the trade one special day, causing him to reminisce about his own father back in Vietnam. An especially warm, poetic text is prefaced with this appropriate Vietnamese proverb: "When you are young, you need your father; when you are old, you need your son." This father represents both strong and tender sides of parenting.

Haseley, Dennis. 1986. *Kite Flier*. Illustrated by David Wiesner. New York: Four Winds Press. A husband and wife share a special relationship flying kites; when she dies giving birth, he shares his kite-making gift with his son.

Hearn, Dawson Diane. 1999. *Dad's Dinosaur Day*. New York: Aladdin Paperbacks. Dad's transformation into a dinosaur yields a day of fantastical fun for father and son.

Heo, Yumi. 1999. *One Sunday Morning*. New York: Scholastic, Inc. In a very detailed dream, Minho spends a wonderful day at the park alone with his father. This book is an obvious wake-up call to negligent, busy, or self-indulgent fathers.

High, Linda Oatman. 2001. *Barn Savers*. Illustrated by Ted Lewin. Honesdale, Penn.: Boyds Mills Press. A father allows his son to feel mature and responsible as they work from dawn to dusk salvaging a barn.

Hort, Lenny. 1997. *How Many Stars in the Sky*. Illustrated by James E. Ransome. New York: Morrow/Avon. Daddy's sense of adventure combines with his son's restlessness to portray a nurturing relationship and an overnight encounter with nature.

Janovitz, Marilyn. 2001. *Good Morning, Little Fox*. New York: North-South Books. Little Fox and his father always spend the weekend together—sleeping late, making breakfast, and doing chores.

Ketteman, Helen. 1998. *I Remember Papa*. Illustrated by Greg Shed. New York: Penguin Putnam Books for Young Readers. The lessons a father taught his son, such as the importance of saving money, of forgiveness, and of parental sacrifices, are remembered for a lifetime in this story about a father and son's passion for baseball.

Lakin, Patricia. 1994. *Dad and Me in the Morning*. Illustrated by Robert G. Steele. Morton Grove, Ill.: Albert Whitman & Company, A child with a hearing impairment wakes his father before dawn to enjoy the sunrise and other sensuous moments at the seashore.

Lauture, Denizé. 1996. *Father and Son*. Illustrated by Jonathan Green. New York: Penguin Putnam Books for Young Readers. The author's dedication to this poem about a father and son is worth mentioning: "To all children who show great respect and love to every decent man they meet down the many roads of life. To all men who understand that they must love, adopt, and give a hand to all children of our poor planet."

London, Jonathan. 1994. *Let's Go, Froggy!* Illustrated by Frank Remkiewicz. New York: Viking. In this repetitious, fun text, Froggy awakes to a beautiful day and the promise of an extra-special picnic and bike ride with his dad; that is, if he gets ready in time.

Martin, David. 2001. *Piggy and Dad*, illustrated by Frank Remkiewicz. Cambridge, Mass.: Candlewick Press. This set of four books designed to help beginning readers captures a truly loving relationship between Piggy and his dad. Titles included are *Piggy's Bath*, *Piggy's Bedtime*, *Piggy's Sandwich*, and *Piggy's Pictures*.

McCleary, William. 1988. *Wolf Story*. Illustrations by Warren Chappell. North Haven, Conn.: Linnet Books. In this now classic book, a father tells his young son stories about Waldo the wolf and the hen named Rainbow that always gets away.

Roy, Ron. 1980. *Breakfast with My Father*. Illustrated by Troy Howell. New York: Houghton Mifflin Company. During a period of marital separation that ultimately ends in reunion, a father and his son meet to have breakfast every Saturday morning.

San Souci, Daniel. 1993. *Country Road*. New York: Doubleday Books for Young Readers. Dad and his generally disinterested son go walking along an old road, coming to appreciate the wildlife and one another along the way.

Sanders, Scott Russell. 1997. *Meeting Trees*. Illustrated by Robert Hynes. Washington, D.C.: National Geographic Society. A father's passions for woodworking, trees, and nature are shared with his son in this story based on the author's life.

Shannon, George. 1993. *Climbing Kansas Mountains*. Illustrated by Thomas B. Allen. New York: Bradbury Press. A creative father helps alleviate his son's summertime boredom as they seek out mountains to climb in Kansas.

Sharmat, Marjorie Weinman. 1976. *Mooch the Messy*. Illustrated by Ben Shecter. New York: Harper & Row Publishers. Mooch the Rat gets a visit from his father, who finds Mooch's hole to be quite unclean and who encourages more healthy habits.

Sharp, N. L. 2001. *Today I'm Going Fishing with My Dad*. Illustrated by Chris L. Demarest. Honesdale, Penn.: Boyds Mills Press. The son, whose honesty and maturity make this an extra-special story, describes the first father-son fishing trip of the season. This is "quality time" with a twist.

Skofield, James. 1993. *'Round and Around*. Illustrated by James Graham Hale. New York: HarperCollins Publishers. While on a walk with his father and their dog, Sam, Dan observes many things in nature that move in circles. But as the sun sets and dad teaches Dan that even the Earth moves in a circle, Dan observes that the best circle of all is a hug.

Smalls-Hector, Irene. 1999. *Kevin and His Dad*. Illustrated by Michael Hays. Boston: Little, Brown and Company. On Saturdays, while Mom is away, a father and son have fun cleaning the house together before engaging in more typically amusing activities.

Smith, Will. 1999. *Just the Two of Us*. Illustrated by Kadir Nelson. New York: Scholastic Press. This book uses the powerful and positive lyrics of Will Smith's song "Just the Two of Us" and beautifully crafted illustrations to depict the growing relationship between a father and his son.

Spohn, David. *Home Field*, *Nate's Treasure*, *Starry Night*, and *Winter Wood*. See **Series**.

Walters, Virginia. 1999. *Are We There Yet, Daddy?* Illustrated by S. D. Schindler. New York: Viking, This rhyming, repetitive text counts down the miles on a 100-mile journey to Grandma's house as a patient father responds to that all-too-frequently asked question.

Weninger, Brigitte. 1995. *Good-Bye, Daddy!* Illustrated by Alan Marks. New York: North-South Books. When Tom's dad leaves after his visit, Tom is inconsolable; only a story from his teddy bear can make things all right. This book deals with familial separation in a softer way by duplicating the theme with a bear family.

Winthrop, Elizabeth. 1998. *As the Crow Flies*. Illustrated by Joan Sandin. New York: Clarion Books. Mikey's parents are divorced; he lives with his mother in Arizona and his father lives in Delaware, "seven states away as the crow flies." Dad's annual visit brings lots of special memories and a wonderful surprise.

Zolotow, Charlotte. 1993. *Peter and the Pigeons*. Illustrated by Martine Gourbault. New York: Greenwillow Books. Dad observes his son's affinity for common park pigeons, and decides to take him to the zoo to introduce him to other more exciting animals.

PORTRAITS OF DADS

ADOLESCENT FATHERS

Cone, Molly. 1983. *Paul David Silverman Is a Father*. Photo-illustrated by Harold Roth. New York: Dutton. Through simple text and photographs, this book outlines the story of teenage parents who decide to get married.

Gravelle, Karen, and Leslie Peterson. 1992. *Teenage Fathers*. Parsippany, N.J.: Silver Burdett Press. This informative, nonfiction book tells the stories of thirteen teenage fathers, but includes very few statistics.

ALTERNATIVE LIFESTYLES

Binch, Caroline. 1998. *Since Dad Left*. Brookfield, Conn.: Millbrook Press, Inc. When Sid visits his dad for the first time after his parents' separation, Dad gives him just enough breathing space to allow for adjustment to the unusual residence and lifestyle.

Lindenbaum, Pija. 1991. *Else-Marie and Her Seven Little Daddies*. New York: Henry Holt & Company. Else-Marie is embarrassed about her seven small fathers, but when it is their turn to pick her up from playgroup, no one seems to notice that they are small or that there are seven of them! The quirky illustrations help tell the story of how Else-Marie learns to appreciate her fathers' uniqueness.

Perkins, Lynne Rae. 1997. *Clouds for Dinner*. New York: HarperCollins Children's Book Group. When Janet is given an opportunity to compare her parents' alternative lifestyle and aesthetic approach to life to relatives with a more mundane lifestyle, their strong influence becomes apparent.

Shepard, Steve. 1991. *Elvis Hornbill: International Business Bird*. New York: Holt & Company. A human couple adopts a young bird they name Elvis who, despite his father's efforts to persuade him to become a musician, is interested only in finance, business, and computer science.

BIOGRAPHICAL AND REAL-LIFE DADS

Greenspun, Adele Aron. 1991. *Daddies*. New York: Philomel Books. This simple book with touching black-and-white photographs captures the many ways fathers love their children.

Hartley, Deborah. 1986. *Up North in Winter*. Illustrated by Lydia Dabcovich. New York: E. P. Dutton. This book, about the author's great-grandfather, recounts tough times during a very cold winter when Grandpa Ole had to walk for miles through the snow to work for his family.

Howard, Elizabeth Fitzgerald. 1995. *Papa Tells Chita a Story*. Illustrated by Floyd Cooper. New York: Simon & Schuster Books for Young Readers. Father and daughter Chita share quality time together after dinner as he recounts his days as a soldier in Cuba during the Spanish-American War.

Lasky, Kathryn. 1997. *Marven of the Great North Woods*. Illustrated by Kevin Hawkes. New York: Harcourt Brace & Company. When an influenza epidemic spread across American in 1918, Marven Lasky was sent to live with French Canadian lumberjacks in the great north woods of Minnesota to be kept safe from the disease. This is the true story of the author's father.

Monjo, F. N. 1961. *The One Bad Thing about Father*. Illustrated by Rocco Negri. New York: Harper & Row. An I CAN READ History Book. Told through the voice of Quentin, Theodore Roosevelt's son, this story captures wonderful family moments shared in the White House.

Morris, Ann. 1993. *Puddle Jumper: How a Toy Is Made*. Photo-illustrated by Ken Heyman. New York: Lothrop, Lee & Shepard Books. Sarah helps her father build a rocking toy in his wood shop.

Moutoussamy-Ashe, Jeanne. 1993. *Daddy and Me: A Photo Story of Arthur Ashe and His Daughter Camera*. New York: Alfred A. Knopf. This photo-essay featuring Arthur Ashe and his daughter, Camera, depicts the true love this famous father shared with his daughter. a wonderful book for discussions about AIDS, unconditional love, and living with illness.

Roop, Peter and Connie. 1994. *Ahyoka and the Talking Leaves*. Illustrated by Yoshi Miyake. New York: Morrow/Avon. This historical book focuses on the legendary Cherokee, Sequoyah, and his quest to decode the English alphabet, which causes much tension and changed relationships in his family.

Sanders, Scott Russell. 1997. *Meeting Trees*. Illustrated by Robert Hynes. Washington, D.C.: National Geographic Society. A father's passions for woodworking, trees, and nature are shared with his son in this story based on the author's life.

Smith, Will. 1999. *Just the Two of Us*. Illustrated by Kadir Nelson. New York: Scholastic Press. This book uses the powerful and positive lyrics of Will Smith's song "Just the Two of Us" and beautifully crafted illustrations to depict the growing relationship between a father and his son.

Stevenson, James. 1996. *I Meant to Tell You*. New York: HarperCollins Children's Book Group. Parents of older children can especially relate to Stevenson's own memories of his daughter's youth—typical things like the day she learned to ride a bike, the beach vacation, the dance classes, and more intimate occasions that he has chosen to share.

Wetzel, JoAnne Stewart. 1995. *The Christmas Box*. Illustrated by Barry Root. New York: Random House Value Publishing, Inc. While Dad is stationed in Japan during the Korean War, he sends home a box full of very special Christmas gifts, which bridges the distance between his family and him.

CONTEMPORARY NONTRADITIONAL DADS

Campbell, Louisa. 1996. *Phoebe's Fabulous Father*. Illustrated by Bridget Starr Taylor. San Diego: Harcourt Brace & Company. As Phoebe and her mother make their way around town completing errands before their concert that evening, Phoebe wonders why her dad is not more like other dads; includes a very surprising ending.

Carson, Jo. 1992. *You Hold Me and I'll Hold You*. Illustrated by Annie Cannon. New York: Orchard Books. Dad, who is a single parent, tenderly comforts his daughter at a family funeral.

Cole, Babette. 1985. *The Trouble with Dad*. New York: G. P. Putnam's Sons: Dad has a rather boring job, so when he comes home he constructs robots that accidentally wreak havoc on the town.

Ketteman, Helen. 1992. *Not Yet, Yvette*. Illustrated by Irene Trivas. Morton Grove, Ill.: Albert Whitman & Company. Yvette and her father clean the house, go shopping, and bake a cake for her mom's birthday. Mom is a veterinarian and dad appears to stay at home with Yvette.

Mandelbaum, Pili. 1990. *You Be Me, I'll Be You*. New York: Kane/Miller Book Publishers. When Anna complains that she does not like her dark skin and curly hair, dad gets creative. This depiction of a biracial family is a beautiful one, marked by one very special child.

Monfried, Lucia. 1993. *The Daddies Boat*. Illustrated by Michele Chessare. New York: Penguin Putnam Books for Young Readers. An island resort is the setting for this story about summer's simple pleasures, enhanced by warm family interactions and a surprise ending.

Munson, Derek. 2000. *Enemy Pie*. Illustrated by Tara Calahan King. San Francisco: Chronicle Books. Dad has just the recipe to take care of his son's new enemy: enemy pie! The father is depicted performing domestic tasks, and appears to be the only parent involved in raising the son.

Ormerod, Jan. *Messy Baby*. See **Series**.

Otey, Mimi. 1990. *Daddy Has a Pair of Striped Shorts*. New York: Farrar, Straus & Giroux. Daddy, a preacher, has a bright, colorful wardrobe full of patterns, which often embarrasses his children at swim class, the movies, and at school; soon they learn to love him and his unique look.

Pedersen, Marika, and Mikele Hall. 2000. *Mommy Works, Daddy Works*. Illustrated by Deirdre Betteridge. Toronto: Annick Press. Depicting mothers and fathers in many nontraditional career roles, this book seeks to provide a diversity of role models for parents and children.

Quinlan, Patricia. 1987. *My Dad Takes Care of Me*. Illustrated by Vlasta van Kampen. Toronto: Annick Press. Luke's father lost his job and takes cares of him at home now; although he continues to look for jobs, this book presents a stay-at-home dad.

Shalev, Meir. 1990. *My Father Always Embarrasses Me*. Translated by Dagmar Herrmann. Illustrated by Yossi Abolafia. Chicago: Wellington Publishing, Inc. Father's unique personality, as well as his role as a stay-at-home father, causes his son, Mortimer, to feel embarrassed (justifiably!), until Dad is given an opportunity for redemption.

Smalls-Hector, Irene. 1999. *Kevin and His Dad*. Illustrated by Michael Hays. Boston: Little, Brown and Company. On Saturdays, while Mom is away, a father and son have fun cleaning the house together before engaging in more typically amusing activities.

Wild, Margaret. 1999. *Tom Goes to Kindergarten*. Illustrated by David Legge. Morton Grove: Albert Whitman & Company. Tom likes kindergarten so much that soon the whole family wants to go too! The illustrations are great depictions of shared parental duties.

Yaccarino, Dan. 1997. *An Octopus Followed Me Home*. New York: Viking. Father refuses to let one more pet into the house when his daughter brings an octopus home to their already zoolike home.

CONTEMPORARY TRADITIONAL DADS

Chorao, Kay. 1998. *Little Farm by the Sea*. New York: Henry Holt & Company. Family members in this traditional rural setting work harmoniously to provide food and other farm goods for their roadside stand and store.

Friend, David. 1990. *Baseball, Football, Daddy and Me*. Illustrated by Rick Brown. New York: Viking. Father and son are the ultimate sports enthusiasts.

Gardella, Tricia. 1997. *Casey's New Hat*. Illustrated by Margot Apple. Boston: Houghton Mifflin Company. Casey's growing out of the cowgirl hat from her toddler days, so on their next trip in to town she and dad seek out the "right" hat. Grandpa joins in on the search in this traditional forming setting and ends up helping his granddaughter find the perfect hat for a growing cowgirl.

Grambling, Lois G. 1998. *Daddy Will Be There*. Illustrated by Walter Gaffney-Kessell. New York: Greenwillow Books. As a young girl becomes more independent—riding her bike all by herself, going to birthday parties, starting kindergarten—she comes to understand that no matter what she does, her father will always be there for her.

Heo, Yumi. 1996. *Father's Rubber Shoes*. New York: Scholastic, Inc. Yungsu's father works long hours so that he can provide his son with a better life than he had growing up in Korea. Immigration, the importance of work, and parental responsibilities are all topics presented here and good for starting discussions.

Mahy, Margaret. 2000. *Down the Dragon's Tongue*. Illustrated by Patricia MacCarthy. New York: Orchard Books. Mr. Prospero, a businessman and orderly man, is reluctant to join his twins on the Dragon's Tongue, the fastest slide at the park, until he realizes that having fun with his children is much more important than keeping his suit neatly pressed.

Manushkin, Fran. 1995. *The Matzah That Papa Brought Home*. Illustrated by Ned Bittinger. New York: Scholastic Inc. The repetitious, rhyming text and detailed illustrations of this book bring to life the culture of a Jewish family celebrating Passover.

Otey, Mimi. *Blue Moon Soup Spoon*. 1993. New York: Farrar, Straus & Giroux. While Ma prepares supper at twilight, a young boy hangs around the kitchen, awaiting the return of his father from work. Especially noteworthy is the contrast depicted between the parents in these traditional roles, with father represented by a pair of well-worn boots and objects associated with his fishing trade.

DADS IN THEIR YOUTH

Brisson, Pat. 1998. *The Summer My Father Was Ten*. Illustrated by Andrea Shine. Honesdale, Penn.: Boyds Mills Press. Each year when father and daughter prepare their garden, he passes on a strong moral lesson in the form of a boyhood story, which concludes with sweet repentance and two examples of intergenerational friendship.

Creech, Sharon. 2000. *Fishing in the Air*. Illustrated by Chris Raschka. New York: Joanna Cotler Books. Father and son embark on a fishing excursion and share many imaginative moments, including a conversation about the father's days as a young boy learning to fish with his father.

Howard, Elizabeth Fitzgerald. 1995. *Papa Tells Chita a Story*. Illustrated by Floyd Cooper. New York: Simon & Schuster Books for Young Readers. Father and Chita share quality time together after dinner as he recounts his days as a soldier in Cuba during the Spanish-American War.

Friedman, Ina R. 1987. *How My Parents Learned to Eat*. Illustrated by Allen Say. New York: Houghton Mifflin Company. This wonderful glimpse of cultural differences will entice children to learn more about their own parents' premarriage lives.

Johnson, Dolores. 1993. *Your Dad Was Just Like You*. New York: Simon & Schuster Children's Publishing. Grandfather shares succinct bits and pieces about his son's childhood with Peter, his grandson, creating more than just memories.

Mochizuki, Ken. 1995. *Heroes*. Illustrated by Dom Lee. New York: Lee & Low Books, Inc. Donnie, who is Asian American, always has to be the "bad guy" when he and his friends play war because his friends will not believe that his father and uncle are decorated military heroes. This book is dedicated to the many people of Asian and Pacific Islander descent who have defended America with little or no recognition.

DADS PROVIDING INSTRUCTION

Bernard, Robin. 1996. *Juma and the Honey-Guide: An African Tale*, illustrated by Nneka Bennett. Parsippany, N.J.: Silver Burdett Press. A Dorobo father teaches his eager son how to follow a *kidege*, or bird, to locate honey, but has much difficulty convincing him of the customary *asante*, or thank-you.

Brown, Margaret Wise. 1998. *The Little Scarecrow Boy*. Illustrated by David Diaz. New York: HarperCollins Publishers. Although this scarecrow dad is mean, fierce, and scary, he also exhibits much sensitivity in dealing with his inexperienced young scarecrow son.

Fowler, Susi Gregg. 1994. *I'll See You When the Moon Is Full*. Illustrated by Jim Fowler. New York: Greenwillow Books. When dad goes out of town on business trips his young son misses him very much. Dad assures his son that he will be home by the time the moon is full, and delivers an impromptu astronomy lesson at the same time!

Garland, Sherry. 1998. *My Father's Boat*. Illustrated by Ted Rand. New York: Scholastic, Inc. A Vietnamese American shrimper teaches his son the tricks of the trade one special day, which causes him to reminisce about his own father back in Vietnam. An especially warm, poetic text is prefaced with this appropriate Vietnamese proverb: "When you are young, you need your father; when you are old, you need your son." This father represents both strong and tender sides of parenting.

George, William T. 1992. *Christmas at Long Pond*. Illustrated by Lindsay Barrett George. New York: Greenwillow. A search for a Christmas tree allows Dad and son to enjoy the woods and Dad to play the role of naturalist.

MacDonald, Margaret Read. 2001. *Mabela the Clever*. Illustrated by Tim Coffey. Morton Grove, Ill.: Albert Whitman & Company. Mabela was once the smallest mouse in the village, but thanks to a lesson in cleverness from her father, she just might save everyone from their worst enemy, the cat.

McCreary, Laura, and Mark Myers. 2001. *Angela Anaconda: The Best Dad*. Based on the scripts by Charlotte Fullerton and Mark Myers. Illustrated by Barry Goldberg. New York: Simon Spotlight. This short chapter book features two stories about Angela Anaconda, her dad, and her eternal enemy Nanette Manoir. The first story sees father and daughter entering a square-dancing competition and the second sees them going fishing.

Peters, Lisa Westberg. 1995. *Meg and Dad Discover Treasure in the Air*. Illustrated by Deborah Durland DeSaix. New York: Henry Holt & Company. Meg is hunting for rubies but only finds "plain, old" rocks, which sparks an impromptu biology lesson from her father about the very first oxygen-producing organisms on Earth.

San Souci, Daniel. 1993. *Country Road*. New York: Doubleday Books for Young Readers. Dad and his generally disinterested son go walking along an old road, coming to appreciate the wildlife and one another along the way.

Sanders, Scott Russell. 1997. *Meeting Trees*. Illustrated by Robert Hynes. Washington, D.C.: National Geographic Society. A father's passions for woodworking, trees, and nature are shared with his son in this story based on the author's life.

Skofield, James. 1993. *'Round and Around*. Illustrated by James Graham Hale. New York: HarperCollins Publishers. While on a walk with his father and their dog, Sam, Dan observes many things in nature that move in circles. But as the sun sets and dad teaches Dan that even the Earth moves in a circle, Dan observes that the best circle of all is a hug.

DADS SHARING HOUSEHOLD CHORES

Browne, Anthony. 1986. *Piggybook*. New York: Alfred A. Knopf. Mr. Piggott and his two sons, Simon and Patrick, are of no help to Mrs. Piggott, who decides to leave and teach them a lesson about helping out. The house goes to ruin, and the male Piggotts turn into pigs and learn a lesson about sharing household chores by the time she returns.

Greenfield, Eloise. 1991. *My Daddy and I*. Illustrated by Jan Spivey Gilchrist. New York: Black Butterfly Children's Books. Cooking, cleaning, reading—daddy and son do everything together in this board book best suited for preschoolers.

Hines, Anna Grossnickle. 1986. *Daddy Makes the Best Spaghetti*. New York: Clarion Books. Corey's Dad creatively shares many domestic and parenting duties with Mom, including making dinner, becoming Bathman at bath time, and tucking in one very loved boy.

Janovitz, Marilyn. 2001. *Good Morning, Little Fox*. New York: North-South Books. Little Fox and his father always spend the weekend together—sleeping late, making breakfast, and doing chores.

Ketteman, Helen. 1992. *Not Yet, Yvette*. Illustrated by Irene Trivas. Morton Grove, Ill.: Albert Whitman & Company. Yvette and her father clean the house, go shopping, and bake a cake for her mom's birthday. Mom is a veterinarian and dad appears to stay at home with Yvette.

Ormerod, Jan. *Messy Baby*. See **Series**.

Quinlan, Patricia. 1987. *My Dad Takes Care of Me*. Illustrated by Vlasta van Kampen. Toronto: Annick Press. Luke's father lost his job and takes cares of him at home now; although he continues to look for jobs, this book presents a stay-at-home dad.

Sharmat, Marjorie Weinman. 1976. *Mooch the Messy*. Illustrated by Ben Shecter. New York: Harper & Row Publishers. Mooch the Rat gets a visit from his father, who finds Mooch's hole to be quite unclean and who encourages more healthy habits.

Smalls-Hector, Irene. 1999. *Kevin and His Dad*. Illustrated by Michael Hays. Boston: Little, Brown and Company. On Saturdays, while Mom is away, a father and son have fun cleaning the house together before engaging in more typically amusing activities.

Wild, Margaret. 1999. *Tom Goes to Kindergarten*. Illustrated by David Legge. Morton Grove, Ill.: Albert Whitman & Company. Tom likes kindergarten so much that soon the whole family wants to go too! The illustrations are great depictions of shared parental duties.

DADS SHARING WORK AND PARENTING RESPONSIBILITIES

Carling, Amelia Lau. 1998. *Mama & Papa Have a Store*. New York: Penguin Putnam Books for Young Readers. Both mother and father share parenting and work responsibilities in this colorful story about a Chinese family operating a retail store in Guatemala.

Catalanotto, Peter. 1999. *The Painter*. New York: Scholastic, Inc. A father balances parenting responsibilities, including imaginative and silly playtime with his young daughter, and work responsibilities in his art studio.

Gilchrist, Jan Spivey. 1997. *Madelia*. New York: Penguin Putnam Books for Young Readers. A preacher father uses the Sunday sermon to inspire his young aspiring artist.

Henkes, Kevin. 2000. *Wemberly Worried*. New York: Greenwillow. When Wemberly is faced with her first day of kindergarten, her mutually supportive parents reassure and comfort her.

Hines, Anna Grossnickle. 1986. *Daddy Makes the Best Spaghetti*. New York: Clarion Books. Corey's Dad creatively shares many domestic and parenting duties with Mom, including making dinner, becoming Bathman at bath time, and tucking in one very loved boy.

Johnson, Dolores. 1994. *Papa's Stories*. New York: Macmillan Publishing Company. An illiterate father realizes that he needs to learn to read when his daughter goes to first grade and discovers that he has been making up the stories in her books all along.

Ketteman, Helen. 1992. *Not Yet, Yvette*. Illustrated by Irene Trivas. Morton Grove, Ill.: Albert Whitman & Company. Yvette and her father clean the house, go shopping, and bake a cake for her mom's birthday. Mom is a veterinarian and dad appears to stay at home with Yvette.

Lindenbaum, Pija. 1991. *Else-Marie and Her Seven Little Daddies*. New York: Henry Holt & Company. Else-Marie is embarrassed about her seven small fathers, but when it is their turn to pick her up from playgroup, no one seems to notice that they are small or that there are seven of them! The quirky illustrations help tell the story of how Else-Marie learns to appreciate her fathers' uniqueness.

Merriam, Eve. 1989. *Daddies at Work*. Illustrated by Eugenie Fernandes. New York: Little Simon. This book and its companion, *Mommies at Work*, depict loving fathers engaged in many parenting and career roles.

Munsch, Robert. 1990. *Something Good*. Illustrated by Michael Martchenko. Toronto: Annick Press. Dad and the kids are grocery shopping, but one very motivated and vocal daughter wants him to buy some "good" food: ice cream and candy.

Quinlan, Patricia. 1987. *My Dad Takes Care of Me*. Illustrated by Vlasta van Kampen. Toronto: Annick Press. Luke's father lost his job and takes cares of him at home now; although he continues to look for jobs, this book presents a stay-at-home dad.

Weidt, Maryann. 1995. *Daddy Played Music for the Cows*. Illustrated by Henri Sorensen. New York: Morrow/Avon. While Daddy milks the cows and tends to other chores, he and his daughter enjoy playful interaction and a love for country music.

Wild, Margaret. 1999. *Tom Goes to Kindergarten*. Illustrated by David Legge. Morton Grove, Ill.: Albert Whitman & Company. Tom likes kindergarten so much that soon the whole family wants to go too! The illustrations are great depictions of shared parental duties.

DADS SUPPORTING MOM

Buehner, Caralyn. 1996. *Fanny's Dream*. Illustrated by Mark Buehner. New York: Dial Books for Young Readers. This story puts a spin on the classic Cinderella fairy tale by presenting Fanny, a girl who never gets to the ball but whose husband is supportive and more wonderful than any prince.

Gliori, Debi. 1999. *Mr. Bear's New Baby*. New York: Scholastic, Inc. Both Mr. and Mrs. Bear share nighttime baby duty, along with many sleepy neighbors, in this latest addition to the Bear family saga.

Hines, Anna Grossnickle. 1986. *Daddy Makes the Best Spaghetti*. New York: Clarion Books. Corey's Dad creatively shares many domestic and parenting duties with Mom, including making dinner, becoming Bathman at bath time, and tucking in one very loved boy.

Janovitz, Marilyn. 2001. *Good Morning, Little Fox*. New York: North-South Books. Little Fox and his father always spend the weekend together—sleeping late, making breakfast, and doing chores.

Ketteman, Helen. 1992. *Not Yet, Yvette*. Illustrated by Irene Trivas. Morton Grove, Ill.: Albert Whitman & Company. Yvette and her father clean the house, go shopping, and bake a cake for her mom's birthday. Mom is a veterinarian and dad appears to stay at home with Yvette.

Lindenbaum, Pija. 1991. *Else-Marie and Her Seven Little Daddies*. New York: Henry Holt & Company. Else-Marie is embarrassed about her seven small fathers, but when it is their turn to pick her up from playgroup no one seems to notice that they are small or that there are seven of them! The quirky illustrations help tell the story of how Else-Marie learns to appreciate her fathers' uniqueness.

Mahy, Margaret. 2000. *Down the Dragon's Tongue*. Illustrated by Patricia MacCarthy. New York: Orchard Books. Mr. Prospero, a businessman and orderly father, is reluctant to join his twins on the Dragon's Tongue, the fastest slide at the park, until he realizes that having fun with his children is much more important than keeping his suit neatly pressed.

McMullan, Kate. 1994. *Good Night, Stella*. Illustrated by Emma Chichester Clark. Cambridge, Mass.: Candlewick Press. Young Stella's imagination overflows at bedtime, making sleep impossible, but Dad, who is the caretaker for the evening, exercises much patience and cleverness in this humorous story.

Miller, Margaret. 1994. *Where's Jenna?* New York: Simon & Schuster Books for Young Readers. While Dad feeds the baby, Jenna plays hide-and-seek with Mom. An ideal depiction of shared parental responsibilities.

Quinlan, Patricia. 1987. *My Dad Takes Care of Me*. Illustrated by Vlasta van Kampen. Toronto: Annick Press. Luke's father lost his job and takes cares of him at home now; although he continues to look for jobs, this book presents a stay-at-home dad.

Smith, Eddie. 1994. *A Lullaby for Daddy*. Illustrated by Susan Anderson. Lawrenceville, N.J.: Africa World Press. Daddy, a musician, and his young daughter compose a lullaby together, which they sing as part of their bedtime ritual.

DADS TEACHING A LESSON OR A MORAL

Booth, David. 1996. *The Dust Bowl*. Illustrated by Karen Reczuch. Toronto: Kids Can Press, Ltd. The struggles of Matthew's grandfather's 20th century farming are detailed in this Canadian story, which also shows lessons and advice being handed down from parent to child, regardless of the age.

Brisson, Pat. 1998. *The Summer My Father Was Ten*. Illustrated by Andrea Shine. Honesdale, Penn.: Boyds Mills Press. Each year when father and daughter prepare their garden, he passes on a strong moral lesson in the form of a boyhood story, which concludes with sweet repentance and two examples of intergenerational friendship.

Bunting, Eve. 1998. *So Far from the Sea*. Illustrated by Chris K. Soentpiet. Boston: Houghton Mifflin Company. While revisiting the internment camp in which he and his family were held during World War II, a Japanese American father impresses upon his children the importance of forgiveness, as well as of patriotism.

Cook, Jean Thor. 1995. *Room for a Stepdaddy*. Illustrated by Martine Gourbault. Morton Grove, Ill.: Albert Whitman & Company. Joey has a very hard time adjusting to a life with three parents—Mom, Dad, and his new stepdaddy, Bill—but ultimately he comes to believe the wisdom his father imparted to him: love is like the sand on the beach; there is always enough to go around.

Heo, Yumi. 1996. *Father's Rubber Shoes*. New York: Scholastic, Inc. Yungsu's father works long hours so that he can provide his son with a better life than he had growing up in Korea. Immigration, the importance of work, and parental responsibilities are all topics presented here and good for starting discussions.

Ketteman, Helen. 1998. *I Remember Papa*. Illustrated by Greg Shed. New York: Penguin Putnam Books for Young Readers. The lessons a father taught his son, such as the importance of saving money, of forgiveness, and of parental sacrifices, are remembered for a lifetime in this story about a father and son's passion for baseball.

MacDonald, Margaret Read. 2001. *Mabela the Clever*. Illustrated by Tim Coffey. Morton Grove, Ill.: Albert Whitman & Company. Mabela was once the smallest mouse in the village, but thanks to a lesson in cleverness from her father, she just might save everyone from their worst enemy, the cat.

Mandelbaum, Pili. 1990. *You Be Me, I'll Be You*. New York: Kane/Miller Book Publishers. When Anna complains that she does not like her dark skin and curly hair, dad gets creative. This depiction of a biracial family is a beautiful one, marked by one very special child.

Medearis, Angela S. 1994. *Our People.* Illustrated by Michael Bryant. New York: Atheneum Books for Young Readers. Father's history lessons are intertwined with play activities, such as building blocks and piggyback riding, providing inspiration for his daughter to imagine and dream.

Mochizuki, Ken. 1995. *Heroes.* Illustrated by Dom Lee. New York: Lee & Low Books, Inc. Donnie, who is Asian American, always has to be the "bad guy" when he and his friends play war because his friends will not believe that his father and uncle are decorated military heroes. This book is dedicated to the many people of Asian and Pacific Islander descent who have defended America with little or no recognition.

Munsch, Robert. 1990. *Something Good.* Illustrated by Michael Martchenko. Toronto: Annick Press. Dad and the kids are grocery shopping, but one very motivated and vocal daughter wants him to buy some "good" food: ice cream and candy.

Munson, Derek. 2000. *Enemy Pie.* Illustrated by Tara Calahan King. San Francisco: Chronicle Books. It was shaping up to be the best summer ever for a young boy, when Jeremy Ross moved to the neighborhood, becoming his first enemy. Fortunately, dad had enemies growing up too, and he has just the recipe to take care of them: enemy pie!

Perkins, Lynne Rae. 1997. *Clouds for Dinner.* New York: HarperCollins Children's Book Group. When Janet is given an opportunity to compare her parents' alternative lifestyle and aesthetic approach to life to relatives with a more mundane lifestyle, their strong influence becomes apparent.

Root, Phyllis. 1998. *Aunt Nancy and Cousin Lazybones.* Illustrated by David Parkins. Cambridge, Mass.: Candlewick Press. Aunt Nancy has just the trick for dealing with her lazy cousin. Alhough this book is not about fathers, it is a useful tool for fathers seeking books with lessons and morals.

————. 1996. *Aunt Nancy and Old Man Trouble.* Illustrated by David Parkins. Cambridge, Mass.: Candlewick Press. When Old Man Trouble pays a visit to Aunt Nancy, she responds with the ultimate optimism. Although this book is not about fathers, it is a useful tool for fathers seeking books with lessons and morals.

Sebastian, John. 1993. *J.B.'s Harmonica.* Illustrated by Garth Williams. San Diego: Harcourt Brace Jovanovich. J.B. plays harmonica well, but constant comparisons to his father, a professional harmonicist, have him considering quitting. Dad ultimately teaches a lesson about self-acceptance.

DADS-IN-TRAINING

Gliori, Debi. 1994. *Mr. Bear Babysits.* New York: Golden Books Publishing Company. In this warm story, Mr. Bear, a novice at parenting, proves his nurturing and caregiving abilities when he is forced to baby-sit the neighbors' children.

Stanley, Diane. 1996, 1999. *Saving Sweetness* and *Raising Sweetness.* Illustrated by G. Brian Karas. New York: The Putnam Publishing Group. In these two zany books, a caring and sensitive but inept sheriff adopts a runaway from an orphanage, Sweetness, and eight other orphans. No other author handles adoption in such a light manner; these books show how love can be found in the most unusual circumstances.

DISCIPLINING IN POSITIVE WAYS

Gray, Nigel. 1996. *Running Away from Home.* Illustrated by Gregory Rogers. New York: Crown Publishing Group. When tension and conflict cause Sam to "run away," Dad relates to him in a respectful, considerate manner.

Root, Phyllis. 1996. *Contrary Bear.* Illustrated by Laura Cornell. New York: HarperCollins Children's Book Group. In this humorous story, Father has many occasions to be irritated with both his daughter and her friend, Contrary Bear, and usually reacts with much patience and effective discipline.

Schertle, Alice. 2000. *Down the Road.* Illustrated by E. B. Lewis. San Diego: Harcourt Children's Books. When Hetty gets sidetracked on her way home from the market and the eggs end up broken, Papa reacts with kindness and understanding, rather than with punishment and lectures.

Walters, Virginia. 1999. *Are We There Yet, Daddy?* Illustrated by S. D. Schindler. New York: Viking. This rhyming, repetitive text counts down the miles on a 100-mile journey to Grandma's house as a patient father responds to that all-too-frequently asked question.

EMBARRASSING DADS

Cole, Babette. 1985. *The Trouble with Dad.* New York: G. P. Putnam's Sons. Dad has a rather boring job, so when he comes home he constructs robots that accidentally wreak havoc on the town.

Lindenbaum, Pija. 1991. *Else-Marie and Her Seven Little Daddies.* New York: Henry Holt & Company. Else-Marie is embarrassed about her seven small fathers, but when it is their turn to pick her up from playgroup, no one seems to notice that they are small or that there are seven of them! The quirky illustrations help tell the story of how Else-Marie learns to appreciate her fathers' uniqueness.

Otey, Mimi. 1990. *Daddy Has a Pair of Striped Shorts.* New York: Farrar, Straus & Giroux. Daddy, a preacher, has a bright, colorful wardrobe full of patterns, which often embarrasses his children at swim class, the movies, and at school; soon they learn to love him and his unique look.

Shalev, Meir. 1990. *My Father Always Embarrasses Me*. Translated by Dagmar Herrmann. Illustrated by Yossi Abolafia. Chicago: Wellington Publishing, Inc. Father's unique personality, as well as his role as a stay-at-home father, causes his son, Mortimer, to feel embarrassed (justifiably!), until Dad is given an opportunity for redemption. This book was originally published in Jerusalem, which demonstrates that embarrassing parents are everywhere!

Silverman, Erica. 1998. *Gittel's Hands*. Illustrated by Deborah Nourse Lattimore. Mahwah, N.J.: Troll Communications, LLC. Yakov, the water carrier, boasts about his daughter's handiwork so much that she is continuously embarrassed, and the boasting leads to additional conflicts.

GAY DADS

Brown, Forman. 1991. *The Generous Jefferson Bartleby Jones*. Illustrated by Leslie Trawin. Boston: Alyson Wonderland. Young Jeff is so pleased to have two dads that he loans them out to his friends who are neglected by their own fathers.

Heron, Ann, and Meredith Maran. 1991. *How Would You Feel if Your Dad Was Gay?* Illustrated by Kris Kovick. Boston: Alyson Wonderland. When Michael's sister, Jasmine, announces in her class that she has three dads, the entire elementary school starts talking about them.

Valentine, Johnny. 1992. *The Daddy Machine*. Illustrated by Lynette Schmidt. Boston: Alyson Wonderland. The children of lesbian parents wish for a dad and, after building a contraption that "manufactures" dads, get more than they bargained for. This is a positive look at what dads are like and what they do.

———. 1994. *One Dad, Two Dads, Brown Dad, Blue Dads*. Illustrated by Melody Sarecky. Boston: Alyson Wonderland. In this Dr. Seuss imitation, fast-paced rhymes about the normalcy of Lou's two blue dads are meant to educate and/or reassure children about gay parents.

Willhoite, Michael. 1991. *Daddy's Roommate*. Boston: Alyson Wonderland. In this now classic portrayal of a boy's gay father and the relationship with his partner, Frank, a variety of typical father-son activities is illustrated, with the emphasis on loving and nurturing behaviors.

HUMOROUS DADS

Browne, Anthony. 1994. *The Big Baby*. New York: Alfred A. Knopf Books for Young Readers. John's father is preoccupied with aging and wakes one day to find himself a baby again.

Lindbergh, Reeve. 1994. *If I'd Known Then What I Know Now*. Illustrated by Kimberly Bulcken Root. New York: Viking. This humorous story tells of the various failed home improvement projects on which dad worked over the years. His family assures the reader at the end, however, that they would have him no other way.

Lindenbaum, Pija. 1991. *Else-Marie and Her Seven Little Daddies*. New York: Henry Holt & Company. Else-Marie is embarrassed about her seven small fathers, but when it is their turn to pick her up from playgroup, no one seems to notice that they are small or that there are seven of them! The quirky illustrations help tell the story of how Else-Marie learns to appreciate her fathers' uniqueness.

Mandelbaum, Pili. 1990. *You Be Me, I'll Be You*. New York: Kane/Miller Book Publishers. When Anna complains that she does not like her dark skin and curly hair, dad gets creative. This depiction of a biracial family is a beautiful one, marked by one very special child.

McCreary, Laura, and Mark Myers. 2001. *Angela Anaconda: The Best Dad*. Based on the scripts by Charlotte Fullerton and Mark Myers. Illustrated by Barry Goldberg. New York: Simon Spotlight. This short chapter book features two stories about Angela Anaconda, her dad, and her eternal enemy Nanette Manoir. The first story sees father and daughter entering a square-dancing competition and the second sees them going fishing.

Otey, Mimi. 1990. *Daddy Has a Pair of Striped Shorts*. New York: Farrar, Straus & Giroux. Daddy, a preacher, has a bright, colorful wardrobe full of patterns, which often embarrasses his children at swim class, the movies, and at school; soon they learn to love him and his unique look.

Patron, Susan. 1994. *Dark Cloud Strong Breeze*. Illustrated by Peter Catalanotto. New York: Orchard Books. In this fun, rhyming text a father locks his keys in the car right before a storm breaks, but his daughter saves the day.

Polacco, Patricia. 1991. *Some Birthday!* New York: Simon & Schuster Books for Young Readers. It is Patricia's birthday and her father, who is divorced from her mother, seems to have forgotten entirely. Little does she know, this birthday will turn into her best ever, complete with monster hunt, camping trip, and the perfect gifts.

Shalev, Meir. 1990. *My Father Always Embarrasses Me*. Translated by Dagmar Herrmann. Illustrated by Yossi Abolafia. Chicago: Wellington Publishing, Inc. Father's unique personality, as well as his role as a stay-at-home father, causes his son, Mortimer, to feel embarrassed (justifiably!), until Dad is given an opportunity for redemption.

Stanley, Diane. 1996, 1999. *Saving Sweetness* and *Raising Sweetness*. Illustrated by G. Brian Karas. New York: The Putnam Publishing Group. In these two zany books, a caring and sensitive but inept sheriff adopts a runaway from an orphanage, Sweetness, and eight other orphans. No other author handles adoption in such a light manner; these books show how love can be found in the most unusual circumstances.

Zimelman, Nathan. 1990. *Treed by a Pride of Irate Lions*. Illustrated by Toni Goffe. Boston: Little, Brown & Company. Father's quest to find an animal that likes him results in his realization that it does not matter if animals like him as long as his family loves him.

LARGER-THAN-LIFE DADS

Ballard, Robin. 1992. *My Father Is Far Away*. New York: Greenwillow Books. While taking part in mundane, everyday activities, a young girl daydreams of all the exciting things her father must be doing while he is away.

Boelts, Maribeth. 2000. *Big Daddy, Frog Wrestler*. Illustrated by Benrei Huang. Morton Grove, Ill.: Albert Whitman & Company. Big Daddy and his son, Curtis, love wrestling, but when Big Daddy gets a chance to wrestle all over the world he must decide between wrestling and his son.

Browne, Anthony. 2000. *My Dad*. New York: Farrar, Straus & Giroux. Dad can do anything and do it well in this cleverly illustrated picture book.

Butterworth, Nick. 1992. *My Dad Is Awesome*. Cambridge, Mass.: Candlewick Press. A young child idolizes his dad for such things as being able to cook three-layer cakes and running as fast as a cheetah. The illustrations depict Dad enthusiastically in this wondrous role.

Campbell, Louisa. 1996. *Phoebe's Fabulous Father*. Illustrated by Bridget Starr Taylor. San Diego: Harcourt Brace & Company. As Phoebe and her mother make their way around town completing errands before their concert that evening, Phoebe wonders why her dad is not more like other dads; includes a very surprising ending.

Carle, Eric. 1986. *Papa, Please Get the Moon for Me*. Natick, Mass.: Picture Book Studio USA. Monica asks dad for the moon and, miraculously, this superdad delivers! But there's a catch: the moon continues to get smaller and smaller.

Graham, Bob. 2000. *Max*. Cambridge, Mass.: Candlewick Press. Max is the super son of superhero parents, but he cannot fly yet! Children will identify with Max's plight and agree that "Everyone's different in *some* way, aren't they?"

Howard, Elizabeth Fitzgerald. 1995. *Papa Tells Chita a Story*. Illustrated by Floyd Cooper. New York: Simon & Schuster Books for Young Readers. Father and Chita share quality time together after dinner as he recounts his days as a soldier in Cuba during the Spanish-American War.

McCreary, Laura, and Mark Myers. 2001. *Angela Anaconda: The Best Dad*. Based on the scripts by Charlotte Fullerton and Mark Myers. Illustrated by Barry Goldberg. New York: Simon Spotlight. This short chapter book features two stories about Angela Anaconda, her dad, and her eternal enemy Nanette Manoir. The first story sees father and daughter entering a square-dancing competition and the second sees them going fishing.

Mochizuki, Ken. 1995. *Heroes*. Illustrated by Dom Lee. New York: Lee & Low Books, Inc. Donnie, who is Asian American, always has to be the "bad guy" when he and his friends play war because his friends will not believe that his father and uncle are decorated military heroes. This book is dedicated to the many people of Asian and Pacific Islander descent who have defended America with little or no recognition.

Munsch, Robert. 1983. *David's Father*. Illustrated by Michael Martchenko. Toronto: Annick Press. David and his father do not look much alike because David was adopted, but David's new friend soon discovers that even giant fathers are fun.

Paradis, Susan. 1999. *My Daddy*. Asheville, N.C.: Front Street, Inc. Daddy is certainly larger than life in the eyes of his toddler son in this book, which depicts a variety of daily activities, tenderness, and playfulness.

SINGLE PARENTING

Booth, David. 1996. *The Dust Bowl*. Illustrated by Karen Reczuch. Toronto: Kids Can Press, Ltd. The struggles of Matthew's grandfather's 20th century farming are detailed in this Canadian story, which also shows lessons and advice being handed down from parent to child, regardless of the age.

Browne, Anthony. 1983. *Gorilla*. New York: Alfred A. Knopf. Hannah's toy gorilla comes to life and takes the place of her father, doing all of the activities he is always too busy to do.

Camp, Lindsay. 1998. *Why?* Illustrated by Tony Ross. New York: The Putnam Publishing Group. A comical look at the typical questioning stage young children go through. Although Lily's Dad, who appears to be parenting solo, does not always exhibit patience, he is learning!

Carson, Jo. 1992. *You Hold Me and I'll Hold You*. Illustrated by Annie Cannon. New York: Orchard Books. Dad, who is a single parent, tenderly comforts his daughter at a family funeral.

Christopher, Matt. 1992. *Centerfield Ballhawk*. Illustrated by Ellen Beier. Boston: Little, Brown & Company. José wants to excel at baseball in order to gain the respect and attention of his emotionally distant father, a widower who once played minor-league baseball.

Egielski, Richard. 1998. *Jazper*. New York: HarperCollins. A Laura Geringer Book. When Jazper comes home to find his father in bandages, he realizes he must go make a living for the two of them and ends up getting mixed up with some magical moths. This is a very cute story with funny illustrations of the bug town.

Grambling, Lois G. 1998. *Daddy Will Be There*. Illustrated by Walter Gaffney-Kessell. New York: Greenwillow Books. As a young girl becomes more independent—riding her bike all by herself, going to birthday parties, starting kindergarten—she comes to understand that no matter what she does, her father will always be there for her.

Guettier, Benedicte. 1999. *The Father Who Had 10 Children*. New York: Penguin Putnam Books for Young Readers. In this humorous glimpse at parental burnout, Dad does it all—cooks, dresses, chauffeurs, bathes, and reads bedtime stories to 10 children—plus goes to work and, in his spare time, builds a boat in which he intends to sail on a solo journey. A surefire hit for fathers.

Haseley, Dennis. 1986. *Kite Flier*. Illustrated by David Wiesner. New York: Four Winds Press. A husband and wife share a special relationship flying kites; when she dies giving birth he shares his kite-making gift with his son.

Hermes, Patricia. 1996. *When Snow Lay Soft on the Mountains*. Illustrated by Leslie Baker. Boston: Little, Brown & Company. Financial hardships, the death of Mama, and father's influenza cause Hallie to keep many wishes to herself while helping to nurse her father back to health in this quiet 1800s story. One special wish comes true on her birthday.

Howard, Ellen. 1997. *The Log Cabin Quilt*. Illustrated by Ronald Himler. New York: Holiday House, Inc. After Mam dies, Pap hustles the family by covered wagon to Michigan, leaving behind all of her possessions and memories, except for some fabric scraps rescued by Granny. These become the chink to the emotional side of this traditional, hard-working, unemotional man.

Lindsay, Jeanne Warren. 1991. *Do I Have a Daddy? A Story About a Single-Parent Child*. Illustrated by Cheryl Boeller. Buena Park, Calif.: Morning Glory Press. In this timely book, young Erik seeks to understand where his daddy is. Mother explains that not all mommies and daddies get married, and encourages him to spend time with his Uncle Bob and grandfather. A resources section at the back of this book might assist in discussions about single-parenthood, absent fathers, or the importance of male role models.

Martin, David. 2001. *Piggy and Dad*. Illustrated by Frank Remkiewicz. Cambridge, Mass.: Candlewick Press. This set of four books designed to help beginning readers captures a truly loving relationship between Piggy and his dad. Titles included are *Piggy's Bath*, *Piggy's Bedtime*, *Piggy's Sandwich*, and *Piggy's Pictures*.

McClintock, Barbara. 1996. *The Fantastic Drawings of Danielle*. New York: Houghton Mifflin Company. Father, a French photographer in the late 1800s, is unable to support his daughter's fantastical approach to art, until her artwork ends up supporting both of them.

Polacco, Patricia. 1999. *My Ol' Man*. New York: Penguin Putnam Books for Young Readers. A nostalgic portrait of a traveling salesman who entertains his children and ends up supporting them with his magical storytelling abilities when he becomes unemployed.

———. 1991. *Some Birthday!* New York: Simon & Schuster Books for Young Readers. It is Patricia's birthday and her father, who is divorced from her mother, seems to have forgotten entirely. Little does she know, this birthday will turn into her best ever, complete with monster hunt, camping trip, and the perfect gifts.

Root, Phyllis. 1996. *Contrary Bear*. Illustrated by Laura Cornell. New York: HarperCollins Children's Book Group. In this humorous story, Father has many occasions to be irritated with both his daughter and her friend, Contrary Bear, and usually reacts with much patience and effective discipline.

Skofield, James. 1993. *'Round and Around*. Illustrated by James Graham Hale. New York: HarperCollins Publishers. While on a walk with his father and their dog, Sam, Dan observes many things in nature that move in circles. But as the sun sets and dad teaches Dan that even the Earth moves in a circle, Dan observes that the best circle of all is a hug.

Smith, Will. 1999. *Just the Two of Us*. Illustrated by Kadir Nelson. New York: Scholastic Press. This book uses the powerful and positive lyrics of Will Smith's song "Just the Two of Us" and beautifully crafted illustrations to depict the growing relationship between a father and his son.

Wolf, Jake. 1998. *Daddy, Could I Have an Elephant?* Illustrated by Marylin Hafner. New York: Penguin Putnam Books for Young Readers. While Dad, who we assume is a single parent, is depicted in a variety of activities such as shaving, cooking, and playing with Tony, they discuss the merits and demerits of keeping a variety of wild animals. This is a fun book in which Dad does it all.

STRONG VERBAL INTERACTION

Bridges, Margaret P. 1999. *If I Were Your Father*. Illustrated by Kady M. Denton. New York: Morrow/Avon. While a father spends the day entertaining and taking care of his young son, they converse about what the son would do if he were the father.

Cazet, Denys. 1993. *Born in the Gravy*. New York: Orchard Books. Margarita tells her papa all about her first day of kindergarten. Features many Spanish words, the meanings of which are translated or implied.

Creech, Sharon. 2000. *Fishing in the Air*. Illustrated by Chris Raschka. New York: Joanna Cotler Books. Father and son embark on a fishing excursion and share many imaginative moments, including a conversation about the father's days as a young boy learning to fish with his father.

Hoberman, Mary Ann. 1991. *Fathers, Mothers, Sisters, Brothers: A Collection of Family Poems*. Illustrated by Marylin Hafner. Boston: Little, Brown & Company. This book of poetry highlights many types of families.

Howard, Elizabeth Fitzgerald. 1995. *Papa Tells Chita a Story*. Illustrated by Floyd Cooper. New York: Simon & Schuster Books for Young Readers. Father and daughter Chita share quality time together after dinner as he recounts his days as a soldier in Cuba during the Spanish-American War.

Quinlan, Patricia. 1987. *My Dad Takes Care of Me*. Illustrated by Vlasta van Kampen. Toronto: Annick Press. Luke's father lost his job and takes cares of him at home now; although he continues to look for jobs, this book presents a stay-at-home dad.

San Souci, Daniel. 1993. *Country Road*. New York: Doubleday Books for Young Readers. Dad and his generally disinterested son go walking along an old road, coming to appreciate the wildlife and one another along the way.

Skofield, James. 1993. *'Round and Around*. Illustrated by James Graham Hale. New York: HarperCollins Publishers. While on a walk with his father and their dog, Sam, Dan observes many things in nature that move in circles. But as the sun sets and dad teaches Dan that even the Earth moves in a circle, Dan observes that the best circle of all is a hug.

Stolz, Mary. 1993. *Say Something*. Illustrated by Alexander Koshkin. New York: HarperCollins Publishers. A young child asks his father to "say something about" many things, revealing his father's spiritual and almost poetic view of the world.

Wolf, Jake. 1998. *Daddy, Could I Have an Elephant?* Illustrated by Marylin Hafner. New York: Penguin Putnam Books for Young Readers. While Dad, who we assume is a single parent, is depicted in a variety of activities such as shaving, cooking, and playing with Tony, they discuss the merits and demerits of keeping a variety of wild animals. This is a fun book in which Dad does it all.

THE WAY THINGS ONCE WERE

Fassler, Joan. 1975. *All Alone With Daddy*. Illustrated by Dorothy Lake Gregory. New York: Human Sciences Press. Ellen dresses up just like her mommy, and wishes for nothing more than to marry a boy just like her daddy.

Puner, Helen Walker. 1946. *Daddies: What They Do All Day*. New York: Lothrop, Lee & Shepard. In this dated text, fathers are depicted in many traditionally masculine careers working "every day for Mommy and you."

QUALITIES OF DADS

ABILITY TO LEARN FROM CHILD

Campbell, Ann-Jeanette. 1998. *Dora's Box*. Illustrated by Fabian Negrin. New York: Alfred A. Knopf Inc. In this tale, based on the Greek mythological character Pandora, a girl grows up without compassion because her parents have prevented her from experiencing evil and sadness. Some parents may see themselves in this overprotective parent role.

Dumbleton, Mike, and Tom Jellett. 1999. *Downsized*. Sydney: Random House Australia. A very shrewd young daughter finds a creative way to get her father out of the slump he has been in since unemployment took over their lives. This upbeat Australian story would be especially therapeutic for families in similar situations.

Ernst, Lisa Campbell. 1993. *Squirrel Park*. New York: Bradbury Press. Stuart's father is an architect and wants his son to follow in his footsteps and think like him. Stuart views life differently, and it takes a crowd of people to get dad to accept and appreciate his son and his son's unique squirrel friend.

Johnson, Dolores. 1994. *Papa's Stories*. New York: Macmillan Publishing Company. An illiterate father realizes that he needs to learn to read when his daughter goes to first grade and discovers that he has been making up the stories in her books all along.

Mahy, Margaret. 2000. *Beaten by a Balloon*. Illustrated by Jonathan Allen. New York: Penguin Putnam Books for Young Readers. Dad's conscientious refusal to buy his son toy weapons, including water pistols, is challenged in this lively story.

Patron, Susan. 1994. *Dark Cloud Strong Breeze*. Illustrated by Peter Catalanotto. New York: Orchard Books. In this fun, rhyming text, a father locks his keys in the car right before a storm breaks, but his daughter saves the day.

Rabe, Berniece. 1988. *Where's Chimpy?* Photo-illustrated by Diane Schmidt. Niles, Ill.: Albert Whitman & Company. Daddy helps his daughter Misty, who has Down Syndrome, find her cherished toy monkey in this book that focuses on bedtime rituals and counting, not on disability.

Silverman, Erica. 1998. *Gittel's Hands*. Illustrated by Deborah Nourse Lattimore. Mahwah, N.J.: Troll Communications, LLC. Yakov, the water carrier, boasts about his daughter's handiwork so much that she is continuously embarrassed; the boasting leads to additional conflicts, which are resolved only when the daughter convinces Yakov to stop lying.

ACCEPTANCE OF CHILD'S INDIVIDUALITY

Curtis, Gavin. 2001. *The Bat Boy & His Violin*. Illustrated by E. B. Lewis. New York: Aladdin Paperbacks. Papa manages a Negro National League team, the Dukes, and assumes that his son will be a talented bat boy, but must accept the fact that Reginald's talent is with the violin instead.

Ernst, Lisa Campbell. 1993. *Squirrel Park*. New York: Bradbury Press. Stuart's father is an architect and wants his son to follow in his footsteps and think like him. Stuart views life differently, and it takes a crowd of people to get dad to accept and appreciate his son and his son's unique squirrel friend.

Friedman, Aileen. 1995. *A Cloak for the Dreamer*. Illustrated by Kim Howard. New York: Scholastic, Inc. A task assigned by a tailor father to his three sons results in very different garments and tests the father's ability to appreciate his sons' individuality.

McClintock, Barbara. 1996. *The Fantastic Drawings of Danielle*. Boston: Houghton Mifflin Company. Father, a French photographer in the late 1800s, is unable to support his daughter's fantastical approach to art, until her artwork ends up supporting both of them.

O'Shaughnessy, Ellen. 1992. *Somebody Called Me a Retard Today . . . and My Heart Felt Sad*. Illustrated by David Garner. New York: Walker & Company. A young girl is called a "retard" at school; her father comforts her and reminds her of her unique and special abilities instead of focusing on her disabilities.

Sebastian, John. 1993. *J.B.'s Harmonica*. Illustrated by Garth Williams. San Diego: Harcourt Brace Jovanovich. J.B. plays harmonica well, but constant comparisons to his father, a professional harmonicist, have him considering quitting.

Shepard, Steve. 1991. *Elvis Hornbill: International Business Bird*. New York: Holt & Company. A human couple adopts a young bird they name Elvis who, despite his father's efforts to persuade him to become a musician, is interested only in finance, business, and computer science.

Spinelli, Eileen. 1993. *Boy, Can He Dance!* Illustrated by Paul Yalowitz. New York: Four Winds Press. Tony loves to dance and seeks nothing more than approval from his father and grandfather, both chefs who encourage him to continue the family business.

PATIENCE

Buckley, Helen E. 1994. *Grandfather and I*. Illustrated by Jan Ormerod. New York: HarperCollins Publishers. A child often told to hurry recounts a special relationship he has with his grandfather, in which they spend quality time together walking, reading, and taking as long as they like.

Camp, Lindsay. 1998. *Why?* Illustrated by Tony Ross. New York: The Putnam Publishing Group. A comical look at the typical questioning stage young children go through, and although Lily's dad, who appears to be parenting solo, does not always exhibit patience, he is learning!

Heap, Sue. 1998. *Cowboy Baby*. Cambridge, Mass.: Candlewick Press. The bedtime routine is extended a bit while Sheriff Pa allows Cowboy Baby to search for his stuffed animals and then continues his playful role in a game of hide-and-seek.

Janovitz, Marilyn. 1998. *Can I Help?* New York: North-South Books, Inc. Father wolf exhibits much patience and love, as his young cub eagerly "assists" with outdoor chores.

Ketteman, Helen. 1992. *Not Yet, Yvette*. Illustrated by Irene Trivas. Morton Grove, Ill.: Albert Whitman & Company. Yvette and her father clean the house, go shopping, and bake a cake for her mom's birthday. Mom is a veterinarian and dad appears to stay at home with Yvette.

Lambert, Paulette Livers. 1995. *Evening: An Appalachian Lullaby*. Niwot, Colo.: Roberts Rinehart Publishers. It is bedtime on the farm; father patiently attends to the extended ritual with his young sons before relaxing on the porch with his fiddle.

London, Jonathan. 1994. *Let's Go, Froggy!* Illustrated by Frank Remkiewicz. New York: Viking. In this repetitious, fun text, Froggy awakes to a beautiful day and the promise of an extra-special picnic and bike ride with his dad; that is, if he gets ready in time.

Martin, David. 2001. *Piggy and Dad*. Illustrated by Frank Remkiewicz. Cambridge, Mass.: Candlewick Press. This set of four books designed to help beginning readers captures a truly loving relationship between Piggy and his dad. Titles included are *Piggy's Bath*, *Piggy's Bedtime*, *Piggy's Sandwich*, and *Piggy's Pictures*.

McMullan, Kate. 1994. *Good Night, Stella*. Illustrated by Emma Chichester Clark. Cambridge, Mass.: Candlewick Press. Young Stella's imagination overflows at bedtime, making sleep impossible, but Dad, who is the caretaker for the evening, exercises much patience and cleverness in this humorous story.

Ormerod, Jan. *Messy Baby*. See **Series**.

Rabe, Berniece. 1988. *Where's Chimpy?* Photo-illustrated by Diane Schmidt. Niles, Ill.: Albert Whitman & Company. Daddy helps his daughter Misty, who has Down Syndrome, find her cherished toy monkey in this book that focuses on bedtime rituals and counting, not on disability.

San Souci, Daniel. 1993. *Country Road*. New York: Doubleday Books for Young Readers. Dad and his generally disinterested son go walking along an old road, coming to appreciate the wildlife and one another along the way.

Wadsworth, Ginger. 1994. *Tomorrow Is Daddy's Birthday*. Illustrated by Maxie Chambliss. Honesdale, Penn.: Boyds Mills Press. Rachel is so excited about the gift she will be giving her father for his birthday that she cannot help but share her secret with those around her.

Waggoner, Karen. 1992. *Lemonade Babysitter*. Illustrated by Dorothy Donohue. Boston: Little, Brown & Company. Neither gender nor generational differences keep spunky young Molly and Mr. Herbert, a grandfatherly neighborhood baby-sitter with a ton of patience, from establishing a wonderful relationship.

Walters, Virginia. 1999. *Are We There Yet, Daddy?* Illustrated by S. D. Schindler. New York: Viking. This rhyming, repetitive text counts down the miles on a 100-mile journey to Grandma's house as a patient father responds to that all-too-frequently asked question.

Wolf, Jake. 1998. *Daddy, Could I Have an Elephant?* Illustrated by Marylin Hafner. New York: Penguin Putnam Books for Young Readers. While Dad, who we assume is a single parent, is depicted in a variety of activities such as shaving, cooking, and playing with Tony, they discuss the merits and demerits of keeping a variety of wild animals. This is a fun book in which Dad does it all.

Ziefert, Harriet. 2001. *No Kiss for Grandpa.* Illustrated by Emilie Boon. New York: Orchard Books. A day at the beach with grouchy Louie is no day at the beach for Grandpa, who has enough patience for himself and for one ornery grandson.

PLAYFULNESS

Anderson, Peggy Perry. 2001. *To the Tub.* Boston: Houghton Mifflin Company. Parents will especially relate to the frustrated father frog's attempts to get junior to the bathtub, and both children and parents will enjoy the ending, in which father's playful side takes over.

Buckley, Helen E. 1999. *Where Did Josie Go?* Illustrated by Jan Ormerod. New York: Morrow/Avon. Readers can participate in the search for Josie, along with Mom and Dad, who indulge in this now classic game of hide-and-seek. Toddlers might ask questions regarding Mom's big stomach!

Catalanotto, Peter. 1999. *The Painter.* New York: Scholastic, Inc. A father balances parenting responsibilities, including imaginative and silly playtime with his young daughter, and work responsibilities in his art studio.

Friend, David. 1990. *Baseball, Football, Daddy and Me.* Illustrated by Rick Brown. New York: Viking. Father and son are the ultimate sports enthusiasts.

Heap, Sue. 1998. *Cowboy Baby.* Cambridge, Mass.: Candlewick Press. The bedtime routine is extended a bit while Sheriff Pa allows Cowboy Baby to search for his stuffed animals and then continues his playful role in a game of hide-and-seek.

Hines, Anna Grossnickle. 1986. *Daddy Makes the Best Spaghetti.* New York: Clarion Books. Corey's Dad creatively shares many domestic and parenting duties with Mom, including making dinner, becoming Bathman at bath time, and tucking in one very loved boy.

Mahy, Margaret. 2000. *Down the Dragon's Tongue.* Illustrated by Patricia MacCarthy. New York: Orchard Books. Mr. Prospero, a businessman and orderly father, is reluctant to join his twins on the Dragon's Tongue, the fastest slide at the park, until he realizes that having fun with his children is much more important than keeping his suit neatly pressed.

Mandelbaum, Pili. 1990. *You Be Me, I'll Be You.* New York: Kane/Miller Book Publishers. When Anna complains that she does not like her dark skin and curly hair, dad gets creative. This depiction of a biracial family is a beautiful one, marked by one very special child.

Manushkin, Fran. 1994. *Peeping and Sleeping.* Illustrated by Jennifer Plecas. New York: Clarion Books. When Barry cannot sleep because of a mysterious and scary "PEEP-peep" he hears outside his window, Daddy promises to stay close as they go exploring outside at night.

McBratney, Sam. 1999. *Guess How Much I Love You/Adivina Cuanto Te Quiero.* Illustrated by Anita Jeram. Nashville: Tommy Nelson. Big Nutbrown Hare and Little Nutbrown Hare try to outdo each other's measures of love while frolicking around in this popular bedtime book.

Pringle, Laurence. 2001. *Octopus Hug.* Illustrated by Kate S. Palmer. Honesdale, Penn.: Boyds Mills Press. While Mom enjoys an evening out, Dad entertains the children with loving, physically interactive games.

Williams, Vera B. 1990. *"More More More," Said the Baby: Three Love Stories.* New York: Greenwillow Books. This wonderfully colorful book will either make you want to be a little baby again, being tossed and tickled and talked to tenderly, or make you want to emulate the loving daddy and other adults providing all the fun.

RESOURCEFULNESS

Brillhart, Julie. 1997. *When Daddy Took Us Camping.* Morton Grove, Ill.: Albert Whitman & Company. Dad has an amazing ability to create an authentic camping experience for his children under unusual circumstances.

Hamanaka, Sheila. 1995. *Bebop-A-Do-Walk!* New York: Simon & Schuster Books for Young Readers. Emi, her friend, Martha, and her father take one very long walk all over the city of New York.

Lemieux, Margo. 1996. *Paul and the Wolf.* Illustrated by Bill Nelson. Parsippany, N.J.: Silver Burdett Press. Having been exposed to *Peter and the Wolf* at school, a boy fears wolves at bedtime, until Dad alleviates his fears with a Native American wolf tale and personal commentary.

Munson, Derek. 2000. *Enemy Pie.* Illustrated by Tara Calahan King. San Francisco: Chronicle Books. It was shaping up to be the best summer ever for a young boy, when Jeremy Ross moved to the neighborhood, becoming his first enemy. Fortunately, dad had enemies growing up too, and he has just the recipe to take care of them: enemy pie!

Shannon, George. 1993. *Climbing Kansas Mountains.* Illustrated by Thomas B. Allen. New York: Bradbury Press. A creative father helps alleviate his son's summertime boredom as they seek out mountains to climb in Kansas.

Soto, Gary. 1998. *Big Bushy Mustache.* Illustrated by Joe Cepeda. New York: Random House, Inc. Father comes to the rescue when his son loses a fake mustache—his paternal identity—in this warm family story.

Steig, William. 1998. *Pete's a Pizza*. New York: HarperCollins Publishers. When rain puts Pete in a bad mood, Dad saves the day by transforming his son into a pizza.

Tunnell, Michael O. 2000. *Mailing May*, Illustrated by Ted Rand. New York: Morrow/Avon. Based on a true story that took place in the early 1900s, a father finds a clever way to circumvent the train fare that otherwise would have prohibited his daughter from visiting Grandma.

SACRIFICE AND UNSELFISHNESS

Brown, Forman. 1991. *The Generous Jefferson Bartleby Jones*. Illustrated by Leslie Trawin. Boston: Alyson Wonderland. Young Jeff is so pleased to have two dads that he loans them out to his friends who are neglected by their own fathers.

Bunting, Eve. 1996. *Going Home*. Illustrated by David Diaz. New York: HarperCollins. Joanna Cotler Books. Carlos and his family are going home to Mexico for Christmas, but how can home be in America *and* in Mexico? This book features extremely self-sacrificing parents who would do anything to provide better opportunities for their children.

Hendershot, Judith. 1987. *In Coal Country*. Illustrated by Thomas B. Allen. New York: Alfred A. Knopf. In this vivid account of life in a small 1930s coal town, Papa is a coal miner who works hard for his family.

Ketteman, Helen. 1998. *I Remember Papa*. Illustrated by Greg Shed. New York: Penguin Putnam Books for Young Readers. The lessons a father taught his son, such as the importance of saving money, of forgiveness, and of parental sacrifices, are remembered for a lifetime in this story about a father and son's passion for baseball.

Posey, Lee. 1999. *Night Rabbits*. Illustrated by Michael G. Montgomery. Atlanta: Peachtree Publishers, Ltd. When a daughter's love of rabbits conflicts with a father's well-tended lawn, the father realizes that the lawn belongs to everyone.

Soto, Gary. 1998. *Big Bushy Mustache*. Illustrated by Joe Cepeda. New York: Random House, Inc. Father comes to the rescue when his son loses a fake mustache—his paternal identity—in this warm family story.

WHEN DAD KNOWS BEST

Barber, Barbara E. 1996. *Allie's Basketball Dream*. Illustrated by Darryl Ligasan. New York: Lee & Low Books, Inc. When Allie gets a new basketball from her father she has hopes of one day becoming a professional basketball player, but first she must combat her peers and their very solidly placed gender ideas that insist basketball is for boys and jumping rope is for girls.

Cook, Jean Thor. 1995. *Room for a Stepdaddy*. Illustrated by Martine Gourbault. Morton Grove, Ill.: Albert Whitman & Company. Joey has a very hard time adjusting to a life with three parents—Mom, Dad, and his new stepdaddy, Bill—but ultimately he comes to believe the wisdom his father imparted to him: love is like the sand on the beach; there is always enough to go around.

Lasky, Kathryn. 1997. *Marven of the Great North Woods*. Illustrated by Kevin Hawkes. New York: Harcourt Brace & Company. When an influenza epidemic spread across American in 1918, Marven Lasky's father decided it would be best if the boy was sent to live with French Canadian lumberjacks in the great north woods of Minnesota to be kept safe from the disease. This is the true story of the author's father.

Marks, Alan. 1993. *The Thief's Daughter*. New York: Farrar, Straus & Giroux. Magpie, whose poor father tells her magnificent stories about royal households, discovers the truth behind her father's life and learns an important lesson about honesty in this fairy-tale-like beginning chapter book.

O'Shaughnessy, Ellen. 1992. *Somebody Called Me a Retard Today . . . and My Heart Felt Sad*. Illustrated by David Garner. New York: Walker & Company. A young girl is called a "retard" at school; her father comforts her and reminds her of her unique and special abilities instead of focusing on her disabilities.

Stanley, Sanna. 1998. *Monkey Sunday: A Story from a Congolese Village*. New York: Farrar, Straus & Giroux. In this humorous African family story, Luzolo, an active young girl, struggles to complete her father's challenge that she remain seated while he preaches.

Wyeth, Sharon Dennis. 1995. *Always My Dad*. Illustrated by Raúl Colón. New York: Knopf. Dad is having problems "getting his life together"; his constant shifting from job to job and his lack of presence in his children's lives have them all upset.

EXCEPTIONALLY POSITIVE DADS—THE BEST!

Brillhart, Julie. 1995. *When Daddy Came to School*. Morton Grove, Ill.: Albert Whitman & Company. On his son's third birthday, Daddy spends the day with him at preschool—a gift more precious than anything money could buy. This book earns four gold stars for patience, humility, humor, and energy!

———. 1997. *When Daddy Took Us Camping*. Morton Grove, Ill.: Albert Whitman & Company. Dad has an amazing ability to create an authentic camping experience for his children under unusual circumstances, which earns him a big "ten."

Gugler, Laurel Dee. 1997. *Muddle Cuddle*. Illustrated by Vlasta van Kampen. Toronto: Annick Press. A young boy and his twin sisters crowd daddy's lap with themselves and their sundry toys; dad remains patient and loving.

Mandelbaum, Pili. 1990. *You Be Me, I'll Be You*. New York: Kane/Miller Book Publishers. When Anna complains that she does not like her dark skin and curly hair, dad gets creative. Dad's positivity and cleverness in the face of an important racial issue wins him this distinction.

Martin, David. 2001. *Piggy and Dad*. Illustrated by Frank Remkiewicz. Cambridge, Mass.: Candlewick Press. This set of four books designed to help beginning readers captures a truly loving relationship between Piggy and his dad. Titles included are *Piggy's Bath*, *Piggy's Bedtime*, *Piggy's Sandwich*, and *Piggy's Pictures*.

Miller, Margaret. 1994. *Where's Jenna?* New York: Simon & Schuster Books for Young Readers. Dad's award-winning smile, easygoing demeanor, and positive parenting skills—while feeding the baby and being "attacked" by a preschooler—win him a place in this category.

O'Shaughnessy, Ellen. 1992. *Somebody Called Me a Retard Today . . . and My Heart Felt Sad*. Illustrated by David Garner. New York: Walker & Company. A young girl is called a "retard" at school; her father comforts her and reminds her of her unique and special abilities instead of focusing on her disabilities.

Wolf, Jake. 1998. *Daddy, Could I Have an Elephant?* Illustrated by Marylin Hafner. New York: Penguin Putnam Books for Young Readers. While Dad, who we assume is a single parent, is depicted in a variety of activities such as shaving, cooking, and playing with Tony, they discuss the merits and demerits of keeping a variety of wild animals. This is a fun book in which Dad does it all.

EXCEPTIONALLY NEGATIVE DADS—THE WORST!

Babbitt, Natalie. 1998. *Ouch! A Tale from Grimm Retold by Natalie Babbitt*. Illustrated by Fred Marcellino. New York: HarperCollins Publishers. Marco, a poor nobody, is destined from birth to marry the princess, but her evil father will hear nothing of it! This is the clever and fun retelling of a lesser-known Grimm tale of a very confident young man's meeting with Devil's Grandmother, and of the evil king's monotonous fate.

Brenner, Barbara. 1995. *Wagon Wheels*. Photo-illustrated by Don Bolognese. New York: HarperCollins Children's Book Group. Father would likely be found guilty of child abuse today for abandoning his young sons for four months with little more than a dugout for shelter and a rifle for hunting their own food. He then expects them to walk 150 miles with just a map for a guide, in this 19th-century story.

Browne, Anthony. 1983. *Gorilla*. New York: Alfred A. Knopf. Hannah's toy gorilla comes to life and takes the place of her father, doing all of the activities he is always too busy to do.

———. 1986. *Piggybook*. New York: Alfred A. Knopf. Mr. Piggott and his two sons, Simon and Patrick, are of no help to Mrs. Piggott, who decides to leave and teach them a lesson about helping out. The house goes to ruin and the male Piggotts turn into pigs by the time she returns.

Ernst, Lisa Campbell. 1993. *Squirrel Park*. New York: Bradbury Press. Stuart's father is an architect and wants his son to follow in his footsteps and think like him. Stuart views life differently, and it takes a crowd of people to get dad to accept and appreciate his son and his son's unique squirrel friend.

Eyvindsom, Peter. 1991. *Old Enough*. Illustrated by Wendy Wolsak. Winnipeg: Pemmican Publications, Inc. A father who neglected his growing son learns from his mistakes and appreciates his newborn grandchild—a bad dad turned good.

Houston, Gloria. 1998. *Littlejim's Gift: An Appalachian Christmas Story*. Illustrated by Thomas B. Allen. New York: Penguin Putnam Books for Young Readers. Readers will find it difficult to empathize with Papa, who tells his son that he "ain't much of a man" and then proceeds to work him all day long without food, until his feet and hands are numb from the cold. For a full portrait of this stern, insensitive father read the chapter book *Littlejim* (1990).

McKenzie, Ellen Kindt. 1993. *The King, the Princess, and the Tinker*. Illustrated by William Low. New York: Henry Holt Books for Young Readers. A king's fathering role consists only of annual inspections of the children to see that they are growing, and at no time are the children or the queen allowed to look at him, which tends to create strained relationships. This fun chapter book will appeal to all ages.

Rathmann, Peggy. 1998. *10 Minutes Till Bedtime*. New York: Penguin Putnam Books for Young Readers. This story is clever, cute, and highly recommended, but the father gets an "F" in "bedtime rituals." Completely immersed in the newspaper, not only is he ignorant of the antics going on, he is totally negligent about teeth brushing and assisting with other hygienic activities. Where's the bathtub rub-a-dub play? Where's the bedtime story? (For better role models, see the section on **Bedtime and Fears**.)

Steptoe, John. 1980. *Daddy Is a Monster . . . Sometimes*. New York: J. B. Lippincott, Daddy sometimes turns into a monster, yelling and spanking, but he insists it is only because he has monsters for children.

Stewig, John Warren. 1999. *King Midas*. Illustrated by Omar Rayyan. New York: Holiday House, Inc. This father's obsession with money detracts a bit from quality time with his daughter, when, like everything else he touches, she turns into gold.

FAMILY PORTRAITS

AFRICAN AMERICAN FAMILIES

Barber, Barbara E. 1996. *Allie's Basketball Dream*. Illustrated by Darryl Ligasan. New York: Lee & Low Books, Inc. When Allie gets a new basketball from her father, she has hopes of one day becoming a professional basketball player, but first she must combat her peers and their very solidly placed gender ideas that insist basketball is for boys and jumping rope is for girls.

Bradby, Marie. 1995. *The Longest Wait*. Illustrated by Peter Catalanotto. New York: Scholastic, Inc. Daddy must deliver mail by horseback in a snowstorm, which creates anxiety in a son awaiting his safe return, and delays snow playing time. A nice family portrait.

Buckley, Helen E. 1994. *Grandfather and I*. Illustrated by Jan Ormerod. New York: HarperCollins Publishers. A child often told to hurry recounts a special relationship he has with his grandfather, in which they spend quality time together walking, reading, and taking as long as they like.

Bunting, Eve. 1998. *Your Move*. Illustrated by James Ransome. San Diego: Harcourt Brace & Company. James always stays home to take care of his little brother, Isaac, at night when his mom goes to work, but tonight the two will experience something much more terrifying. This riveting book offers a glimpse into an extremely positive and responsible brotherly relationship, and would be great for discussions about gangs, violence, or guns.

Caines, Jeannette. 1977. *Daddy*. Illustrated by Ronald Himler. New York: Harper & Row. This is a simple, charming story of a noncustodial father and the time he shares with his daughter, Windy, on Saturdays.

Carter, Dorothy. 1999. *Wilhe'mina Miles After the Stork Night*. Illustrated by Harvey Stevenson. New York: Farrar, Straus & Giroux. While working in New York City, Daddy regularly sends home letters and money, which are appreciated, but his presence cannot be replaced so easily, especially the night that Wilhe'mina becomes a big sister.

Clifton, Lucille. 1977. *Amifika*. Illustrated by Thomas DiGrazia. New York: E. P. Dutton. Amifika hears his mother discussing his father's homecoming and the lack of room in their small apartment and becomes afraid that he will be one of the things thrown out to make room for daddy.

———. 1983. *Everett Anderson's Goodbye*. Illustrated by Ann Grifalconi. New York: Henry Holt & Company. This book outlines the five stages of grief—denial, anger, bargaining, depression, and acceptance—through the use of a child whose father has just died.

Cooke, Trish. 2000. *The Grandad Tree*. Illustrated by Sharon Wilson. Cambridge, Mass.: Candlewick Press. Focusing on life cycles, this book depicts growth and remembrance through the symbol of the family apple tree. After their Grandad dies, Leigh and Vin cherish even more dearly the apple tree and the wonderful times they had there with him.

Cummings, Pat. 1994. *Carousel*. New York: Simon & Schuster Children's Publishing. Not even a toy carousel, a special gift from Daddy, can dull the anger that a young girl feels when he accidentally misses her birthday.

Curtis, Gavin. 2001. *The Bat Boy & His Violin*. Illustrated by E. B. Lewis. New York: Aladdin Paperbacks. Papa manages a Negro National League team, the Dukes, and assumes that his son will be a talented bat boy, but must accept the fact that Reginald's talent is with the violin instead.

Gilchrist, Jan Spivey. 1997. *Madelia*. New York: Penguin Putnam Books for Young Readers. A preacher father uses the Sunday sermon to inspire his young aspiring artist.

Greenfield, Eloise. 1993. *First Pink Light*. Illustrated by Jan Spivey Gilchrist. New York: Writers & Readers Publishing, Inc. A young boy awaits the return of his father, who is expected home in early morning. The illustrations especially convey the love and admiration felt between the boy and his father.

———. 1993. *Lisa's Daddy and Daughter Day*. Illustrated by Jan Spivey Gilchrist. Littleton, Mass.: Sundance Publishing. Spending the whole day with daddy, talking and taking it easy, is special for his daughter.

———. 1991. *My Daddy and I*. Illustrated by Jan Spivey Gilchrist. New York: Black Butterfly Children's Books. Cooking, cleaning, reading—daddy and son do everything together in this board book best suited for preschoolers.

Greenspun, Adele Aron. 1991. *Daddies*. New York: Philomel Books. This simple book with touching black-and-white photographs captures the many ways fathers love their children.

Grifalconi, Ann. 1999. *Tiny's Hat*. New York: HarperCollins Children's Book Group. Tiny's father is a blues musician who travels a lot; when he is away for long periods, she gets the blues herself.

Haskins, James. 1994. *The Headless Haunt and Other African-American Ghost Stories*. Illustrated by Ben Otero. New York: HarperCollins Publishers. With special emphasis on stories influenced by African and African American traditions, this book is perfect for the older, thrill-seeking reader.

Heron, Ann, and Meredith Maran. 1991. *How Would You Feel If Your Dad Was Gay?* Illustrated by Kris Kovick. Boston: Alyson Wonderland. When Michael's sister, Jasmine, announces in her class that she has three dads, the entire elementary school starts talking about them.

Hoberman, Mary Ann. 1991. *Fathers, Mothers, Sisters, Brothers: A Collection of Family Poems*. Illustrated by Marylin Hafner. Boston: Little, Brown & Company. This book of poetry highlights many types of families.

Hoffman, Mary. 2000. *Boundless Grace*. Illustrated by Caroline Binch. New York: Penguin Putnam Books for Young Readers. When Grace visits her remarried father in Africa, he and his family help to dispel Grace's limited notions about families, fathers, and stepmothers, culled from reading fairy tales. This is the sequel to *Amazing Grace* (1998).

Hort, Lenny. 1997. *How Many Stars in the Sky*. Illustrated by James E. Ransome. New York: Morrow/Avon. Daddy's sense of adventure combines with his son's restlessness to portray a nurturing relationship and an overnight encounter with nature.

Howard, Elizabeth Fitzgerald. 1995. *Papa Tells Chita a Story*. Illustrated by Floyd Cooper. New York: Simon & Schuster Books for Young Readers. Father and Chita share quality time together after dinner as he recounts his days as a soldier in Cuba during the Spanish-American War.

Johnson, Angela. 2000. *Daddy Calls Me Man*. Illustrated by Rhonda Mitchell. New York: Scholastic, Inc. The secure and loving environment that his parents have provided are demonstrated in a young boy's poetic enthusiasm for life, and daddy's statement is like icing on a cake.

———. 1994. *Joshua's Night Whispers*. Illustrated by Rhonda Mitchell. New York: Orchard Books. Joshua is awakened by night whispers and finds comfort in his father's arms in this board book.

———. 1990. *When I Am Old with You*. Illustrated by David Soman. New York: Orchard Books. A little boy imagines all the fun he and his granddaddy will have spending quality time together in the future while having a wonderful time in the present.

Johnson, Dolores. 1994. *Papa's Stories*. New York: Macmillan Publishing Company. An illiterate father realizes that he needs to learn to read when his daughter goes to first grade and discovers that he has been making up the stories in her books all along.

———. 1993. *Your Dad Was Just Like You*. New York: Simon & Schuster Children's Publishing. Grandfather shares succinct bits and pieces about his son's childhood with Peter, his grandson, creating more than just memories.

Ketteman, Helen. 1992. *Not Yet, Yvette*. Illustrated by Irene Trivas. Morton Grove, Ill.: Albert Whitman & Company. Yvette and her father clean the house, go shopping, and bake a cake for her mom's birthday. Mom is a veterinarian and dad appears to stay at home with Yvette.

May, Kathy L. 2000. *Molasses Man*. Illustrated by Felicia Marshall. New York: Holiday House. Grandpa works with his family to make fresh molasses, paying special attention to a young grandson who will be the next Molasses Man.

Medearis, Angela S. 1994. *Our People*. Illustrated by Michael Bryant. New York: Atheneum Books for Young Readers. Father's history lessons are intertwined with play activities, such as building blocks and piggyback riding, providing inspiration for his daughter to imagine and dream.

Moutoussamy-Ashe, Jeanne. 1993. *Daddy and Me: A Photo Story of Arthur Ashe and His Daughter Camera*. New York: Alfred A. Knopf. This photo-essay featuring Arthur Ashe and his daughter, Camera, depicts the true love this famous father shared with his daughter. A wonderful book for discussions about AIDS, unconditional love, and living with illness.

Patrick, Denise Lewis. 1993. *The Car Washing Street*. Illustrated by John Ward. New York: Morrow/Avon. Matthew and his father share quality time together while also participating in a bit of boisterous neighborhood camaraderie.

Pringle, Laurence. 2001. *Octopus Hug*. Illustrated by Kate S. Palmer. Honesdale, Penn.: Boyds Mills Press. While Mom enjoys an evening out, Dad entertains the children with loving, physically interactive games.

Schertle, Alice. 2000. *Down the Road*. Illustrated by E. B. Lewis. San Diego: Harcourt Children's Books. When Hetty gets sidetracked on her way home from the market and the eggs end up broken, Papa reacts with kindness and understanding, rather than with punishment and lectures.

Smalls-Hector, Irene. 1999. *Kevin and His Dad*. Illustrated by Michael Hays. Boston: Little, Brown and Company. On Saturdays, while Mom is away, a father and son have fun cleaning the house together before engaging in more typically amusing activities.

Smith, Eddie. 1994. *A Lullaby for Daddy*. Illustrated by Susan Anderson. Lawrenceville, N.J.: Africa World Press. Daddy, a musician, and his young daughter compose a lullaby together, which they sing as part of their bedtime ritual.

Smith, Will. 1999. *Just the Two of Us*. Illustrated by Kadir Nelson. New York: Scholastic Press. This book uses the powerful and positive lyrics of Will Smith's song "Just the Two of Us" and beautifully crafted illustrations to depict the growing relationship between a father and his son.

Steptoe, Javaka, illustrator. 2001. *In Daddy's Arms I Am Tall: African Americans Celebrating Fathers*. New York: Lee & Low Books, Inc. A captivating picture book anthology of poems that portray as many different feelings about fathers as there are authors. There is something here for all age groups.

Steptoe, John. 1980. *Daddy Is a Monster . . . Sometimes*. New York: J. B. Lippincott. Daddy sometimes turns into a monster, yelling and spanking, but he insists it is only because he has monsters for children.

Williams, Sherley Anne. 1992. *Working Cotton*. Illustrated by Carole Byard. San Diego: Harcourt Brace Jovanovich. This story about migrant workers features a family working hard together and a father whose children are proud of his speed and skill at cotton-picking.

Wyeth, Sharon Dennis. 1995. *Always My Dad*. Illustrated by Raúl Colón. New York: Knopf. Dad is having problems "getting his life together"; his constant shifting from job to job and his lack of presence in his children's lives have them all upset.

ASIAN AMERICAN FAMILIES

Greenspun, Adele Aron. 1991. *Daddies*. New York: Philomel Books. This simple book with touching black-and-white photographs captures the many ways fathers love their children.

Hamanaka, Sheila. 1995. *Bebop-A-Do-Walk!* New York: Simon & Schuster Books for Young Readers. Emi, her friend, Martha, and her father take one very long walk all over the city of New York.

Hoberman, Mary Ann. 1991. *Fathers, Mothers, Sisters, Brothers: A Collection of Family Poems*. Illustrated by Marylin Hafner. Boston: Little, Brown & Company. This book of poetry highlights many types of families.

Garland, Sherry. 1998. *My Father's Boat*. Illustrated by Ted Rand. New York: Scholastic, Inc. A Vietnamese American shrimper teaches his son the tricks of the trade one special day, causing him to reminisce about his own father back in Vietnam. An especially warm, poetic text is prefaced with this appropriate Vietnamese proverb: "When you are young, you need your father; when you are old, you need your son." This father represents both strong and tender sides of parenting.

Mochizuki, Ken. 1995. *Heroes*. Illustrated by Dom Lee. New York: Lee & Low Books, Inc. Donnie, who is Asian American, always has to be the "bad guy" when he and his friends play war because his friends will not believe that his father and uncle are decorated military heroes. This book is dedicated to the many people of Asian and Pacific Islander descent who have defended America with little or no recognition.

BIRACIAL FAMILIES

Hoberman, Mary Ann. 1991. *Fathers, Mothers, Sisters, Brothers: A Collection of Family Poems*. Illustrated by Marylin Hafner. Boston: Little, Brown & Company. This book of poetry highlights many types of families.

Kandel, Bethany. 1997. *Trevor's Story: Growing Up Biracial*. Photo-illustrated by Carol Halebian. Minneapolis: Lerner Publishing Group. Fifth grader Trevor, who has an African American father and a Caucasian mother, narrates the pros and cons of growing up in a biracial family and how he copes with outside attitudes, such as racism.

Mandelbaum, Pili. 1990. *You Be Me, I'll Be You*. New York: Kane/Miller Book Publishers. When Anna complains that she does not like her dark skin and curly hair, dad gets creative. This depiction of a biracial family is a beautiful one, marked by one very special child.

Munsch, Robert. 1990. *Something Good*. Illustrated by Michael Martchenko. Toronto: Annick Press. Dad and the kids are grocery shopping, but one very motivated and vocal daughter wants him to buy some "good" food: ice cream and candy. Although the story is not about being biracial, the illustrations depict a biracial family.

Senisi, Ellen B. 1998. *For My Family, Love, Allie*. Morton Grove, Ill.: Albert Whitman & Company. In this extended family gathering, which is a celebration of Jamaican food and culture, grandfathers, uncles, and fathers all share cooking and parenting responsibilities with the women. Photographs depict Allie's biracial parents and the upbeat occasion.

Spohn, David. *Home Field*, *Nate's Treasure*, *Starry Night*, and *Winter Wood*. See **Series**.

Turner, Ann. 1990. *Through Moon and Stars and Night Skies*. Illustrated by James Graham Hale. New York: Harper & Row. A Charlotte Zolotow Book, A young boy enjoys retelling his mother the story of his adoption and fearful journey to live with his new parents.

Winthrop, Elizabeth. 1998. *As the Crow Flies*. Illustrated by Joan Sandin. New York: Clarion Books. Mikey's parents are divorced; he lives with his mother in Arizona and his father lives in Delaware, "seven states away as the crow flies." Dad's annual visit brings lots of special memories and a wonderful surprise. The illustrations depict a biracial family.

EXTENDED FAMILIES

Carson, Jo. 1992. *You Hold Me and I'll Hold You*. Illustrated by Annie Cannon. New York: Orchard Books. Dad, who is a single parent, tenderly comforts his daughter at a family funeral.

Eversole, Robyn H. 1998. *The Gift Stone*. Illustrated by Allen Garns. New York: Alfred A. Knopf Books for Young Readers. Dad has found work in an opal mine, which means living underground, and Jean misses her old house with real windows and grass outside, or wishes she could live with Grandma and Granddad, who are unable to support her. This Australian story blends hardships with hope, and depicts various types of family relationships.

Hoberman, Mary Ann. 1991. *Fathers, Mothers, Sisters, Brothers: A Collection of Family Poems*. Illustrated by Marylin Hafner. Boston: Little, Brown & Company. This book of poetry highlights many types of families.

Rylant, Cynthia. 1985. *The Relatives Came*. Illustrated by Stephen Gammell. New York: Bradbury Press. The relatives come to visit in this humorous tale, crowding the house and bringing with them many joyful family moments.

Senisi, Ellen B. 1998. *For My Family, Love, Allie*. Morton Grove, Ill.: Albert Whitman & Company. In this extended family gathering, which is a celebration of Jamaican food and culture, grandfathers, uncles, and fathers all share cooking and parenting responsibilities with the women. Photographs depict Allie's biracial parents and the upbeat occasion.

FAMILIES AROUND THE WORLD

Aliki. 1998. *Marianthe's Story: Painted Words and Spoken Memories*. New York: HarperCollins Children's Book Group. The males, including Marianthe's father and her new teacher, are depicted in nurturing roles in these two stories about a young immigrant girl adjusting to school in America.

Anaya, Rudolfo. 1998. *The Farolitos of Christmas*. Illustrated by Edward Gonzalez. New York: Hyperion Paperbacks for Children. In this warm World War II-era story, father is wounded and hospitalized, and Grandfather (Abuelo) is too ill to create the traditional luminarias, which forces Luz, her friends, and her family to prepare for Christmas on their own.

Bernard, Robin. 1996. *Juma and the Honey-Guide: An African Tale*. Illustrated by Nneka Bennett. Parsippany, N.J.: Silver Burdett Press. A Dorobo father teaches his eager son how to follow a *kidege*, or bird, to locate honey, but has much difficulty convincing him of the customary *asante*, or thank-you.

Carling, Amelia Lau. 1998. *Mama & Papa Have a Store*. New York: Penguin Putnam Books for Young Readers. Both mother and father share parenting and work responsibilities in this colorful story about a Chinese family operating a retail store in Guatemala.

Carney, Margaret. 1998. *At Grandpa's Sugar Bush*. Illustrated by Janet Wilson. Toronto: Kids Can Press, Ltd. During Spring Break, Grandpa gets extra help with sugaring from his enthusiastic nephew, who narrates the story, thus providing a new generation with sugaring know-how.

Eversole, Robyn H. 1998. *The Gift Stone*. Illustrated by Allen Garns. New York: Alfred A. Knopf Books for Young Readers. Dad has found work in an opal mine, which means living underground, and Jean misses her old house with real windows and grass outside, or wishes she could live with Grandma and Granddad, who are unable to support her. This Australian story blends hardships with hope.

Hanson, Regina. 1995. *The Tangerine Tree*. Illustrated by Harvey Stevenson. Boston: Houghton Mifflin Company. Papa must leave his impoverished Jamaican family for work in New York, but a book given to his young daughter, along with reading goals, will help to shorten the time that he is away.

Hoberman, Mary Ann. 1991. *Fathers, Mothers, Sisters, Brothers: A Collection of Family Poems*. Illustrated by Marylin Hafner. Boston: Little, Brown & Company. This book of poetry highlights many types of families.

Isadora, Rachel. 2000. *At The Crossroads*. New York: Morrow/Avon. The emotions that Zolani, his siblings, and his friends feel for their fathers, who have been away for 10 months working in the South African mines, are strongly indicative of the importance of fathers in children's lives.

Lewin, Hugh. 1994. *Jafta: The Homecoming*. Illustrated by Lisa Kopper. New York: Knopf. Things are changing in South Africa; soon Jafta's father will be able to come home from the city where he has been working. See also *Jafta's Father*.

McKay, Lawrence Jr. 1995. *Caravan*. Illustrated by Darryl Ligasan. New York: Lee & Low Books, Inc. Based on the lifestyle of Kirghiz caravaneers in Afghanistan, this story is about a 10-year-old son who literally travels in his father's footsteps.

Mennen, Ingrid. 1994. *One Round Moon and a Star for Me*. Illustrated by Niki Daly. New York: Orchard Books. When a new baby is born into the family, Papa must reassure his son of his love. This story is set in a Lesotho village and features many words from Lesotho, South Africa.

Riecken, Nancy. 1996. *Today Is the Day*. Illustrated by Catherine Stock. Boston: Houghton Mifflin Company. Yesenia, a young Mexican girl, awaits the return of her father who has been working away from home, in the hopes that he will have brought enough money for her to attend school.

Seeger, Pete. 1986. *Abiyoyo: Based on a South African Lullaby and Folk Story*. Illustrated by Michael Hays. New York: Macmillian Publishing Company. The townsfolk ostracize a magician and his musician son until the day the pair defeats Abiyoyo the giant. The illustrations depict a town of incredibly diverse people.

Senisi, Ellen B. 1998. *For My Family, Love, Allie*. Morton Grove, Ill.: Albert Whitman & Company. In this extended family gathering, which is a celebration of Jamaican food and culture, grandfathers, uncles, and fathers all share cooking and parenting responsibilities with the women. Photographs depict Allie's biracial parents and the upbeat occasion.

Shalev, Meir. 1990. *My Father Always Embarrasses Me*. Translated by Dagmar Herrmann. Illustrated by Yossi Abolafia. Chicago: Wellington Publishing, Inc. Father's unique personality, as well as his role as a stay-at-home father, causes his son, Mortimer, to feel embarrassed (justifiably!), until Dad is given an opportunity for redemption.

Stanley, Sanna. 1998. *Monkey Sunday: A Story from a Congolese Village*. New York: Farrar, Straus & Giroux. In this humorous African family story, Luzolo, an active young girl, struggles to complete her father's challenge that she remain seated while he preaches.

Tompert, Ann. 1990. *Grandfather Tang's Story: A Tale Told with Tangrams*. Illustrated by Robert Andrew Parker. New York: Crown Publishers, Inc. Grandfather Tang and his granddaughter, Little Soo, construct a story together using tangrams.

Tsubakiyama, Margaret Holloway. 1999. *Mei-Mei Loves the Morning*. Illustrated by Cornelius Van Wright and Ying-hwa Hu. Morton Grove, Ill.: Albert Whitman & Company. Before her parents wake, a young girl and her grandfather enjoy breakfast and a special trip to the park in this warm Chinese story.

Van Laan, Nancy. 1995. *Mama Rocks, Papa Sings*. Illustrations by Roberta Smith. New York: Alfred A. Knopf Books for Young Readers. Based on a true story about Haitian missionaries who adopted 28 children, this book depicts, in Creole and English, parents who welcome children with loving, open arms and who support each other. The rhythmic, repetitive text makes a fun read-aloud and would be a good selection for classroom participation.

FAMILIES IN RURAL SETTINGS

Booth, David. 1996. *The Dust Bowl*. Illustrated by Karen Reczuch. Toronto: Kids Can Press, Ltd. The struggles of Matthew's grandfather's 20th-century farming are detailed in this Canadian story, which also shows lessons and advice being handed down from parent to child, regardless of the age.

Bunting, Eve. 1996. *Going Home*. Illustrated by David Diaz. New York: HarperCollins. Joanna Cotler Books. Carlos and his family are going home to Mexico for Christmas, but how can home be in America *and* in Mexico? This book features extremely self-sacrificing parents who would do anything to provide better opportunities for their children.

Chorao, Kay. 1998. *Little Farm by the Sea*. New York: Henry Holt & Company. Family members in this traditional rural setting work harmoniously to provide food and other farm goods for their roadside stand and store.

Donovan, Mary Lee. 1993. *Papa's Bedtime Story*. Illustrated by Kimberly Bulcken Root. New York: Alfred A. Knopf Books for Young Readers. Fathers throughout the animal world comfort their babies with bedtime stories, while a log cabin family does the same.

Estes, Kristyn Rehling. 1999. *Manuela's Gift*. Illustrated by Claire B. Cotts. San Francisco: Chronicle Books. Times are hard for Manuela's Mama, Papa, and Abuela, but on her birthday she realizes there is still much to celebrate. This book contains many Spanish words.

Gardella, Tricia. 1997. *Casey's New Hat*. Illustrated by Margot Apple. Boston: Houghton Mifflin Company. Casey's growing out of the cowgirl hat from her toddler days, so on their next trip in to town she and dad seek out the "right" hat. Grandpa joins in on the search and ends up helping his granddaughter find the perfect hat for a growing cowgirl.

———. 1996. *Just Like My Dad*. Illustrated by Margot Apple. New York: HarperCollins Children's Book Group. Dad and his young cowhand work together from morning to night on the ranch.

Hartley, Deborah. 1986. *Up North in Winter*. Illustrated by Lydia Dabcovich. New York: E. P. Dutton. This book, about the author's great-grandfather, recounts tough times during a very cold winter when Grandpa Ole had to walk for miles through the snow to work for his family.

Hendershot, Judith. 1987. *In Coal Country*. Illustrated by Thomas B. Allen. New York: Alfred A. Knopf. In this vivid account of life in a small 1930s coal town, Papa is a coal miner who works hard for his family.

Johnson, Angela. 1990. *When I Am Old with You*. Illustrated by David Soman. New York: Orchard Books. A little boy imagines all the fun he and his granddaddy will have spending quality time together in the future while having a wonderful time in the present.

Jukes, Mavis. 1984. *Like Jake and Me*. Illustrated by Lloyd Bloom. New York: Dragonfly Books. Alex, who loves ballet, does not have much in common with his stepfather, Jake, a cowboy. A funny misunderstanding about a spider helps them bond.

Kinsey-Warnock, Natalie. 1994. *On a Starry Night*. Illustrated by David M. McPhail. New York: Scholastic, Inc. Papa joins his daughter and wife on the hillside above their farm for stargazing; when Papa tosses his daughter up into the sky, she pretends that she is interacting with the constellations.

Lambert, Paulette Livers. 1995. *Evening: An Appalachian Lullaby*. Niwot, Colo.: Roberts Rinehart Publishers. It is bedtime on the farm; father patiently attends to the extended ritual with his young sons before relaxing on the porch with his fiddle.

Leavy, Una. 1996. *Good-Bye, Papa*. Illustrated by Jennifer Eachus. New York: Orchard Books. Two young boys mourn the passing of their farmer grandfather.

Lewin, Hugh. 1994. *Jafta: The Homecoming*. Illustrated by Lisa Kopper. New York: Knopf. Things are changing in South Africa; soon Jafta's father will be able to come home from the city where he has been working. See also *Jafta's Father*.

Lindbergh, Reeve. 1994. *If I'd Known Then What I Know Now*. Illustrated by Kimberly Bulcken Root. New York: Viking. This humorous story tells of the various failed home improvement projects on which dad worked over the years. His family assures the reader at the end, however, that they would have him no other way.

MacLachlan, Patricia. 1985. *Sarah, Plain and Tall*. New York: Harper & Row, Publishers. When Papa invited a mail-order bride to live with his family on the prairie, he could not have known the joy she would bring back to the mourning household. See also the sequel, *Skylark*.

McPhail, David M. 1990. *Ed and Me*. San Diego: Harcourt Brace Jovanovich, Publishers. This telling of a special father-daughter relationship is told with respect to Ed, the cherished old pickup truck in which the two share many happy memories.

Riecken, Nancy. 1996. *Today Is the Day*. Illustrated by Catherine Stock. Boston: Houghton Mifflin Company. Yesenia, a young Mexican girl, awaits the return of her father who has been working away from home, in the hopes that he will have brought enough money for her to attend school.

Root, Phyllis. 1998. *What Baby Wants*. Illustrated by Jill Bartow. Cambridge, Mass.: Candlewick Press. Big Brother knows just how to calm Baby down.

Schertle, Alice. 2000. *Down the Road*. Illustrated by E. B. Lewis. San Diego: Harcourt Children's Books. When Hetty gets side-tracked on her way home from the market and the eggs end up broken, Papa reacts with kindness and understanding, rather than with punishment and lectures.

Shannon, George. 1993. *Climbing Kansas Mountains*. Illustrated by Thomas B. Allen. New York: Bradbury Press. A creative father helps alleviate his son's summertime boredom as they seek out mountains to climb in Kansas.

Wadsworth, Ginger. 1994. *Tomorrow Is Daddy's Birthday*. Illustrated by Maxie Chambliss. Honesdale, Penn.: Boyds Mills Press. Rachel is so excited about the gift she will be giving her father for his birthday that she cannot help but share her secret with those around her.

Wallace, Ian. 1999. *Boy of the Deeps*. New York: DK. In this recounting of the author's grandfather's hard childhood, James accompanies his father down into "the deeps" of a coal mine for his first day on the job.

Weidt, Maryann. 1995. *Daddy Played Music for the Cows*. Illustrated by Henri Sorensen. New York: Morrow/Avon. While Daddy milks the cows and tends to other chores, he and his daughter enjoy playful interaction and a love for country music.

Williams, Sherley Anne. 1992. *Working Cotton*. Illustrated by Carole Byard. San Diego: Harcourt Brace Jovanovich. This story about migrant workers features a family working hard together and a father whose children are proud of his speed and skill at cotton-picking.

FAMILIES IN URBAN SETTINGS

Banks, Kate. 2000. *The Night Worker*. Illustrated by Georg Hallensleben. New York: Farrar, Straus & Giroux. Alex is surprised and thrilled when his Papa, who is a night worker at a construction site, takes him along to work while the rest of the city sleeps.

Bradman, Tony. 1990. *The Sandal*. Illustrated by Philippe Dupasquier. New York: Penguin Putnam Books for Young Readers. A child's lost sandal provides the bridge to connect past, present, and future dads enjoying a day in the city with the children.

Hamanaka, Sheila. 1995. *Bebop-A-Do-Walk!* New York: Simon & Schuster Books for Young Readers. Emi, her friend, Martha, and her father take one very long walk all over the city of New York.

Hughes, Shirley. 1997. *Alfie and the Birthday Surprise*. New York: Lothrop, Lee & Shepard Books. After Bob's cherished cat dies, his daughter, Maureen, enlists the help of Alfie and his family to plan a birthday party with one very special surprise. A good book for discussions about death.

Patrick, Denise Lewis. 1993. *The Car Washing Street*. Illustrated by John Ward. New York: Morrow/Avon. Matthew and his father share quality time together while also participating in a bit of boisterous neighborhood camaraderie.

Rush, Ken. 1994. *Friday's Journey*. New York: Orchard Books. While riding the subway to spend the weekend at his dad's place, a young boy remembers fondly places he and his parents used to go together, and asks his father to return to them.

Zolotow, Charlotte. 1993. *Peter and the Pigeons*. Illustrated by Martine Gourbault. New York: Greenwillow Books. Dad observes his son's affinity for common park pigeons, and decides to take him to the zoo to introduce him to other more exciting animals.

LATINO FAMILIES

Bunting, Eve. 1996. *Going Home*. Illustrated by David Diaz. New York: HarperCollins. Joanna Cotler Books. Carlos and his family are going home to Mexico for Christmas, but how can home be in America *and* in Mexico? This book features extremely self-sacrificing parents who would do anything to provide better opportunities for their children.

Cazet, Denys. 1993. *Born in the Gravy*. New York: Orchard Books. Margarita tells her papa all about her first day of kindergarten. Features many Spanish words, the meanings of which are translated or implied.

Christopher, Matt. 1992. *Centerfield Ballhawk*. Illustrated by Ellen Beier. Boston: Little, Brown & Company. José wants to excel at baseball in order to gain the respect and attention of his emotionally distant father, a widower who once played minor-league baseball.

Figueredo, D. H. 1999. *When This World Was New*. Illustrated by Enrique O. Sanchez. New York: Lee & Low Books, Inc. A Latino father, new to the United States and facing many uncertainties, takes time to enjoy a snowfall with his son, which ends up being therapeutic as well as fun.

Heide, Florence Parry, and Roxanne Heide Pierce. 1998. *Tío Armando*. Illustrated by Ann Grifalconi. Lothrop, New York: Lee & Shepard Books. A young girl develops a very special relationship with her philosophical great-uncle in this story featuring Spanish words.

Johnston, Tony. 2001. *Uncle Rain Cloud*. Illustrated by Fabricio VandenBroeck. Watertown, Mass.: Talewinds. Carlos's uncle, who is extremely involved in his life, is often grumpy because he has difficulty with the English language. One day he tells Carlos that he is afraid and needs help. The two agree to work together: Carlos will teach his uncle English, and his uncle will tell him stories about Mexico in Spanish. There are many untranslated Spanish words.

Sáenz, Benjamin Alire. 1997. *A Gift from Papá Diego/Un Regalo de Papá Diego*. Illustrated by Geronimo Garcia. El Paso: Cinco Puntos Press. In this Spanish/English book, the ties between grandfather, Big Diego, and his grandson, Little Diego, are stronger than the Mexican–U.S. border that separates them, and Father is very supportive in his liaison role.

NATIVE AMERICAN FAMILIES

James, Betsy. 1998. *The Mud Family*. Illustrated by Paul Morin. New York: Oxford University Press, Inc. Tension in an Anasazi family, caused by a drought and other hardships, causes the parents, especially father, to overlook their sensitive young daughter's needs until an emergency brings her into the limelight of his love.

Roop, Peter and Connie. 1994. *Ahyoka and the Talking Leaves*. Illustrated by Yoshi Miyake. New York: Morrow/Avon. This short historical novel focuses on the legendary Cherokee, Sequoyah, and his quest to decode the English alphabet, which causes much tension and changed relationships in his family.

VARIETY OF DADS

Bailey, Debbie. 1991. *My Dad*. Photo-illustrated by Susan Huszar. Willowdale, Ontario: Annick Press. This simple board book highlights visually and through simple text the relationship toddlers and fathers have, and features fathers of many ethnicities.

Greenspun, Adele Aron. 1991. *Daddies*. New York: Philomel Books. This simple book with touching black-and-white photographs captures the many ways fathers love their children.

Hausherr, Rosmarie. 1997. *Celebrating Families*. New York: Scholastic, Inc. Families with stepparents, incarcerated fathers, and biracial parents are among the many different families presented in this nonfiction book.

Lindenbaum, Pija. 1991. *Else-Marie and Her Seven Little Daddies*. New York: Henry Holt & Company. Else-Marie is embarrassed about her seven small fathers, but when it is their turn to pick her up from playgroup, no one seems to notice that they are small or that there are seven of them! The quirky illustrations help tell the story of how Else-Marie learns to appreciate her fathers' uniqueness.

Merriam, Eve. 1989. *Daddies at Work*. Illustrated by Eugenie Fernandes. New York: Little Simon. This book and its companion, *Mommies at Work*, depicts loving fathers engaged in many parenting and career roles.

Micklos, John. 2000. *Daddy Poems*. Illustrated by Robert Casilla. Foreword by Jim Trelease. Honesdale, Penn.: Boyds Mills Press. This poetic celebration of fathers depicts dads of many ethnicities.

Miller, Margaret. 1998. *Big and Little*. New York: Greenwillow Books. The fun of relative size is emphasized in this book with colorful photographic images and simple text; many types of families and people are featured.

Morris, Ann. 1995. *The Daddy Book*. Photo-illustrated by Ken Heyman. Parsippany, N.J.: Silver Burdett Press. Many kinds of dads are depicted loving, playing, and working with their children in this multicultural photo-essay; thumbnail photos and additional notes are in the "Index to Daddies."

———. *Loving*. 1990. Photo-illustrated by Ken Heyman. New York: Lothrop, Lee & Shepard Books. Depicting families from all over the world, this book of photographs is perfect for younger children.

Numeroff, Laura. 1998. *What Mommies Do Best/What Daddies Do Best*. Illustrated by Lynn Munsinger. New York: Simon & Schuster Books for Young Readers. Using a variety of animal characters, this book illustrates the similarities and differences, and the strengths and weaknesses, between mothers and fathers and their parenting interactions with young children.

Pedersen, Marika, and Mikele Hall. 2000. *Mommy Works, Daddy Works*. Illustrated by Deirdre Betteridge. Toronto: Annick Press. Depicting mothers and fathers in many nontraditional career roles, this book seeks to provide a diversity of role model for parents and children.

Regan, Dian Curtis. 1996. *Daddies*. Illustrated by Mary Morgan. New York: Scholastic Inc. Babies' and toddlers' voices express, in gentle rhymes, the various activities enjoyed with their daddies.

Rotner, Shelley, and Sheila M. Kelly. 2000. *Lots of Dads*. Photo-illustrated by Shelley Rotner. New York: Penguin Putnam Books for Young Readers. Babies and young children are shown with their fathers in a variety of positive nurturing situations.

Scharlotte, Rich. 1997. *I Love My Daddy*. Illustrated by Linda Weller. Grand Rapids, Mich.: Zondervan Publishing House. Of interest especially to Christian families, this preschool book presents a multicultural selection of fathers and children engaged in many activities, including a passage of Biblical wisdom.

Valentine, Johnny. 1992. *The Daddy Machine*. Illustrated by Lynette Schmidt. Boston: Alyson Wonderland. The children of lesbian parents wish for a dad and, after building a contraption that "manufactures" dads, get more than they bargained for. This is a positive look at what dads are like and what they do.

Ziefert, Harriet. 1999. *Daddies Are for Catching Fireflies*. Illustrated by Cynthia Jabar. New York: Penguin Putnam Books for Young Readers. This is a paperback, lift-the-flap book that depicts different fathers in traditional roles and activities with young children.

CELEBRATING GRANDFATHERS

GRANDFATHER AND GRANDCHILDREN SHARING WORK

Carney, Margaret. 1998. *At Grandpa's Sugar Bush*. Illustrated by Janet Wilson. Toronto: Kids Can Press, Ltd. During Spring Break, Grandpa gets extra help with sugaring from his enthusiastic nephew, who narrates the story, thus providing a new generation with sugaring know-how.

DiSalvo-Ryan, DyAnne. 2000. *Grandpa's Corner Store*. New York: HarperCollins Publishers. Lucy must come up with a solution when a brand-new supermarket being built down the street threatens her grandpa's cozy, landmark grocery store. Good for discussions about change and community.

High, Linda Oatman. 2001. *Beekeepers*. Illustrated by Doug Chayka. Honesdale, Penn.: Boyds Mills Press. Grandpa and his granddaughter share quality time while tending to beehives.

Leavy, Una. 1996. *Good-Bye, Papa*. Illustrated by Jennifer Eachus. New York: Orchard Books. Two young boys mourn the passing of their farmer grandfather.

May, Kathy L. 2000. *Molasses Man*. Illustrated by Felicia Marshall. New York: Holiday House. Grandpa works with his family to make fresh molasses, paying special attention to a young grandson who will be the next Molasses Man.

Ogburn, Jacqueline K. 1998. *The Jukebox Man*. Illustrated by James Ransome. New York: Penguin Putnam Books for Young Readers. A young girl not only enjoys making the rounds with her grandfather who tends to jukeboxes, but also learns that he can be a giving, sensitive man.

Sathre, Vivian. 1997. *On Grandpa's Farm*. Illustrated by Anne Hunter. New York: Houghton Mifflin Company. In this simple book, a girl assists Grandpa with farm chores all day long, then they relax at the fishing pond.

GRANDFATHER AND GRANDDAUGHTER SHARING QUALITY TIME

Chocolate, Debbi. 1998. *The Piano Man*. Illustrated by Eric Velasquez. New York: Walker & Company. A granddaughter highlights the exciting life of her Broadway and vaudeville pianist grandfather; the story also illustrates the warm relationship between the two.

DiSalvo-Ryan, DyAnne. 2000. *Grandpa's Corner Store*. New York: HarperCollins Publishers. Lucy must come up with a solution when a brand-new supermarket being built down the street threatens her grandpa's cozy, landmark grocery store. Good for discussions about change and community.

Doyle, Malachy. 1999. *Jody's Beans*. Illustrated by Judith Allibone. Cambridge, Mass.: Candlewick Press. This story features a warm relationship between a grandfather and granddaughter; readers also learn about growing scarlet runner beans.

Gardella, Tricia. 1997. *Casey's New Hat*. Illustrated by Margot Apple. Boston: Houghton Mifflin Company. Casey's growing out of the cowgirl hat from her toddler days, so on their next trip in to town she and dad seek out the "right" hat. Grandpa joins in on the search and ends up helping his granddaughter find the perfect hat for a growing cowgirl.

Griffith, Helen V. 2001. *Grandaddy and Janetta Together: The Three Stories in One Book*. Illustrated by James Stevenson. New York: Greenwillow Books. Janetta's never known her grandaddy, but in this beginning chapter book (originally published as separate picture books), she will learn to love him.

Hest, Amy. 1986. *The Purple Coat*. Illustrated by Amy Schwartz. New York: Four Winds Press. Gabrielle's annual trip to see her grandfather, a tailor, for a new navy blue coat is turned topsy-turvy when she declares that this year she wants a purple coat.

Ogburn, Jacqueline K. 1998. *The Jukebox Man*. Illustrated by James Ransome. New York: Penguin Putnam Books for Young Readers. A young girl not only enjoys making the rounds with her grandfather who tends to jukeboxes, but also learns that he can be a giving, sensitive man.

Sathre, Vivian. 1997. *On Grandpa's Farm*. Illustrated by Anne Hunter. Boston: Houghton Mifflin Company. In this simple book, a girl assists Grandpa with farm chores all day long, then they relax at the fishing pond.

Tompert, Ann. 1990. *Grandfather Tang's Story: A Tale Told with Tangrams*. Illustrated by Robert Andrew Parker. New York: Crown Publishers, Inc. Grandfather Tang and his granddaughter, Little Soo, construct a story together using tangrams.

Tsubakiyama, Margaret Holloway. 1999. *Mei-Mei Loves the Morning*. Illustrated by Cornelius Van Wright and Ying-hwa Hu. Morton Grove, Ill.: Albert Whitman & Company. Before her parents wake, a young girl and her grandfather enjoy breakfast and a special trip to the park in this warm Chinese story.

GRANDFATHER AND GRANDSON SHARING QUALITY TIME

Buckley, Helen E. 1994. *Grandfather and I*. Illustrated by Jan Ormerod. New York: HarperCollins Publishers. A child often told to hurry recounts a special relationship he has with his grandfather, in which they spend quality time together walking, reading, and taking as long as they like.

Carney, Margaret. 1998. *At Grandpa's Sugar Bush*. Illustrated by Janet Wilson. Toronto: Kids Can Press, Ltd. During Spring Break, Grandpa gets extra help with sugaring from his enthusiastic nephew, who narrates the story, thus providing a new generation with sugaring know-how.

de Paola, Tomie. 1980. *Now One Foot, Now the Other*. New York: G. P. Putnam's Sons. Bob, little Bobby's grandfather, namesake, and best friend, suffers a physically and mentally debilitating stroke. The student becomes the teacher as young Bobby returns the favor Bob long ago taught him, and helps his grandfather relearn how to walk. Great for discussions about aging, sickness, and memory loss.

Grindley, Sally. 1998. *A Flag for Grandma*. Illustrated by Jason Cockcroft. New York: Dorling Kindersley Publishing, Inc. A visit to Grandpa's seaside home yields a playful and tender day for both grandson and Grandpa, with touching memorials for Grandma.

High, Linda Oatman. 2001. *Beekeepers*. Illustrated by Doug Chayka. Honesdale, Penn.: Boyds Mills Press. Grandpa and his granddaughter share quality time while tending to beehives.

Johnson, Angela. 1990. *When I Am Old with You*. Illustrated by David Soman. New York: Orchard Books. A little boy imagines all the fun he and his granddaddy will have spending quality time together in the future while having a wonderful time in the present.

Matze, Claire Sidhom. 1999. *The Stars in My Geddoh's Sky*. Illustrated by Bill Farnsworth. Morton Grove, Ill.: Albert Whitman & Company. While visiting, Alex's *geddoh*, which means grandfather in Arabic, shares many traditions from his Middle Eastern culture as well as quality time with his grandson.

Mills, Claudia. 1999. *Gus and Grandpa*. Photo-illustrated by Catherine Stock. New York: Farrar, Straus & Giroux. A warm intergenerational relationship between a seven-year-old grandchild and his 70-year-old grandfather is depicted in this old-fashioned series for newly independent readers. Other titles include *Gus and Grandpa and the Christmas Cookies* (1997), *Gus and Grandpa at the Hospital* (1998), *Gus and Grandpa Ride the Train* (1998), *Gus and Grandpa and the Two-Wheeled Bike* (1999), and *Gus and Grandpa and Show-and-Tell* (2000).

Stevenson, James. 2000. *Sam the Zamboni Man*. Illustrated by Harvey Stevenson. Collingdale, Penn.: DIANE Publishing Company. In this collaborative effort by father and son, a young boy and his grandfather share some very exciting, special times at the ice arena.

Stiles, Martha Bennett. 1999. *Island Magic*. Illustrated by Daniel San Souçi. New York: Atheneum Books for Young Readers. When Grandad sells his farm to move in with his son's family on an island, his grandson, David, tries tenderly to help him to stop missing his cows.

Waboose, Jan Bourdeau. 1998. *Morning on the Lake*. Illustrated by Karen Reczuch. Toronto: Kids Can Press, Ltd. An Ojibway grandfather shares his knowledge of the natural world with his grandson on an outing together.

Ziefert, Harriet. 2001. *No Kiss for Grandpa*. Illustrated by Emilie Boon. New York: Orchard Books. A day at the beach with grouchy Louie is no day at the beach for Grandpa, who has enough patience for himself and for one ornery grandson.

GRANDFATHER AS CUSTODIAL CAREGIVER

Blos, Joan. 1999. *Hello Shoes!* Illustrated by Ann Boyajian. New York: Simon & Schuster Children's Publishing. Grandfather helps his young grandson get ready in the morning; when it is time to go outside, he exercises much patience while the grandson searches for his shoes.

Hänel, Wolfram. 1997. *The Gold at the End of the Rainbow*. Translated by Anthea Bell. Illustrated by Loek Koopmans. New York: North-South Books, Inc. Grandpa is the primary caregiver of his grandson, and when he tells a story intended to dispel their financial difficulties, the story moves into the fantasy realm.

Helmer, Marilyn. 2000. *Fog Cat*. Illustrated by Paul Mombourquette. Toronto: Kids Can Press, Ltd. When Hannah moves in with her grandfather, a quietly supportive man, their unique relationship unfolds as a stray cat also becomes part of their lives.

Lewin, Ted. 1998. *The Storytellers*. New York: HarperCollins Children's Book Group. Abdul accompanies his grandfather to the colorful Moroccan city, Fez, where his grandfather earns a living as a storyteller.

Medearis, Angela Shelf. 1995. *Poppa's New Pants* and *Poppa's Itchy Christmas*. Illustrated by John Ward. New York: Holiday House. In these humorous family stories, a young boy lives with his grandparents and enjoys a special relationship with his grandfather, who comes to his rescue in more ways than one.

GRANDFATHER AS TEMPORARY CAREGIVER

DiSalvo-Ryan, DyAnne. 2000. *Grandpa's Corner Store*. New York: HarperCollins Publishers. Grandpa watches Lucy after school, but is unaware of her plans. Lucy must come up with a solution when a brand-new supermarket being built down the street threatens her grandpa's cozy, landmark grocery store.

Hest, Amy. 1986. *The Purple Coat*. Illustrated by Amy Schwartz. New York: Four Winds Press. Gabrielle's annual trip to see her grandfather, a tailor, for a new navy blue coat is turned topsy-turvy when she declares that this year she wants a purple coat.

Leavy, Una. 1996. *Good-Bye, Papa*. Illustrated by Jennifer Eachus. New York: Orchard Books. Two young boys mourn the passing of their farmer grandfather.

Paul, Ann Whitford. 1999. *Everything to Spend the Night from A to Z*. Illustrated by Maggie Smith. New York: Dorling Kindersley Publishing, Inc. An energetic preschooler packs just about everything she could possibly need to entertain Grandpa and herself overnight, and Grandpa indulges in her imaginative play and antics.

Rael, Elsa Okoon. 1997. *When Zaydeh Danced on Eldridge Street*. Illustrated by Marjorie Priceman. New York: Simon & Schuster Children's Publishing. While Mama is having a baby, Grandfather Zaydeh and his granddaughter, Zeesie, come to a deeper appreciation of each other after a special visit to the synagogue.

Van Leewen, Jean. 1998. *The Tickle Stories*. Illustrated by Mary Whyte. New York: Penguin Putnam Books for Young Readers. Grandpop, the caregiver for the evening, does not get off easy at bedtime with three demanding children, who encourage his storytelling abilities.

GRANDFATHER NURTURING SMALL CHILDREN AND BABIES

de Paola, Tomie. 1980. *Now One Foot, Now the Other*. New York: G. P. Putnam's Sons. Bob, little Bobby's grandfather, namesake, and best friend, suffers a physically and mentally debilitating stroke. The student becomes the teacher as young Bobby returns the favor Bob long ago taught him, and helps his grandfather relearn how to walk. Great for discussions about aging, sickness, and memory loss.

Eyvindsom, Peter. 1991. *Old Enough*. Illustrated by Wendy Wolsak. Winnipeg: Pemmican Publications, Inc. A father who neglected his growing son learns from his mistakes and appreciates his newborn grandchild—a bad dad turned good.

Hest, Amy. 1999, 1997, 1996, 1995. *Off to School, Baby Duck*; *You're the Boss, Baby Duck!*; *Baby Duck and the Bad Eyeglasses*; and *In the Rain with Baby Duck*. Illustrated by Jill Barton. Cambridge, Mass.: Candlewick Press. When Baby Duck needs it the most, Grampa Duck is there to brighten the day or to provide support and companionship in this series for young children.

GRANDFATHER PROVIDING INSPIRATION OR INDIRECT LESSONS

Bunting, Eve. 1999. *I Have an Olive Tree*. Illustrated by Karen Barbour. New York: HarperCollins Children's Book Group. Before he dies, Grandfather gives his granddaughter a priceless gift for her birthday, an olive tree and a trip to Greece where the tree, a symbol of her heritage, is located.

Cooke, Trish. 2000. *The Grandad Tree*. Illustrated by Sharon Wilson. Cambridge, Mass.: Candlewick Press. Focusing on life cycles, this book depicts growth and remembrance through the symbol of the family apple tree. After their Grandad dies, Leigh and Vin cherish even more dearly the apple tree and the wonderful times they had there with him.

Garland, Sherry. 1998. *My Father's Boat*. Illustrated by Ted Rand. New York: Scholastic, Inc. A Vietnamese American shrimper teaches his son the tricks of the trade one special day, causing him to reminisce about his own father back in Vietnam. An especially warm, poetic text is prefaced with this appropriate Vietnamese proverb: "When you are young, you need your father; when you are old, you need your son." This father represents both strong and tender sides of parenting.

Johnston, Tony. 1996. *Fishing Sunday*. Illustrated by Barry Root. New York: Morrow/Avon. The cultural and generational differences, which alienate a grandson from his elderly grandfather, also unite them when the boy gains appreciation for his grandfather's kindnesses and individuality.

Michelson, Richard. *Grandpa's Gamble*. Illustrated by Barry Moser. New York: Marshall Cavendish. In this touching tale, Grandpa tells his grandchildren of his past, including immigration from Poland to escape Nazi persecution, life in America as a gambler, and the biggest gamble he ever made.

Waddell, Martin. 1999. *The Toymaker*. Illustrated by Terry Milne. Cambridge, Mass.: Candlewick Press. The lessons learned from a sensitive, creative father who made very special dolls for his daughter last a lifetime and more.

GRANDFATHER SHARING WISDOM OR PROVIDING INSTRUCTION

Antle, Nancy. 1997. *Staying Cool*. Illustrated by E. B. Lewis. New York: Penguin Putnam Books for Young Readers. Curtis is learning how to box from his grandfather and hopes to follow in his footsteps as a professional boxer and gain his grandfather's respect.

Booth, David. 1996. *The Dust Bowl*. Illustrated by Karen Reczuch. Toronto: Kids Can Press, Ltd. The struggles of Matthew's grandfather's 20th-century farm are detailed in this Canadian story, which also shows lessons and advice being handed down from parent to child, regardless of the age.

Carney, Margaret. 1998. *At Grandpa's Sugar Bush*. Illustrated by Janet Wilson. Toronto: Kids Can Press, Ltd. During Spring Break, Grandpa gets extra help with sugaring from his enthusiastic nephew, who narrates the story, thus providing a new generation with sugaring know-how.

de Paola, Tomie. 1980. *Now One Foot, Now the Other*. New York: G. P. Putnam's Sons. Bob, little Bobby's grandfather, namesake, and best friend, suffers a physically and mentally debilitating stroke. The student becomes the teacher as young Bobby returns the favor Bob long ago taught him, and helps his grandfather relearn how to walk. Great for discussions about aging, sickness, and memory loss.

Doyle, Malachy. 1999. *Jody's Beans*. Illustrated by Judith Allibone. Cambridge, Mass.: Candlewick Press. This story features a warm relationship between a grandfather and granddaughter; readers also learn about growing scarlet runner beans.

Hest, Amy. 1986. *The Purple Coat*. Illustrated by Amy Schwartz. New York: Four Winds Press. Gabrielle's annual trip to see her grandfather, a tailor, for a new navy blue coat is turned topsy-turvy when she declares that this year she wants a purple coat.

High, Linda Oatman. 2001. *Beekeepers*. Illustrated by Doug Chayka. Honesdale, Penn.: Boyds Mills Press. Grandpa and his granddaughter share quality time while tending to beehives.

Matze, Claire Sidhom. 1999. *The Stars in My Geddoh's Sky*. Illustrated by Bill Farnsworth. Morton Grove, Ill.: Albert Whitman & Company. While visiting, Alex's *geddoh*, which means grandfather in Arabic, shares many traditions from his Middle Eastern culture as well as quality time with his grandson.

May, Kathy L. 2000. *Molasses Man*. Illustrated by Felicia Marshall. New York: Holiday House. Grandpa works with his family to make fresh molasses, paying special attention to a young grandson who will be the next Molasses Man.

Michelson, Richard. *Grandpa's Gamble*. Illustrated by Barry Moser. New York: Marshall Cavendish. In this touching tale, Grandpa tells his grandchildren of his past, including immigration from Poland to escape Nazi persecution, life in America as a gambler, and the biggest gamble he ever made.

Oberman, Sheldon. 1997. *By the Hanukkah Light*. Illustrated by Neil Waldman. Honesdale, Penn.: Boyds Mills Press. Grandfather tells two stories of Hanukkah to his expectant grandchildren: the miraculous first Hanukkah with the Macabees, and the fearful, secretive Hanukkahs of his youth in Nazi Europe.

Onyefulu, Ifeoma. 1998. *Grandfather's Work: A Traditional Healer in Nigeria*. Brookfield, Conn.: Millbrook Press, Inc. This photo-essay introduces the author's extended family, and explores the grandfather's traditional, natural medicine knowledge. As stated by the author, "I have written this book to keep alive the memory of my grandfather."

Rael, Elsa Okoon. 1997. *When Zaydeh Danced on Eldridge Street*. Illustrated by Marjorie Priceman. New York: Simon & Schuster Children's Publishing. While Mama is having a baby, Grandfather Zaydeh and his granddaughter, Zeesie, come to a deeper appreciation of each other after a special visit to the synagogue.

Waboose, Jan Bourdeau. 1998. *Morning on the Lake*. Illustrated by Karen Reczuch. Toronto: Kids Can Press, Ltd. An Ojibway grandfather shares his knowledge of the natural world with his grandson on an outing together.

Wood, Douglas. 1999. *Grandad's Prayers for the Earth*. Illustrated by P.J. Lynch. Cambridge, Mass.: Candlewick Press. The spiritual lessons that Grandfather provides to his grandson while on nature walks later prove their value when the grandson grows older.

GRANDFATHER'S DEATH

Cooke, Trish. 2000. *The Grandad Tree*. Illustrated by Sharon Wilson. Cambridge, Mass.: Candlewick Press. Focusing on life cycles, this book depicts growth and remembrance through the symbol of the family apple tree. After their Grandad dies, Leigh and Vin cherish even more dearly the apple tree and the wonderful times they had there with him.

Leavy, Una. 1996. *Good-Bye, Papa*. Illustrated by Jennifer Eachus. New York: Orchard Books. Two young boys mourn the passing of their farmer grandfather.

Wood, Douglas. 1999. *Grandad's Prayers for the Earth*. Illustrated by P. J. Lynch. Cambridge, Mass.: Candlewick Press. The spiritual lessons that Grandfather provides to his grandson while on nature walks later prove their value when the grandson grows older.

Zalben, Jane Breskin. 1997. *Pearl's Marigolds for Grandpa*. New York: Simon & Schuster Books for Young Readers. When Pearl's grandfather dies, her father steps in to take part in activities the pair had shared. This book includes information at the back regarding Jewish mourning customs.

GRANDFATHER, PARENT, AND CHILD: MULTIGENERATIONAL

Booth, David. 1996. *The Dust Bowl*. Illustrated by Karen Reczuch. Toronto: Kids Can Press, Ltd. The struggles of Matthew's grandfather's 20th-century farm are detailed in this Canadian story, which also shows lessons and advice being handed down from parent to child, regardless of the age.

Couture, Susan Arkin. 1997. *The Biggest Horse I Ever Did See*. Illustrated by Claire Ewart. New York: HarperCollins Publishers. This sweet, simple tale tells two stories; the text speaks of the beauty of horses galloping over the mountains, but the images speak of nurturing father/son/grandson relationships.

Creech, Sharon. 2000. *Fishing in the Air*. Illustrated by Chris Raschka. New York: Joanna Cotler Books. Father and son embark on a fishing excursion and share many imaginative moments, including a conversation about the father's days as a young boy learning to fish with his father.

Eyvindsom, Peter. 1991. *Old Enough*. Illustrated by Wendy Wolsak. Winnipeg: Pemmican Publications, Inc. A father who neglected his growing son learns from his mistakes and appreciates his newborn grandchild—a bad dad turned good.

Gardella, Tricia. 1997. *Casey's New Hat*. Illustrated by Margot Apple. Boston: Houghton Mifflin Company. Grandpa joins his son in helping his granddaughter find the perfect hat for a growing cowgirl.

Garland, Sherry. 1998. *My Father's Boat*. Illustrated by Ted Rand. New York: Scholastic, Inc. A Vietnamese American shrimper teaches his son the tricks of the trade one special day, causing him to reminisce about his own father back in Vietnam. An especially warm, poetic text is prefaced with this appropriate Vietnamese proverb: "When you are young, you need your father; when you are old, you need your son." This father represents both strong and tender sides of parenting.

Graham, Bob. 2000. *Max*. Cambridge, Mass.: Candlewick Press. Max is the super son of superhero parents and grandparents, but he cannot fly yet! Children will identify with Max's plight and agree that "Everyone's different in *some* way, aren't they?"

Hartley, Deborah. 1986. *Up North in Winter*. Illustrated by Lydia Dabcovich. New York: E. P. Dutton. This book, about the author's great-grandfather, recounts tough times during a very cold winter when Grandpa Ole had to walk for miles through the snow to work for his family.

Johnson, Dolores. 1993. *Your Dad Was Just Like You*. New York: Simon & Schuster Children's Publishing. Grandfather shares succinct bits and pieces about his son's childhood with Peter, his grandson, creating more than just memories.

May, Kathy L. 2000. *Molasses Man*. Illustrated by Felicia Marshall. New York: Holiday House. Grandpa works with his family to make fresh molasses, paying special attention to a young grandson who will be the next Molasses Man.

Paxton, Tom. 1996. *The Marvelous Toy*. Illustrated by Elizabeth Sayles. New York: Morrow Junior Books. A father gives his son an extraordinary and unique new toy; later in life the son goes on to give a similar toy to his son. This clever book would be great for reading aloud, and includes a song to sing the repeating text.

Pettigrew, Eileen. 1992. *Night-Time*. Illustrated by William Kimber. Toronto: Annick Press. Michael's dad takes him on a very special nighttime walk around the neighborhood, recounting his own fond memories of his father.

Sáenz, Benjamin Alire. 1997. *A Gift from Papá Diego/Un Regalo de Papá Diego*. Illustrated by Geronimo Garcia. El Paso: Cinco Puntos Press. In this Spanish/English book, the ties between grandfather, Big Diego, and his grandson, Little Diego, are stronger than the Mexican–U.S. border that separates them, and Father is very supportive in his liaison role.

Spinelli, Eileen. 1993. *Boy, Can He Dance!* Illustrated by Paul Yalowitz. New York: Four Winds Press. Tony loves to dance and seeks nothing more than approval from his father and grandfather, both chefs who encourage him to continue the family business.

MISCELLANEOUS GRANDFATHER BOOKS

Bowdish, Lynea. 2000. *Brooklyn, Bugsy, and Me*. Illustrated by Nancy Carpenter. New York: Farrar, Straus & Giroux. It is 1953, and Sam and his mother move from West Virginia to Brooklyn after the death of Sam's father. There they live with grandfather Bugsy, who wants little to do with his hurting grandson.

Clement, Rod. 1997. *Grandpa's Teeth*. Sydney: HarperCollins Publishers. Grandpa awakes in the middle of the night to find his teeth stolen, sending the entire town into a smiling frenzy.

Hartley, Deborah. 1986. *Up North in Winter*. Illustrated by Lydia Dabcovich. New York: E. P. Dutton. This book, about the author's great-grandfather, recounts tough times during a very cold winter when Grandpa Ole had to walk for miles through the snow to work for his family.

OTHER MALE CAREGIVERS

BROTHERS

Bunting, Eve. 1998. *Your Move*. Illustrated by James Ransome. San Diego: Harcourt Brace & Company. James always stays home to take care of his little brother, Isaac, at night when his mom goes to work, but tonight the two will experience something much more terrifying. This riveting book offers a glimpse into an extremely positive and responsible brotherly relationship, and would be great for discussions about gangs, violence, or guns.

Dunbar, Joyce. 1998. *Tell Me Something Happy Before I Go to Sleep*. Illustrated by Debi Gliori. San Diego: Harcourt Brace & Company. Big brother Willoughby soothes his little sister, Willa, who is too afraid of bad dreams to fall asleep, by reminding her of many happy things.

Hiatt, Fred. 1999. *Baby Talk*. Illustrated by Mark Graham. New York: Margaret K. McElderry Books. Young Joey learns to love his new baby brother when they develop a special language and become inseparable. Although not in a custodial role, Joey is regardless a wonderful brotherly caregiver.

Root, Phyllis. 1998. *What Baby Wants*. Illustrated by Jill Bartow. Cambridge, Mass.: Candlewick Press. Big Brother knows just how to calm Baby down.

Wishinsky, Frieda. 1998. *Oonga Boonga*. Illustrated by Carol Thompson. New York: Dutton Children's Books. Big brother Daniel is able to quiet his screaming infant sister, Louise, when no one else can.

NEIGHBORS, MENTORS, AND VOLUNTEERS

Cole, Kenneth. 2001. *No Bad News*. Photo-illustrated by John Ruebartsch. Morton Grove, Ill.: Albert Whitman & Company. A walk alone through the urban streets of his neighborhood to get a haircut causes young Marcus to reflect only on the negatives in his environment; a community of positive male role models at the barbershop changes his mind. The retouching of the photography in this book is beautiful.

Grimes, Nikki. 1999. *My Man Blue*. Illustrated by Jerome Lagarrigue. New York: Penguin Putnam Books for Young Readers. A fatherless boy meets Blue, a father who has lost his son "to the streets," and the two begin a father-son type of friendship. The story is presented in poetry geared for older readers.

Hughes, Shirley. 1997. *Alfie and the Birthday Surprise*. New York: Lothrop, Lee & Shepard Books. After Bob's cherished cat dies, his daughter, Maureen, enlists the help of Alfie and his family to plan a birthday party with one very special surprise. A good book for discussions about death.

Lasky, Kathryn. 1997. *Marven of the Great North Woods*. Illustrated by Kevin Hawkes. New York: Harcourt Brace & Company. When an influenza epidemic spreads across American in 1918, Marven Lasky was sent to live with French Canadian lumberjacks in the great north woods of Minnesota to be kept safe from the disease. While living there, Marven develops a special relationship with a father-figure lumberjack named Jean Louis. This is the true story of the author's father.

London, Jonathan. 1998. *The Candystore Man*. Illustrated by Kevin O'Malley. New York: Lothrop, Lee & Shepard Books. The fun and eccentric owner of the neighborhood candy store serves as a positive male role model for many children in the community.

Sansone, Adele. 2001. *The Little Green Goose*, illustrated by Alan Marks. New York: North-South Books, Inc. A perfect book for preschool story times. A male goose goes out of his way to demonstrate his nurturing abilities; his adopted offspring learns that dads can be every bit as warm and loving as moms.

Waggoner, Karen. 1992. *Lemonade Babysitter*. Illustrated by Dorothy Donohue. Boston: Little, Brown & Company. Neither gender nor generational differences keep spunky young Molly and Mr. Herbert, a grandfatherly neighborhood baby-sitter with a ton of patience, from establishing a wonderful relationship.

Wojciechowski, Susan. 1995. *The Christmas Miracle of Jonathan Toomey*. Illustrated by P. J. Lynch. Cambridge, Mass.: Candlewick Press. Jonathan Toomey, a wood-carver known as Mr. Gloomy to the village children, experiences the miracle of love when carving a special nativity for widow McDowell and her son.

UNCLES

DiSalvo-Ryan, DyAnne. 1997. *Uncle Willie and the Soup Kitchen*. New York: Morrow/Avon. Uncle Willie is the after-school caregiver; on a school vacation day, he provides his nephew with moral and civic lessons during a visit to the soup kitchen where he volunteers.

Fowler, Susi Gregg. 1998. *Beautiful*. Illustrated by Jim Fowler. New York: HarperCollins Children's Book Group. The garden, which Uncle George tenderly taught his nephew to tend, is the lifeline between the two during the uncle's terminal illness.

Gretz, Susanna. 2001. *Rabbit Food*. Cambridge, Mass.: Candlewick Press. When Uncle Bunny takes care of the niece and nephew bunnies one weekend, he tries very hard to be a role model for his picky-eater nephew.

Heide, Florence Parry, and Roxanne Heide Pierce. 1998. *Tío Armando*. Illustrated by Ann Grifalconi. New York: Lothrop, Lee & Shepard Books. A young girl develops a very special relationship with her philosophical great-uncle in this story featuring Spanish words.

Johnston, Tony. 2001. *Uncle Rain Cloud*. Illustrated by Fabricio VandenBroeck. Watertown, Mass.: Talewinds. Carlos's uncle, who is extremely involved in his life, is often grumpy because he has difficulty with the English language. One day he tells Carlos that he is afraid and needs help; the two agree to work together: Carlos will teach his uncle English, and his uncle will tell him stories about Mexico in Spanish. There are many untranslated Spanish words.

Mochizuki, Ken. 1995. *Heroes*. Illustrated by Dom Lee. New York: Lee & Low Books, Inc. Donnie, who is Asian American, always has to be the "bad guy" when he and his friends play war because his friends will not believe that his father and uncle are decorated military heroes. This book is dedicated to the many people of Asian and Pacific Islander descent who have defended America with little or no recognition.

Roberts, Bethany. 1993. *The Two O'Clock Secret*. Illustrated by Robin Kramer. Morton Grove, Ill.: Albert Whitman & Company. The family has the perfect surprise for daddy's birthday—his twin brother home from the Navy—but it is hard to keep a secret!

OTHER PICTURE BOOKS

ANIMAL CHARACTERS

Anderson, Peggy Perry. 2001. *To the Tub*. Boston: Houghton Mifflin Company. Parents will especially relate to the frustrated father frog's attempts to get junior to the bathtub, and both children and parents will enjoy the ending in which father's playful side takes over.

Asch, Frank. 1984. *Just Like Daddy*. New York: Simon & Schuster Books for Young Readers. A young bear emulates Daddy bear as they prepare for a fishing trip that ends with a surprise.

Boelts, Maribeth. 2000. *Big Daddy, Frog Wrestler*. Illustrated by Benrei Huang. Morton Grove, Ill.: Albert Whitman & Company. Big Daddy and his son, Curtis, love wrestling, but when Big Daddy gets a chance to wrestle all over the world, he must choose between wrestling and his son.

Browne, Anthony. 1983. *Gorilla*. New York: Alfred A. Knopf. Hannah's toy gorilla comes to life and takes the place of her father, doing all of the activities he is always too busy to do.

———. 1986. *Piggybook*. New York: Alfred A. Knopf. Mr. Piggott and his two sons, Simon and Patrick, are of no help to Mrs. Piggott, who decides to leave and teach them a lesson about helping out. The house goes to ruin and the male Piggotts turn into pigs by the time she returns.

Carmichael, Clay. 1996. *Bear at the Beach*. New York: North-South Books. Bear longs for a father, and discovers him in the night sky.

de Brunhoff, Laurent. *The Rescue of Babar, Babar and Father Christmas, Babar and His Children*. See **Series**.

Egielski, Richard. 1998. *Jazper*. New York: HarperCollins. A Laura Geringer Book. When Jazper comes home to find his father in bandages, he realizes he must go make a living for the two of them and ends up getting mixed up with some magical moths. This is a very cute story with funny illustrations of the bug town.

Fox, Mem. 1996. *Zoo-Looking*. Illustrated by Candace Whitman. Greenvale, N.Y.: Mondo Publishing. Flora and her dad explore the zoo in this simple rhyming book.

Gliori, Debi. 1994. *Mr. Bear Babysits*. New York: Golden Books Publishing Company. In this warm story, Mr. Bear, a novice at parenting, proves his nurturing and caregiving abilities when he is forced to baby-sit the neighbors' children.

———. 1999. *Mr. Bear's New Baby*. New York: Scholastic, Inc. Both Mr. and Mrs. Bear share nighttime baby duty, along with many sleepy neighbors, in this latest addition to the Bear family saga.

Hearn, Dawson Diane. 1999. *Dad's Dinosaur Day*. New York: Aladdin Paperbacks. Dad's transformation into a dinosaur yields a day of fantastical fun for father and son.

Horn, Peter. 1999. *When I Grow Up . . . .* Illustrated by Christina Kadmon. New York: North-South Books, Inc. A turtle father gently supports his young son's late-night thoughts about growing up.

Janovitz, Marilyn. 1998. *Can I Help?* New York: North-South Books, Inc. Father wolf exhibits much patience and love, as his young cub eagerly "assists" with outdoor chores.

———. 2001. *Good Morning, Little Fox*. New York: North-South Books. Little Fox and his father always spend the weekend together—sleeping late, making breakfast, and doing chores.

———. 1994. *Is It Time?* New York: North-South Books. In this cumulative rhyming story, father wolf lovingly helps his young cub prepare for bed.

London, Jonathan. 1994. *Let's Go, Froggy!* Illustrated by Frank Remkiewicz. New York: Viking. In this repetitious, fun text, Froggy awakes to a beautiful day and the promise of an extra-special picnic and bike ride with his dad; that is, if he gets ready in time.

MacDonald, Margaret Read. 2001. *Mabela the Clever*. Illustrated by Tim Coffey. Morton Grove, Ill.: Albert Whitman & Company. Mabela was once the smallest mouse in the village, but thanks to a lesson in cleverness from her father, she just might save everyone from their worst enemy, the cat.

Martin, David. 2001. *Piggy and Dad*. Illustrated by Frank Remkiewicz. Cambridge, Mass.: Candlewick Press. This set of four books designed to help beginning readers captures a truly loving relationship between Piggy and his dad. Titles included are *Piggy's Bath*, *Piggy's Bedtime*, *Piggy's Sandwich*, and *Piggy's Pictures*.

McBratney, Sam. 1999. *Guess How Much I Love You/Adivina Cuanto Te Quiero*. Illustrated by Anita Jeram. Nashville: Tommy Nelson. Big Nutbrown Hare and Little Nutbrown Hare try to outdo each other's measures of love while frolicking around in this popular bedtime book.

———. 2000. *Just You and Me*. Illustrated by Ivan Bates. Cambridge, Mass.: Candlewick Press. Big Gander Goose, whether intended to represent a father or other male caregiver, plays both protector and nurturer to Little Goosey in this warm story.

McCleary, William. 1988. *Wolf Story*. Illustrations by Warren Chappell. North Haven, Conn.: Linnet Books. In this now classic book, a father tells his young son stories about Waldo the wolf and the hen named Rainbow that always gets away.

McMullan, Kate. 2000. *Papa's Song*. Illustrated by Jim McMullan. New York: Farrar, Straus & Giroux. After Granny Bear, Grandpa Bear, and Mama Bear all give it a try, Papa Bear finds the perfect melody to put Baby Bear to sleep.

Miyamoto, Tadao. 1994. *Papa and Me*. Minneapolis: The Lerner Publishing Group. While Papa bear and baby bear fish, father reassures his son that they are, in fact, father and son, because of special memories they share together. Adults will especially like the ending.

Numeroff, Laura. 1998. *What Mommies Do Best/What Daddies Do Best*. Illustrated by Lynn Munsinger. New York: Simon & Schuster Books for Young Readers. Using a variety of animal characters, this book illustrates the similarities and differences, and the strengths and weaknesses, between mothers and fathers and their parenting interactions with young children.

Sansone, Adele. 2001. *The Little Green Goose*. Illustrated by Alan Marks. New York: North-South Books, Inc. A perfect book for preschool story times, a male goose goes out of his way to demonstrate his nurturing abilities; his adopted offspring learns that dads can be every bit as warm and loving as moms.

Sebastian, John. 1993. *J.B.'s Harmonica*. Illustrated by Garth Williams. San Diego: Harcourt Brace Jovanovich. J.B. plays harmonica well, but constant comparisons to his father, a professional harmonicist, have him considering quitting.

Sharmat, Marjorie Weinman. 1976. *Mooch the Messy.* Illustrated by Ben Shecter. New York: Harper & Row Publishers. Mooch the Rat gets a visit from his father, who finds Mooch's hole to be quite unclean and who encourages more healthy habits.

Shepard, Steve. 1991. *Elvis Hornbill: International Business Bird.* New York: Holt & Company. A human couple adopts a young bird they name Elvis who, despite his father's efforts to persuade him to become a musician, is interested only in finance, business, and computer science.

Tompert, Ann. 1990. *Grandfather Tang's Story: A Tale Told with Tangrams.* Illustrated by Robert Andrew Parker. New York: Crown Publishers, Inc. Grandfather Tang and his granddaughter, Little Soo, construct a story together using tangrams.

Weninger, Brigitte. 1995. *Good-Bye, Daddy!* Illustrated by Alan Marks. New York: North-South Books. When Tom's dad leaves after his visit, Tom is inconsolable; only a story from his teddy bear can make things all right. This book deals with familial separation in a softer way by duplicating the theme with a bear family.

Wood, Jakki. 1992. *Dads Are Such Fun.* Illustrated by Rog Bonner. New York: Simon & Schuster Books for Young Readers. This simple book shows through the use of human and animal fathers and their children that dads are wonderful for many different reasons.

Zalben, Jane Breskin. 1994. *Papa's Latkes.* New York: Henry Holt. When Mama Bear tires of making latkes, and the cubs' attempts fail, Papa salvages the holiday tradition with delicious results.

———. 1997. *Pearl's Marigolds for Grandpa.* New York: Simon & Schuster Books for Young Readers. When Pearl's grandfather dies, her father steps in to take part in activities the pair had shared. This book includes information at the back regarding Jewish mourning customs.

FOLKTALES, FAIRYTALES, AND TALL TALES

Babbitt, Natalie. 1998. *Ouch! A Tale from Grimm Retold by Natalie Babbitt.* Illustrated by Fred Marcellino. New York: HarperCollins Publishers. Marco, a poor nobody, is destined from birth to marry the princess, but her evil father will hear nothing of it! This is the clever and fun retelling of a lesser-known Grimm tale of a very confident young man's meeting with Devil's Grandmother, and of the evil king's monotonous fate.

Buehner, Caralyn. 1996. *Fanny's Dream.* Illustrated by Mark Buehner. New York: Dial Books for Young Readers. This story puts a spin on the classic Cinderella fairy tale by presenting Fanny, a girl who never gets to the ball, but whose husband is supportive and more wonderful than any prince.

Cole, Brock. 2000. *Buttons.* New York: Farrar, Straus & Giroux. In this humorous and fairy-tale-like story, father has burst his buttons and it is up to his three young daughters to scheme up plans to find more.

Davol, Marguerite W. 1995. *Papa Alonzo Leatherby: A Collection of Tall Tales from the Best Storyteller in Carroll County.* New York: Simon & Schuster Books for Young Readers. Papa Alonzo Leatherby is renowned in his county for being the best storyteller around, but when an especially vicious winter freeze comes along, he will need to find a way to thaw out his freezing stories.

Jackson, Ellen. 1995. *The Impossible Riddle.* Illustrated by Alison Winfield. Watertown, Mass.: Charlesbridge Publishing, Inc. Unable to let go of his beloved daughter and her delicious potato pancakes, Tsar Nicholas uses a riddle to stump potential suitors, while Katarina conjures up ways to make her potato pancakes less palatable. Fathers will especially appreciate the warm humor and the wise message encased in this tale.

Marks, Alan. 1993. *The Thief's Daughter.* New York: Farrar, Straus & Giroux. Magpie, whose poor father tells her magnificent stories about royal households, discovers the truth behind her father's life and learns an important lesson about honesty in this fairy-tale-like beginning chapter book.

Sawyer, Ruth. 1997. *The Remarkable Christmas of the Cobbler's Sons.* Illustrated by Barbara Cooney. New York: Viking Penguin. In this Austrian tale, a poor, widowed cobbler demonstrates a playful manner in raising his three sons despite their poverty; they experience Christmastime prosperity thanks to a surprise visit from an eccentric goblin king.

PUZZLES AND PLAY BOOKS

Burnie, Richard. 1999. *Monumental Mazes: Around-the-World Puzzling Mazes, from Ancient Egypt to the Skyscrapers of Manhattan.* New York: Alfred A. Knopf. This is a book of architectural mazes that feature structures from across the globe.

Tompert, Ann. 1990. *Grandfather Tang's Story: A Tale Told with Tangrams.* Illustrated by Robert Andrew Parker. New York: Crown Publishers, Inc. Grandfather Tang and his granddaughter, Little Soo, construct a story together using tangrams.

Walker, Lester. 1995. *Block Building for Children: Making Buildings of the World with the Ultimate Construction Toy.* Preface by Witold Rybczynski. Woodstock, N.Y.: The Overlook Press. This book about block building contains innovative plans for recreating with architectural structures.

SCARY STORIES FOR KIDS WHO DON'T HAVE NIGHTMARES

Bunting, Eve. 1987. *Ghost's Hour, Spook's Hour.* Illustrated by Donald Carrick. New York: Clarion Books. A young boy and his dog are frightened by nighttime sounds, and are further distressed by a ghost sighting.

DeFelice, Cynthia. 2000. *Cold Feet*. Illustrated by Robert Andrew Parker. New York: Dorling Kindersley Publishing, Inc. When Willie McPhee, a bagpiper journeying through the forest on a frigid winter night, takes a pair of boots from a dead man he finds in the woods, he never considers that the man might come looking for them.

Gorog, Judith. 1996. *In a Creepy, Creepy Place and Other Scary Stories*, Illustrated by Kimberly Bulcken Root. New York: HarperCollins Publishers. With five stories about especially creepy places, this book contains a good balance of silliness and scariness. See also *In a Messy, Messy Room and Other Strange Stories* (Philomel Books, 1990).

Haskins, James. 1994. *The Headless Haunt and Other African-American Ghost Stories*, Illustrated by Ben Otero. New York: HarperCollins Publishers. With special emphasis on stories influenced by African and African American traditions, this book is perfect for the older, thrill-seeking reader.

Heide, Florence Parry. 2000. *Some Things Are Scary*. Illustrated by Jules Feiffer. Cambridge, Mass.: Candlewick Press. The quirky illustrations bring to life the text of this book that highlights things that are scary in the lives of young people. Although it's about fearful moments in life, the book itself is quite a funny read.

Martin, Bill, Jr. 1993. *Old Devil Wind*. Illustrated by Barry Root. San Diego: Harcourt Brace & Company. In this compounding story, various everyday objects assume more spooky demeanors and are forbidden to act so until Halloween.

Schwartz, Alvin. 1984. *More Scary Stories to Tell in the Dark*. Illustrated by Stephen Gammell. New York: HarperCollins Publishers. Depicting tales about such terrifying topics as being buried alive, this chapter-style book is not for the faint of heart. For further reading, see also *In a Dark, Dark Room and Other Scary Stories* (1984).

SERIES

de Brunhoff, Laurent. 1993, 1991, 1989. *The Rescue of Babar, Babar and Father Christmas*, and *Babar and His Children*. New York: Random House. These are just a few of the books in the now classic series following the adventures of Babar the elephant.

Gauthier, Bertrand. 1993. *Zachary in I'm Zachary!* Illustrated by Daniel Sylvestre. Milwaukee: Gareth Stevens, Inc. This first book in a French-Canadian series introduces the divorced, custodial father, David, and his exuberant son, Zach, in a very warm and positive but realistic relationship, which frequently tests the father's patience. The comic-book-style illustrations and humorous scenarios make for an upbeat series. Other titles include *Zachary in Camping Out, Zachary in the Winner, Zachary in the Present,* and *Zachary in the Championship.*

Hest, Amy. 1999, 1997, 1996, 1995. *Off to School, Baby Duck; You're the Boss, Baby Duck!; Baby Duck and the Bad Eyeglasses;* and *In the Rain with Baby Duck*. Illustrated by Jill Barton. Cambridge, Mass.: Candlewick Press. When Baby Duck needs it the most, Grampa Duck is there to brighten the day or to provide support and companionship in this series for young children.

Koller, Jackie French. 1995. *The Dragonling*. Illustrated by Judith Mitchell. New York: Pocket Books. This first book in a fantasy series that includes *A Dragon in the Family* (1993) through *Dragons and Kings* (1998), introduces the aggressive, authoritative father in a major conflict with his approval-seeking nine-year-old son.

Le Saux, Alain. 1992. *King Daddy, Daddy Scratches, Daddy Sleeps,* and *Daddy Shaves*. New York: Henry Holt & Company. These four simple books for toddlers recall in colorful and quirky illustrations the many activities of daddy.

Mills, Claudia. 1999. *Gus and Grandpa*. Photo-illustrated by Catherine Stock. New York: Farrar, Straus & Giroux. A warm intergenerational relationship between a seven-year-old grandchild and his 70-year-old grandfather is depicted in this old-fashioned series for newly independent readers. Other titles include *Gus and Grandpa and the Christmas Cookies* (1997), *Gus and Grandpa at the Hospital* (1998), *Gus and Grandpa Ride the Train* (1998), *Gus and Grandpa and the Two-Wheeled Bike* (1999), and *Gus and Grandpa and Show-and-Tell* (2000).

Ormerod, Jan. 1985. *Messy Baby*. New York: Lothrop, Lee & Shepard Books. This picture book for toddlers features a father who, after discovering that his small child has undone all the tidying up he has done, responds with momentary frustration, but ultimately with love and patience. Other titles in the series include *Reading, Dad's Back,* and *Sleeping.*

Rylant, Cynthia. 1987. *Henry and Mudge*. Illustrated by Sucie Stevenson. New York: Simon & Schuster. This beginning reader series with more than 20 titles is still going strong. It includes *Henry and Mudge and the Forever Sea (1989), Henry and Mudge in the Family Trees (1997),* and *Henry and Mudge and the Funny Lunch (1999).* Although Dad is not a strong presence in all the books, his role is that of a contemporary father and husband, sharing most parenting responsibilities with Mom and, miraculously, never aging a bit.

Spohn, David. 1991, 1991, 1992, 1993. *Winter Wood, Nate's Treasure, Starry Night,* and *Home Field*. New York: Lothrop, Lee & Shepard. These books follow Matt, Nate, and their father as they spend quality time together outdoors. The text does not focus on the biracial nature of their relationship as do the illustrations, but on the love between a father and his sons.

Stevenson, James. 1986. *When I Was Nine*. New York: Greenwillow Books. In this charming book from his series, the author recounts life when he was nine, from never quite being able to learn arithmetic, to getting a cowboy hat—what he always wanted. Other books in Stevenson's autobiographical series include *Higher on the Door* (1987), *July* (1990), *Don't You Know There's a War On?* (1992), and *Fun, No Fun* (1994).

Waddell, Martin. 1999, 1996, 1993, 1992. *Good Job, Little Bear; You and Me, Little Bear; Let's Go Home, Little Bear;* and *Can't You Sleep, Little Bear?* Illustrated by Barbara Firth. Cambridge, Mass.: Candlewick Press. This warm series depicts an especially nurturing, supportive father, Big Bear, interacting with his young son, Little Bear, although Big Bear could represent any caring male adult, such as a Big Brother. These books are especially good for preschoolers.

SILLY STORIES DADS WILL LIKE

Feiffer, Jules. 1999. *Bark, George.* New York: Scholastic. George and his mother visit the vet because somehow George cannot seem to be able to bark; he can only meow, moo, quack, and oink. The crazy illustrations and surprise ending in this book make for a great read.

Heide, Florence Parry. 2000. *Some Things Are Scary.* Illustrated by Jules Feiffer. Cambridge, Mass.: Candlewick Press. The quirky illustrations bring to life the text of this book that highlights things that are scary in the lives of young people. Although it's about fearful moments in life, the book itself is quite a funny read.

Scieszka, Jon. 1998. *Squids Will Be Squids: Fresh Morals, Beastly Fables.* Illustrated by Lane Smith. Designed by Molly Leach. New York: Viking. These quirky, albeit hysterical, moralistic fables are sure to please many a father and child reading together.

———. 1992. *The Stinky Cheese Man and Other Fairly Stupid Tales.* Illustrated by Lane Smith. New York: Viking. This clever collection of reinvented classic fairy tales features the Stinky Cheese Man, a retelling of the Gingerbread Man tale.

———. 1989. *The True Story of the Three Little Pigs!* Illustrated by Lane Smith. New York: Viking. This wonderfully funny book recounts the story of the three little pigs through the eyes of Alexander T. Wolf, who insists that, being neither big nor bad, he was framed.

Shannon, Margaret. 1998. *Gullible's Troubles.* Boston: Houghton Mifflin Company. Gullible Guineapig believes all the stories about monsters his relatives tell him, and it turns out that they should too!

Sturges, Philemon. 1999. *The Little Red Hen (Makes a Pizza).* Illustrated by Amy Walrod. New York: Dutton Children's Books. In this clever retelling of the classic tale, Little Red Hen wants to make a pizza, but her companions, duck, cat, and dog, are extremely unhelpful.

Yaccarino, Dan. 1997. *An Octopus Followed Me Home.* New York: Viking. Father refuses to let one more pet into the house when his daughter brings an octopus home to their already zoolike home.

SPANISH/ENGLISH BOOKS

Appelt, Kathi. 1999. *Cowboy Dreams: Sleep Tight, Little Buckaroo.* Illustrated by Barry Root. New York: HarperCollins Publishers. This whimsical look at bedtime follows a little buckaroo as he mimics the other cowboys and settles in for a refreshing sleep under the stars; includes some Spanish words.

Cazet, Denys. 1993. *Born in the Gravy.* New York: Orchard Books. Margarita tells her papa all about her first day of kindergarten; features many Spanish words, the meanings of which are translated or implied.

Estes, Kristyn Rehling. 1999. *Manuela's Gift.* Illustrated by Claire B. Cotts. San Francisco: Chronicle Books. Times are hard for Manuela's Mama, Papa, and Abuela, but on her birthday she realizes there is still much to celebrate. This book contains many Spanish words.

Heide, Florence Parry, and Roxanne Heide Pierce. 1998. *Tío Armando.* Illustrated by Ann Grifalconi. New York: Lothrop, Lee & Shepard Books. A young girl develops a very special relationship with her philosophical great-uncle in this story featuring Spanish words.

Howard, Elizabeth Fitzgerald. 1995. *Papa Tells Chita a Story.* Illustrated by Floyd Cooper. New York: Simon & Schuster Books for Young Readers. Father and Chita share quality time together after dinner as he recounts his days as a soldier in Cuba during the Spanish-American War.

Johnston, Tony. 2001. *Uncle Rain Cloud.* Illustrated by Fabricio VandenBroeck. Watertown, Mass.: Talewinds. Carlos's uncle, who is extremely involved in his life, is often grumpy because he has difficulty with the English language. One day he tells Carlos that he is afraid and needs help; the two agree to work together: Carlos will teach his uncle English, and his uncle will tell him stories about Mexico in Spanish. There are many untranslated Spanish words.

Sáenz, Benjamin Alire. 1997. *A Gift from Papá Diego/Un Regalo de Papá Diego.* Illustrated by Geronimo Garcia. El Paso: Cinco Puntos Press. In this Spanish/English book, the ties between grandfather, Big Diego, and his grandson, Little Diego, are stronger than the Mexican–U.S. border that separates them, and Father is very supportive in his liaison role.

TOY AND MOVABLE BOOKS

Dijs, Carla. 1990. *Are You My Daddy?* New York: Simon & Schuster. This simple pop-up book is a surefire hit with preschoolers, who will surely love the silliness of the concept that a polar bear, turtle, ostrich, or crocodile could be a baby tiger's daddy!

———. 1996. *Daddy, Would You Love Me If . . . ?* New York: Little Simon. Daddy penguin eases a young penguin's concerns about growing up different from him, thus losing his love, in this pop-up story. See also *Mommy, Would You Love Me If . . . ?* (1996).

Ehlert, Lois. *Hands*. 1997. San Diego: Harcourt Brace & Company. Cutout shapes such as father's work gloves, along with illustrations of collages and tools, provide a tactile portrait of a young child's creative parents and their influence on the child's developing artistic ambitions.

Reasoner, Charles. 1997. *Whose Daddy Does This?* New York: Penguin Putnam Books for Young Readers. Adults and toddlers will have fun sliding apart this board book to discover the animal answers to questions such as "Whose daddy baby-sits all day long?" and "Whose daddy leads the pack?"

REFERENCES

Only children's books presented as incomplete text citations are presented in the reference list; all other children's books are cited fully the first time they appear in the book.

10 + 1 Tips for Father Involvement. 1999. From *Dads Can: Building Father Involvement*. Retrieved September 11, 1999, from www.dadscan.org.

Armas, G. C. 2001. "Census: Single-father Homes on the Rise." *Centre Daily Times* (May 18): A4.

Bandura, A. 1989. Social Cognitive Theory. In *Annals of Child Development. Theories of Child Development: Revised Formulations and Current Essues*, edited by R. Vasta. Greenwich, Conn.: JAI Press.

———. 1977. *Social Learning Theory*. Englewood Cliffs, N.J.: Prentice-Hall.

Beitel, A., and R. Parke. 1998. "Paternal Involvement in Infancy: The Role of Maternal and Paternal Attitudes." *Journal of Family Psychology* 12 (2): 268-288.

Belsky, J., and J. Kelly. 1994. *The Transition to Parenthood: How a First Child Changes a Marriage, Why Some Couples Grow Closer and Others Apart*. New York: Dell.

Biller, H. B., and R. J. Trotter. 1994. *The Father Factor: What You Need to Know to Make a Difference*. New York: Pocket Books.

Bly, C. 1991. "The Six Uses of Story." *The Journal of the Children's Literature Council of Pennsylvania,* 6 (1).

Bower, D., and V. K. Wright. 1986. *The Rubberband Syndrome: Family Life with a Child with a Disability.* Lincoln, Neb.: Nebraska Department of Education; Des Moines, Iowa: Iowa Department of Public Instruction.

Bowers, M. 1993. "The Storyteller's Corner: Personal Stories, Personal Myths: Pathways to Understanding." *The Journal of the Children's Literature Council of Pennsylvania* 7 (1): 13-17.

Brazelton, T. B. 1992. *Touchpoints*. Reading, Mass.: Addison-Wesley.

Brock, D. R., and E. Dodd. 1994. "A Family Lending Library: Promoting Early Literacy Development." *Young Children,* 49 (3): 16-21.

Bronfenbrenner, U. 1979. *The Ecology of Human Development: Experiments by Nature and Design*. Cambridge, Mass.: Harvard University Press.

Browne, A. 1986. *Piggybook*. New York: Alfred Knopf.

Bruner, J. S. 1983. *Child's Talk: Learning to Use Language*. New York: W.W. Norton.

Buehner, C. 1996. *Fanny's Dream*. Illustrated by M. Buehner. New York: Dial Books for Young Readers.

Bunting, E. 1997. *Twinnies*. Illustrated by N. Carpenter. San Diego, Calif.: Harcourt Brace.

Byars, B. C. 1991. *The Seven Treasure Hunts*. Illustrated by Jennifer Barrett. New York: HarperCollins.

Carnegie Corporation of New York. 1994. *Starting Points: Meeting the Needs of Our Youngest Children*. Abr. ed. New York: Carnegie Corporation of New York.

Carroad, D. L. 1994. "Getting Men Involved with Childrearing: An Interview with Jim Levine." *Children Today* 23 (1): 24-28.

Children's Defense Fund. 1995. *The State of America's Children Yearbook*. Washington, D.C.: The Children's Defense Fund.

———. 1999. *Take Action for Children* [Online]. Available: www.childrensdefense.org/takeaction/. [4 September 1999].

Clarke-Stewart, K. A. 1978. "And Daddy Makes Three: The Father's Impact on Mother and Young Child." *Child Development* 49 (2): 466-478.

Cole, M., and S. R. Cole. 1996. *The Development of Children*, 3rd ed. New York: W. H. Freeman.

Curtis, J. 1995. *F.A.T.H.E.R.S. Program Guide*. Sacramento, Calif.: State Library of California.

Daly, K. 1993. "Reshaping Fatherhood: Finding the Models." *Journal of Family Issues* 14 (4): 510-530.

Delamare, D. 1993. *Cinderella*. New York: Simon & Schuster.

Dickinson , D. K., J. M. DeTemple, J. Hirschler, and M. W. Smith. 1992. "Book Reading with Preschoolers: Co-construction of Text at Home and at School. *Early Childhood Research Quarterly* 7 (3): 323-346.

Dinnebeil, L. A., L. Hale, and S. Rule. 1999. "Early Intervention Program Practices that Support Collaboration." *Topics in Early Childhood Special Education* 19 (4): 225-235.

Dolmetsch, P., and A. Shih 1985. *The Kids' Book about Single-parent Families.* Garden City, N.Y.: Doubleday.

Edelman, H. 1994. *Motherless Daughters: The Legacy of Loss.* New York: Dell.

Edwards, P. A. 1991. Fostering Early Literacy through Parent Coaching. In *Literacy for a Diverse Society: Perspectives, Programs and Policies*, edited by E. Hiebert. New York: Teachers College Press.

Elliot, I. 1996. "Dads by the Dozen." *Teaching K-8* 26 (5): 54-55.

Engel, S. 1995. *The Stories Children Tell: Making Sense of the Narratives of Childhood.* New York: W. H. Freeman.

Fowler, S. G. 1994. *I'll See You When the Moon Is Full.* Illustrated by Jim Fowler. New York: Greenwillow Books.

Frank, R. 1998. Yikes, That's My Boy! from "Frankly Speaking." *Centre Daily Times* (March 8): 1C.

Garbarino, J. 1999. *Lost Boys: Why Our Sons Turn Violent and How We Can Save Them.* New York: The Free Press.

Genisio, M. H. 1996. "Breaking Barriers with Books: A Fathers' Book-sharing Program from Prison." *Journal of Adolescent & Adult Literacy* 40 (2): 92-100.

Gilbert, R., and P. Gilbert. 1998. *Masculinity Goes to School.* London: Routledge.

Gray, C. A. 1998. Social Stories and Comic Strip Conversations with Students with Asperger Syndrome and High Functioning Autism. In *Asperger Syndrome or High-Functioning Autism?*, edited by E. Schopler, G. B. Mesibov, and L. J. Kunce. New York: Plenum Press.

Hamburg, D. A. 1994. *Today's Children: Creating a Future for a Generation in Crisis.* New York: Times Books.

Hart, B., and T. R. Risley. 1995. *Meaningful Differences in the Everyday Experience of Young American Children.* Baltimore: Paul H. Brookes.

Heller, C. 1994. "Fathers, Children and Books: Selecting Picture Books that Portray Nurturing Fathers." *Texas Child Care* 18 (3): 14-19.

Herb, S. L. 1987. "The Effects of a Storyhour and Book Borrowing Strategy on Emergent Reading Behavior in First-grade Children." Ph.D. diss., Pennsylvania State University.

Herb, S. 1990. "The Storyteller's Corner: Some Stories about Storytelling." *The Journal of the Children's Literature Council of Pennsylvania* 4 (2): 9-12.

Herb, S., and S. Willoughby-Herb. 1994. *Using Children's Books in Preschool Settings.* New York: Neal-Schuman Publishers.

———. 2001. "Preschool Education through Public Libraries." *School Library Media Research Online* 4. Available: www.ala.org/ aasl/SLMR/vol4/content/html [20 July 2001].

Hines, A. G. 1986. *Daddy Makes the Best Spaghetti.* New York: Clarion.

Hoffman, M. 1995. *Boundless Grace.* Illustrated by C. Binch. New York: Dial Books for Young Readers.

Jennings, T. 1986. "Storytelling: A Nonliterate Approach to Teaching Reading." *Journal of the Children's Literature Council of Pennsylvania* 1 (2): 16-18.

Kantrowitz, B., and C. Kalb. 1998. "Boys Will Be Boys." *Newsweek.* May 11: 54-61.

Kortenhaus, C. M., and J. Demarest. 1993. "Gender Role Stereotyping in Children's Literature: An Update." *Sex-Roles: A Journal of Research* 28 (3-4): 219-232.

Lancy, D. F. 1994. "Libraries Can Serve Homeless Children: Cambridge Public Library Outreach Project." *Journal of Youth Services in Libraries* 7 (3): 268-272.

Levine, J. A., and E. W. Pitt. 1995. *New Expectations: Community Strategies for Responsible Fatherhood.* New York: Families & Work Institute.

Levine, J. A., and T. L. Pittinsky. 1997. *Working Fathers: New Strategies for Balancing Work and Family.* Reading, Mass.: Addison-Wesley.

Lyytinen, P., M. Laakso, and A. Poikkeus. 1998. "Parental Contribution to Child's Early Language and Interest in Books." *European Journal of Psychology of Education* 13 (3): 297-308.

Mason, J. M., and B. M. Kerr. 1992. Literacy Transfer from Parents to Children in the Preschool Years. In *The Intergenerational Transfer of Cognitive Skills: Vol. II. Theory and Research in Cognitive Science*, edited by T. G. Sticht, M. J. Beeler, and B. A. McDonald. Norwood, N.J.: Heinemann.

Masson, J. M. 1999. *The Emperor's Embrace: Reflections on Animal Families and Fatherhood.* New York: Simon & Schuster.

Mathews, V. H. 1996. *Kids Can't Wait . . . Library Advocacy Now!* Chicago: American Library Association.

Miedzian, M. 1991. *Boys Will Be Boys: Breaking the Link between Masculinity and Violence.* New York: Doubleday.

Miller, P. H. 1993. *Theories of Developmental Psychology.* New York: W. H. Freeman.

Morrow, L. M. 1993. *Literacy Development in the Early Years: Helping Children Read and Write.* Boston: Allyn and Bacon.

National Center for Educational Statistics. 1998. In *The Condition of Education* [Online]. Available: http://nces.ed.gov/edstats/ new_Pubsindex.html [4 September 1999].

Nelson, R. 1997. *My Hero.* Manuscript in preparation.

Nord, C. W., D. A. Brimhall, and J. West. 1997. *Fathers' Involvement in Their Children's Schools* (Report No. NCES 98-091). Washington, D.C.: U.S. Department of Education, National Center for Education Statistics. (ERIC Document Reproduction Service No. ED409125).

Norman-Jackson, J. 1982. "Family Interactions, Language Development, and Primary Reading Achievement of Black Children in Families of Low Income." *Child Development* 53 (2): 349-358.

Nugent, J. K. 1991. "Cultural and Psychological Influences on the Father's Role in Infant Development." *Journal of Marriage and the Family* 53: 475-485.

Numeroff, L. J. 1998. *What Daddies Do Best.* Illustrated by L. Munsinger. New York: Simon & Schuster.

Olmsted, P. P., and D. P. Weikart. 1995. *Families Speak: Early Childhood Care and Education in 11 Countries.* Ypsilanti, Mich.: High/Scope Press.

Ortiz, R. W. 1994. "Fathers and Children Explore Literacy." *The Kamehameha Journal of Education* 5 (Fall): 131-134.

Otstott, M. 1984. "The Role of the American Father as Revealed in Selected Fiction Books for Children in the Elementary Grades: An Historical Overview and Content Analysis." Ph.D. diss., Texas Woman's University.

Palfrey, J. S. 1994. *Community Child Health: An Action Plan for Today.* Westport, Conn.: Praeger.

Palm, G. F. 1996. "Understanding the Parent Education Needs of Incarcerated Fathers." Paper presented at the annual conference of the National Council on Family Relations, Kansas City, Mo. (ERIC Document Reproduction Service No. ED 407112).

Papalia, D. E., and S. W. Olds. 1996. *A Child's World: Infancy through Adolescence*, 7th ed. New York: McGraw-Hill.

Parke, R. D. 1996. *Fatherhood.* Cambridge, Mass.: Harvard University Press.

Parke, R. D., and A. A. Brott. 1999. *Throwaway Dads.* Boston: Houghton Mifflin.

Parke, R. D., and P. Stearns. 1993. Fathers and Child Rearing. In *Children in Time and Place: Developmental and Historical Insights*, edited by G. H. Elder, Jr., J. Modell, and R. D. Parke. Cambridge, Mass.: Cambridge University Press.

Pellegrini, A. D., and L. Galda. 1994. Not by Print Alone: Oral Language Supports for Early Literacy Development. In *Children's Emergent Literacy: From Research to Practice*, edited by D. F. Lancy. Westport, CT: Praeger.

Phillips, A. 1994. *The Trouble with Boys: A Wise and Sympathetic Guide to the Risky Business of Raising Sons.* New York: Basic Books.

Pipher, M. 1994. *Reviving Ophelia: Saving the Selves of Adolescent Girls.* New York: G. P. Putnam's Sons.

Pritchard, D. 1983/1984. "Daddy, Talk!" Thoughts on reading early picture books. *The Lion and the Unicorn* 7/8: 64-69.

Rak, C., and L. Patterson. 1996. "Promoting Resilience in At-Risk Children." *Journal of Counseling & Development* 74 (4): 368-373.

Ray, A. 2000. "Q & A." *Applied Research in Child Development* 2 [Brochure]. Chicago: Herr Research Center at Erikson Institute.

Rex, M. 1999. *My Fire Engine.* New York: Scholastic.

Rothenberg, D. 1996. Grandparents as Parents: A Primer for Schools. (Report: EDO-PS-96-8). Urbana, Ill.: ERIC Clearinghouse on Elementary and Early Childhood Education, ERIC Digest (073). (ERIC Document Reproduction No. ED401044).

Sacks, O. W. 1987. *The Man Who Mistook His Wife for a Hat and Other Clinical Tales.* New York: Perennial Library.

Sáenz, B. A. 1998. *A Gift from Pápa Diego.* Illustrated by G. Garcia. El Paso: Cinco Puntos Press.

Scarborough, H. S., W. Dobrich, and M. Hager. 1991. "Preschool Literacy Experience and Later Reading Achievement." *Journal of Learning Disabilities* 24 (8): 508-511.

Scarr, S., R. A. Weinberg, A. Levine, and J. Kagan. 1986. *Understanding Development.* San Diego, Calif.: Harcourt Brace Jovanovich.

Schickedanz, J. A. 1993. Designing the Early Childhood Classroom Environment to Facilitate Literacy Development. In *Language and Literacy in Early Childhood Education, Yearbook in Early Childhood Education 4*, edited by B. Spodek and O. N. Saracho. New York: Teachers College Press.

Seifert, K., and R. Hoffnung. 1997. *Child and Adolescent Development*, 4th ed. Boston: Houghton Mifflin.

Silber, S. 1989. "Family Influences on Early Development." *Topics in Early Childhood Special Education* 8 (4): 1-23.

Smith, D. D., and R. Luckasson. 1995. *Introduction to Special Education: Teaching in an Age of Challenge.* Boston: Allyn and Bacon.

Snow, C. E., S. M. Burns, and P. Griffin, eds. 1998. *Preventing Reading Difficulties in Young Children.* Washington, D.C.: National Academy Press.

Spink, J. C., C. Spink, and J. K. Spink. 2000. "Dads and Sons: Sharing Good Books and Good Times." *The New Advocate* 13 (1): 16.

Stewig, J. W. 1988. "Fathers: A Presence in Picture Books?" *Journal of Youth Services in Libraries* 1 (Summer): 301-305.

Story, P. 1999. "High Infant Death Rate Tied to Teen Moms." *Centre Daily Times* (July 15): A4.

Sturges, P. 1999. *I Love Trucks.* Illustrated by S. Halpern. New York: HarperCollins.

Sulzby, E., and P. A. Edwards. 1993. Role of Parents in Supporting Literacy Development of Young Children. In *Language and Literacy in Early Childhood Education, Yearbook in Early Childhood Education 4*, edited by B. Spodek and O. N. Saracho. New York: Teachers College Press.

Taylor, D., and D. S. Strickland. 1989. Learning from Families: Implications for Educators and Policy. In *Risk Makers Risk Takers Risk Breakers: Reducing the Risks for Young Literacy Learners*, edited by J. Allen and J. M. Mason. Portsmouth, N.H.: Heinemann.

Teale, W. H. 1995. Public Libraries and Emergent Literacy: Helping Set the Foundation for School Success. In *Achieving School Readiness: Public Libraries and National Education Goal No. 1*, edited by B. R. Immroth and V. Ash-Geisler. Chicago: American Library Association.

Thurston, D. P. 1999. "Grandfathers Matter, Too." *Mature Outlook* (April): 65-68.

Tichenor, M., A. M. Bock, and M. A. Sumner. 1999. "Enhancing Literacy of an At-Risk Group: A Reading Incentive Program for Teen Parents and Their Babies." *Reading Improvement* 36 (3): 134-142.

Trelease, J. 1982. *The Read-Aloud Handbook*. New York: Penguin.

Vygotsky, L. S. 1978. *Mind in Society, the Development of Higher Psychological Processes*. Edited by M. Cole, V. John-Steiner, S. Scribner, and E. Souberman. Cambridge, Mass.: Harvard University Press.

Wallerstein, J. S., and S. Blakeslee. 1989. *Second Chances: Men, Women, and Children a Decade after Divorce*. New York: Ticknor & Fields.

Weissbourd, R. 1996. *The Vulnerable Child: What Really Hurts America's Children and What We Can Do About It*. Reading, Mass.: Addison-Wesley.

Wells, G. 1985. Preschool Literacy-related Activities and Success in School. In *Literacy, Language, and Learning: The Nature and Consequences of Reading and Writing*, edited by D. Olson, N. Torrance, and A. Hildyard. Cambridge: Cambridge University Press.

Willoughby-Herb, S., and S. Herb. 1992. "The Importance of Men as Role Models in Literacy." *The Bookmark* 50 (3): 231-235.

Willoughby-Herb, S., and Vaughan, E. 1996. "Children's Literature for Children with Disabilities." *Journal of the Children's Literature Council of Pennsylvania* 10: 16-22.

Winthrop, E. 1998. *As the Crow Flies*. Illustrated by J. Sandin. New York: Clarion.

Yogman, M. W., S. Doxin, E. Tronick, H. Als, L. Adamson, B. Lester, et al. 1977. "The Goals and Structure of Face-to-Face Interaction between Infants and Fathers." Paper presented at the biannual meeting of the Society for Research in Child Development, New Orleans, La.

INDEX

Note: All italicized entries represent sidebar or text box titles

ABOUT THE AUTHORS

SARA WILLOUGHBY-HERB

Sara Willoughby-Herb was professor of Teacher Education at Shippensburg University for 20 years until her retirement at the end of 1999. She is currently on the special education faculty at Penn State University, where she supervises practicum students and graduate student teachers.

The author or coauthor of a dozen books, Dr. Willoughby-Herb was the lead teacher and curriculum designer for the HICOMP Preschool Project in the mid-1970s, the first preschool program and curriculum in the nation to integrate nondisabled with disabled and developmentally delayed children.

She is the lead author of a Poetry Big Book series published by Continental Press and the coauthor of Neal-Schuman's *Using Children's Books in Preschool Settings* (with husband Steven).

Sara's first job after graduate school was as a Head Start teacher in its initial year of 1965. Except for a depressing year or two, she has been teaching children under age eight ever since.

STEVEN HERB

Steven Herb is head of the Education and Behavioral Sciences Library and affiliate professor of Language and Literacy Education at Penn State University.

He has a special interest in storytelling and the power stories hold. Dr. Herb is the coauthor of the history of Penn State's school mascot: *The Nittany Lion: An Illustrated Tale* (Penn State Press). His course "Stories and Storytelling: How Humans Become People" resulted in Herb being named Penn State's most innovative faculty member of 2000. He also received the University Libraries Award in 2000, an annual peer award recognizing library faculty and staff for their professional contributions to Penn State and the library science community.

Herb is the past president of the Association for Library Service to Children (ALSC), one of the eleven divisions of the American Library Association. He is the immediate past chair of the American Library Association's Intellectual Freedom Committee, and is also the director of the Pennsylvania Center for the Book.